Measuring the Distance

Dai Smith was born in the Rhondda in 1945. His writing has encompassed history, biography, essays, fiction and criticism. He was was made a CBE for services to arts and culture in Wales in 2016. His memoir *Off the Track* was published in 2023 and followed in 2025 by *Street Fighting* and *Other Past Times* is his debut collection of poetry.

Measuring the Distance

DAI SMITH

Parthian, Cardigan SA43 1ED
www.parthianbooks.com

ISBN 9781917140393
Edited by Daryl Leeworthy
Typeset by Elaine Sharples
Printed by 4edge Limited
Published with the financial support of the Books Council of Wales
British Library Cataloguing in Publication Data
A cataloguing record for this book is available from the British Library.

Printed on FSC accredited paper

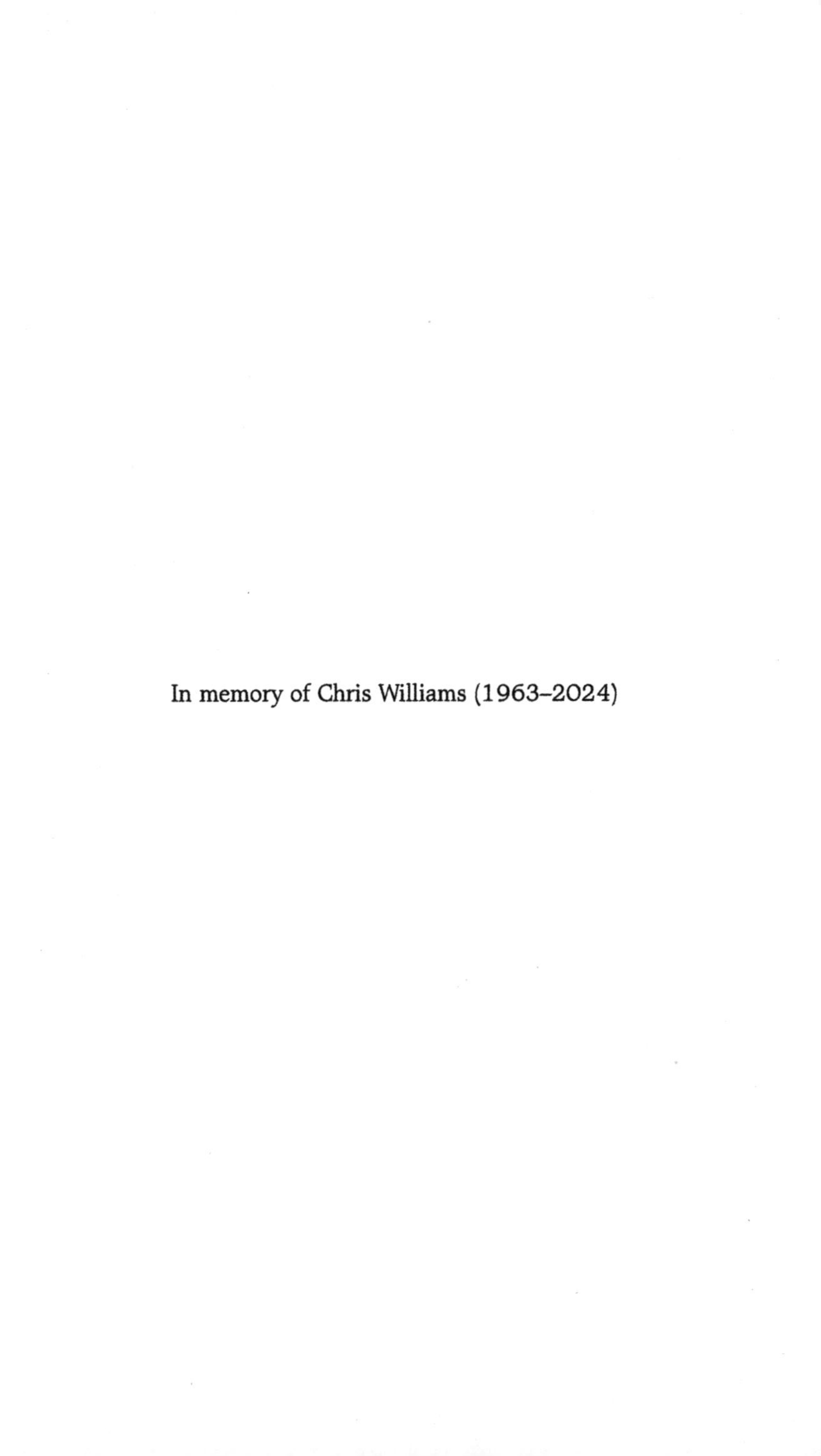

In memory of Chris Williams (1963–2024)

‘By measuring the distance, we come home.’

Raymond Williams, *Border Country* (1960)

CONTENTS

PRELIMINARIES

WELSH WATER

Against our lean-to's house wall
Set square on redbrick columns
A white ceramic sink agape,
        and
Plumb above its plughole
        a
  Brass tap.

The tap's two-handled head twisted
  Just the one way left for water
  Lead piped from mountain to tank,
        gushing
Gravity dropped, violently
        cold
  To splash.

Coming down from summer's play
Grass stained and prickled by heat
T-shirt soaked by ludic sweat
        I'd
Slake a day's thirst
        and
Drink direct.

Strained upwards on tiptoes
Mouth clamped over the spout
Sucking inwards channelled streams
        Till

Glacial melt filled to
          Tautness
          Belly's drum.

One such day of drymouthed swelter
Cup or glass scorned to swallow
Fast the quick pulse of icewater
          I
Gulped and felt its squirm
          Wriggle,
     Hawked out

Into the Belfast box's whirl
A comma in the swirling pool,
Coppery gleamed and flickering
          Alive
A shiver in its shared surprise
   A snake.

I had tasted its metallic otherness
A presence slithered tap to gob,
And filled a glass now to rinse
          Memory.
To scramble its netherworld message
          Through
        Tepid spit.

Then, scooped elastic in a tumbler,
A-writhe around its glassy walls
The snake curled in confinement
          Under
My hand over the meniscus curve
          Before
     Waterfalled
                    Earthwards.

RINGING THE BELL

When you come out for the bell aged eighty you have no choice but to employ a late style. This is mine. A mix of deceitfully plain reportage; fictive history and fictional forays into the past; personalised reflections and more shaded perspectives from others; some poetry and polemics; glances of delight at the playfulness of sport and the charisma of personalities; taking a stance, whether orthodox or southpaw, in the courage to live with what you are given no matter what is put in front of you. And the illusion of random repetition, the rat tat tat bam bam, before any change in the angle of attack. But that's enough bobbing out of reach, jabbing and sliding away with pretty dancing around the ring.

I still want to punch out at idiocy in public places and to land blows, left hooks and right-handed uppercuts, on the socially myopic and the culturally self-serving. Real opponents need to be faced down in the real world. There must, beyond shadow-boxing, be a recognition of the enemy before us: of the way Cymru as a concept can be made to serve as a fig leaf against the actuality of Wales. Both these contenders for a future claim on the title deeds of our country have to take a grip on who the Welsh once were and who the people of Wales may yet become. The going could yet be tough.

As to that, I have a continuing and unconquerable faith in the efficacy of historical enquiry and the necessary accompanying gravity of an appropriate style for the changing occasion. Here I choose both insistent pools of light to illuminate the gloom of any deliberated obfuscation and, for contrast, call for the blinding dazzle of confrontational flashbulbs to dispel, however temporarily, the dark pall of any ethnic and linguistic mythos to which, in our uncertainty, we may have fallen prey.

In all of this I am encouraged by the necessary prioritisation of intellect over sentiment which can be detected wherever the practice of historical analysis comes up against the smother tactics of public memory. It is definitely present as a thematic motif running through the life and work of Seamus Heaney who, ever, demanded of himself an independence of the creative spirit as witness within that wider obligation which he acknowledged had to be 'faithful to a collective historical experience'. When, early and late, the poet on his divided and troubled island was accused of a lack of grounded patriotism, a spurning of blood and soil and religion and language, he turned back to his great forbear W. B. Yeats, that patrician patriot and cold-eyed Protestant, and to Yeats' spirited defence of Sean O'Casey, Catholic apostate and rebellious proletarian, after the riotous outcry in 1926 which had greeted *The Plough and the Stars*, the Dubliner's defiantly unsentimental play on the Easter Rising of 1916. Yeats scornfully rejected that species of vanity which was implicit in self-preening public memory as being no more than an unthinking national chest-thumping undertaken to win the plaudits of others. Instead, he reserved his praise for that intellectual maturity explicit in self-pride, and which stemmed from national indifference to the judgement of others. These divergent streams of thought and of action ran particularly deep in Ireland and their tributary gouging of a culture carry warning marks for significant others.

Seamus Heaney, native Ulsterman and generational Republican, had with a searing indignation rejected the (near) injunction that he should commit to the instruction of a cause and make writing in Irish a primary rallying call for cultural autonomy; on the contrary, he insisted that his tongue to speak of his people to his people, and beyond them, was that particular English language which, for him and those he came from, had been historically imbricated with an inescapable Irish dimension. To do other, personally or publicly, he said, would be 'to obliterate history'. Both Irish poets, Nobel prize-winners from either side of that real and yet nominal border in their island, nurtured to the discomfort of the tribal life-giving seeds of their multivalent creativity. W. B. Yeats had long proposed, and Seamus Heaney ardently seconded, that 'as a nation came to intellectual maturity it realised that the only thing that did it any credit was its intellect'. That last encapsulates the vision which I felt Wales needed to capture and cherish, not out of vanity but from pride, from its own divergent history as this new century began. Our politics and our society had been, was, distinctive. But streams could be diverted if they were not channelled.

It was why, when I was asked to give the annual Welsh Political Archive Lecture for the National Library of Wales in Aberystwyth in 2000, that I chose to concentrate on the single most significant, and surviving, political institution of the twentieth century in Wales: the Labour Party. The subtitle of my lecture, *Out of the People*, was 'A Century in Labour'. I intended the punning, for I was intent on casting the future runes of that hybrid and hobbled organisation just as much as I was choosing to quiz its less than immaculate conception and question its ability to ever fructify its cultural destiny beyond a febrile electoralism. I had prefaced the printed edition of the lecture with a quote from Raymond Williams on whose biography I was then working. Raymond, at that time not fully and retrospectively drafted into a cut-and-paste version of post-hoc nationalist exegesis, a fate textually more than contextually derived, had been an erstwhile, and consistently uneasy, supporter of Labour as an electoral machine for radical politics based upon the collective interests of the British working class as historically defined. However, his realistic ambitions for an outcome of truly profound social change were more honed than that as my quote emphasised: 'the task of a successful socialist movement will be one of feeling and imagination quite as much as one of fact and organisation.'

Twenty-five years have since passed and so I begin here with a backward, historical glance from a hopeful time by presenting a fuller version of that intervention, and one for whose continuing questions this present book seeks further definitions along with renewed hope for their replenishment by feeling and imagination. It is the privilege of old age to be present whilst a future is revealed and a past still unfolds. It is a condition which Edward Said describing the expressiveness of a late style of articulation called 'a form of exile' in which state the witness is 'in but oddly apart from the present'. By measuring the distances, we build the bridges to allow us to find home.

OUT OF THE PEOPLE

For most of the last century the Labour Party, methodically and maddeningly, first aroused Welsh expectations and then, having satisfied immediate Welsh needs, doused Welsh desires; and all to a rhythmic calendar the Vatican could have recognised. In part this was because of the perennial gap between a rhetoric of socialism and the reality of post-electoral delivery; in part because of the umbilical connection, originally necessary and constantly broken, between a Labour Party as such and a wider Labour movement; in part because what was advanced in Wales often stalled in both England *and* Scotland – it was only the phalanx of Welsh MPs elected in 1931 which kept the post-MacDonald party afloat in that disastrous year and as one of them, Aneurin Bevan, wrote in 1947, in the still-socialist heyday of the Attlee government in which he so conspicuously served: 'Wales (has) ... an excitement for things of the mind and spirit, which are wholly different from England and English ways'; and, in part, because Bevan also recognised it was not Labour which had created and shaped the culture of modern Wales but, rather, that culture which flowed in and around Labour activism until the latter had become buoyant and a bearer, one among many, of that culture's hopes. For, as Bevan insisted, looking back on the connection between the progress of Labour and the support it had won: 'abstract ideas which ignite [the] mind are those to which ... experience provides a reference.' Labour, in other words, had come out of the people.

More particularly, its ability to act as a social agent for change relied as much, if not more, on the nature of that people than it did on its own institutional and ideological configurations. Let us go back and ask, again, why Keir Hardie was elected as the second member for Merthyr Boroughs in October 1900. The answers routinely given are psephological, ideological and accidental but the underlying reason is cultural.

We know that Keir Hardie had scarcely given Merthyr Tydfil a second thought until, in a staggered campaign, his earlier defeat at Preston was clear. Only then did he fully embrace the tricky concept of riding two horses in the election for, only then, had his favoured mount fallen. Besides, he was only in the race because the small yet earnest and organised ILP faction in the twinned constituencies of Aberdare and Merthyr had effectively rigged a nomination conference for a Labour candidate in late September by causing the numerically dominant miners' lodges, whose votes were to be counted by delegates rather than proportionate to their membership, to withdraw in disgust. The miners would have preferred a Liberal candidate with Labourite sympathies. Yet the growing dissatisfaction, even among the Liberals, with the yoked pairing since 1888 of the progressive coal owner D. A. Thomas and the freewheeling speculator Pritchard Morgan, meant voter alienation from the erstwhile working man's champion, Morgan, would create a near-perfect cameo of the Lib-Lab politics that dominated all Welsh constituencies i.e. the return of D. A. Thomas and whoever was the larger second-choice candidate in conjunction with Thomas. That, in this method of voting in a two-member constituency, meant Hardie was elected on the coat-tails of D. A. Thomas; Hardie whose individual poll was the lowest, by far, of the three candidates. So, a combination of backroom tactics, ideology-driven activists, the luck of timing, a Liberal split and the electoral quirks of 1900 had led to the unlikely return to Parliament of Wales' first avowed socialist MP. Not that socialism had had very much to do with it, or even the concept of independent Labour representation.

Yet Hardie's election remains an epiphany – a revelation, if you like, of the political outcome that cannot be read off from social trends and economic data but is, nonetheless, waiting, within a particular culture, to be given a new focus.

At this point Hardie was to be that focus. He was the focus for the economic discontent that was still gathering in the mining workforce after the defeat of the six-months' strike of 1898. Out of which that key institution the South Wales Miners' Federation would emerge. He was the focus of the diffused politics and energies that had crackled fitfully around ILP missionary work in South Wales since 1894. Out of which, via the trades councils and the redirected trade union movement, the institutional force of the Labour Party would come in the two decades that followed. He was the focus for the civic resentment felt by working men against Liberal elites who acknowledged the interests of Labour and the right to vote but not the right to nominate before the ballot was cast. Out of which came successive challenges such as that which saw a miners' agent like Vernon Hartshorn stand twice in the Labour cause against Liberals in Mid Glamorgan in 1910 and be defeated both times only to win, unopposed, in 1918. Above all, this carpet-bagging Scottish chancer was the focus for that limited electorate and the wider inchoate cultural formation in the making. This was a place and a time where, however fitfully, a social being can be seen to begin to attain a glimpse of social consciousness. The core of the matter was that Hardie, ex-miner and selfless champion of the socially excluded, of the poor, the dispossessed and the aspirational, was palpably out of the people, and of their kind.

Fortunately, we have first-hand testimony of this in the autobiography of Wil Jon Edwards, *From the Valley I Came* (1956), an unjustly neglected classic account of those cusp years to 1914. Looking back from the 1950s on his young collier boy self, Wil Jon probes for the reasons for Hardie's popularity in Aberdare and Merthyr and recollects how at a break underground he had asked an older collier to explain. The heroic synthesis of Hardie's life that followed was patently culled from newspapers of the day but it ended with 'the thought that that day (Hardie's election to Westminster for West Ham in 1894) was the most important day in working-class history: because Keir Hardie was 'one of us', and that he always would be 'one of us'.'

Wil Jon goes to hear Hardie speak in Aberaman – the year is 1900:

> There was a large crowd already gathered on the Plough Tip when I arrived. At such meetings it was usually not difficult to isolate the speaker, the really important person present, the centre of a fussy entourage; but now there seemed nobody of any significance at the highest point of the tip, certainly not one who could 'sway multitudes'.

When, eventually, the chairman called on Keir Hardie to speak, my mind flew back to the Heading and Dai Bobby's words 'just like one of us'. And this, I saw, and felt, was simply true; he was indeed just like one of us but, I knew, he had in him a power and, to us, a glory which raised him to the skies in our thinking.

(The message was simple and exciting) ... We should have a political party of our own... It is true that (in 1898) a trade union had been born; but it was still young, still incoherent and still struggling towards maturity. It could, indeed, recognise and express feelings of frustration and anxiety; but it was still without aspirations based on a plan of action...

This man Keir Hardie came into the midst of our confusion and showed us a way out of it. This is how it looked to me, a mere youth in years. Keir Hardie's plan was based on a long-term policy; but then the union had no plan at all. At any rate he had captured the imagination of the workers in the Valleys; for days afterwards his name was on everybody's lips. I always tried to work out things in my own mind, and I asked myself why it was that he, a stranger, could drive home a message of hope when the same message from another might mean little. I found an answer, I thought. It was Keir Hardie's complete integrity, an integrity made the more forceful by the fact that he had no oratorical tricks ... no desire to mould events or even conditions into points of eloquence: he offered complete sincerity; he was without guile and told the truth, and this went straight to the hearts and minds of even the more ignorant miners in the Valleys.

In 1907, Wil Jon Edwards, aged nineteen and with seven years' work underground behind him, won a miners' scholarship to Ruskin College, Oxford. On the train out of the valley his mind turned towards it.

All this thought of the valley and the lives then lived by my people finally concentrated into the picture of a stoutly built little man in a Scotch tweed suit and a cloth cap above a bearded face, Keir Hardie. Keir Hardie was just 'one of us' and he would never be anything else...

I was now going to Oxford to be educated and I would, I be-

> lieved, gain much; but whatever I gained it would be shared with my people as I worked to raise their status. Like Keir Hardie, I would be 'just one of us'....

This journey 'out of the people' would prove, in many individual cases, more a one-way ticket than a round trip as idealistic vows cracked under unforeseen pressures. But the impulse of identification with 'the people' as both initial motive and driven purpose was, indeed, at the heart of this first generation's politics. Hardie's own Election Handbill of 1910 begins by thanking the 'Electors of the Merthyr Boroughs' for returning him with 'a great majority' and ends by acknowledging the 'toil and sacrifice' of Labour Party members which were 'the Chief Agents in bringing about Victory' but sandwiched between those mutual pillars of gratitude is the simple declaration that he will work 'in and out of Parliament on behalf of the People'.

But who were these people? For sure, they were not empty vessels waiting to be filled with the pure milk of socialism. In his own family Wil Jon Edwards had gamblers, drinkers and street fighters a-plenty – his brother Twm was even arraigned on a manslaughter charge after one such bare-knuckle bout – and the Merthyr and Aberdare that took up Hardie, even in the late Victorian days of municipal improvement such as parks and libraries, had not entirely civilised its urban spaces where the openly raucous spectacle of street life – often violent, often drunken, consistently challenging – shaded into the lively popular culture of Edwardian Wales, its champion boxers, its aggressively competitive male voice choirs, its bribed and triumphant rugby teams, its resonating chapels and its vibrating music halls, and out again into both riotous demonstrations that could indict the motives of a whole society, as with the world-turned-upside-down in Tonypandy in 1910, and into the sharp-edged ideological conflict between mass industrial unionism, or Welsh syndicalism, and the parliamentary approach. And sometimes in the fast-flowing waters of this culture, now as much immigrant as it had been rooted, people could put on and take off all those garments of wishful identity with bewildering rapidity. Not all chronology of individual life is lived at the same calendar's measured pace. For some generations, life really is more intensely experienced.

In turbulent times just prior to the unheralded, lurking carnage of the First World War, contemporary perceptions of the extent of what social violence might unfold were more material than spectral. In the days immediately prior to and following the shocking disorder on the streets of Tonypandy in 1910 on 7 and 8 November, the Deputy Chief Constable of Glamorgan was reporting that mandril handles were being sold at double the normal price and that there was 'Great demand for revolvers and any firearms at Tonypandy' where tradesmen received over 100 applications for revolvers within a week, none of which were supplied since 'the necessary gun licences' were not produced. The seven revolvers which were sold undoubtedly went to the tradesmen themselves. Yet revolvers and rifles, carried and used by the troops sent to Rhondda and to Llanelli in 1911, where two men died when soldiers opened up with indiscriminate fire, were no more the artillery of the working class than were cannons or field guns. *That* was dynamite. Proletarian artillery was ready to hand in the explosives and through the expertise to use them which could be found all over the coalfield.

At this time an unpopular mine manager's residence in Cwmllynfell in the Swansea Valley was indeed dynamited and General Macready, officer in charge of the troops billeted and deployed in the Rhondda, warned the Home Office that there were rumours of strikers manufacturing bombs 'by packing four or five explosive cartridges in tobacco boxes with a fuse attached' and advised jittery mine managers that 'live wires for the protection of colliery property was illegal'. As late as March 1911 the violence had not abated in mid-Rhondda as troops and police move through 'clouds of stones' and are 'pelted from steep side streets' or from the altitudes of coal tips by crowds in excess of 5,000 people. *This* people, that month, burned the Clydach Vale slaughterhouse of a wholesale butcher who was supplying the occupying army.

The stress needs to be on underlying cultural continuity as much as the immediacy of social fracture, because those involved in the disturbance would also be the electors, the voters, the supporters who would see the Labour Party, within a decade, as another means of organising opposition to the forces that oppressed them. When open disorder on such a scale breaks out, all manner of things may have failed, but the revelatory significance of protest on that scale should not be waylaid in the historical slipstream of teleological outcome. It, too, fuelled change. And would be seen to do so again via the fierce guerrilla conflicts of the 1926 lockout, in the defiance implicit in 1933 in the very maw of European despair as shown by Bevan's Workers' Freedom Groups and in the very rebuilding of the SWMF confronted by coal-owner aggression and the virus of company unionism.

A Labour Party coming to a coherent form after 1918, winning what would prove to be an irresistible Westminster majority from 1922 in Wales, was not immune from such storms. It stressed, however, and with increasing insistence, its own respectability and its responsibility. Its clothes, too, were often borrowed. Thus, the late Victorian habit of the Whit Walks – the nonconformist chapels en fête, on holiday and on foot – persisted into the interwar period but saw their processions and their parading purposes hijacked by the secular religion of Labour. In 1912 the annual conference of the ILP was actually held in Merthyr and, along with luminaries like Hardie and Sylvia Pankhurst, the proceedings spilled out onto the streets to be greeted, ritually, by the mayor (now Labour of course) and cheered on by crowds of well-wishers.

> Over 1,000 members of the ILP and trade unionists wearing red ties, red rosettes or badges assembled with a picturesque array of banners and bannerettes outside the ILP institute, and headed by a band, marched to the Tabernacle Church, Brecon Road, where a sermon was preached by the Revd. Rowland Jones on the 'Message of Jesus'.

The delegates who marched, miners, ironworkers, railwaymen, shop assistants, and suffragettes were all in a procession headed by a large banner inscribed with the words 'God Save the People'. Many of these same people would have read in *The Merthyr Pioneer* of January that year, 1912, that 'every member of the ILP' would need 'a smart suit' and that they could get one from the 500 cloth patterns held by J. Hughes Evans in The London Warehouse, Dowlais. On those pages the causes of Irish independence, Welsh spiritualism, the case for a General Strike and support for the Bolshevik revolution would jostle, and the slippage between one and the other was not always as clear-cut as later sectarian divides would seem to establish. In some individual cases the general impetus, to fall eventually on one side or other of a dividing line, can, however, be more abruptly discerned.

Take the case of the Merthyr grocer's boy and shop assistant who, aged sixteen in 1910, was winning a reputation inside Merthyr's boxing rings as a whirlwind puncher and within Merthyr's Church of Christ as a fiery evangelist. In *The Pioneer* in 1913 he could read articles on the anarchist thinker Kropotkin, postulating a complete alternative cultural life to that under capitalism, or peruse a debate as to whether Jesus was a revolutionary.

By 1915 the twenty-one-year-old, trained for missionary work at Birmingham, was the chair of an Easter Conference of the Church of Christ in South Wales just as he had acted previously as recording secretary of several Divisional Conferences. At the end of that same year he avowed that too many preachers were able to abandon too easily the 'Promise of Peace' for the 'God of Patriotism'. He would look elsewhere. Before the end of the Great War, this future president of the South Wales Miners' Federation was court-martialled for refusing to obey orders on military service and given six months' imprisonment. 'I live alone to destroy the (capitalist) system, the cause of so much sorrow and misery to my class,' he told the court. Two years later in September 1920, the Christian activist turned Rhondda socialist was reported in *The Pioneer*, in his capacity as the newly elected checkweighman of the Maerdy Lodge, as attacking all conventional outlooks. Arthur Lewis Horner now called for a class-conscious mentality *and* morality since, he argued, being 'in the Fight without Might' was a useless stance.

Horner's political trajectory was an extreme one, taking him outside the orbit of the people whose 'awakening ... to a true understanding of their interests' would prove, for him, to be only a fitful stirring. His allegiance to the Communist Party as his chosen political vehicle to the future proved to be of lesser significance than his embrace of trades unionism as the collective bedrock for any advance at all. Indeed, culturally, by being 'just one of us', only a hairsbreadth separated him, even beyond the Second World War and certainly in terms of that reforming Labour government, from his predecessor as president of the SWMF, Jim Griffiths, whose later avuncularity belied his own youthful socialist fervour as a self-proclaimed 'class warrior' in the Anthracite coalfield or from their other near contemporary, Aneurin Bevan, whose kick-over-the-traces rebelliousness was, even in the 1920s, much tempered by the possibilities available in practice. A learned process of structural control was a more vital component for the broad front of working-class political culture than any ideological thrashing about. And nowhere is this clearer than in the centrality of trades and labour councils.

Prior to 1914, albeit in a patchy and diverse manner, trades and labour councils were catalytic agencies in connecting up the local interests of working-class people in all manner of economic, social and cultural concerns with the nascent organisations, from the ILP to other and varied Labour Party associations, intent on achieving electoral success for unambiguously Labour candidates. The TLCs consisted of trades union delegates, and others from affiliated bodies, organised into a convened body meeting mostly monthly, serviced by a chair and secretary, and dedicated to giving direct voice to people still largely muted as to their electoral representation. They were, then, both lightning rods to express grievances as they arose and conduits for access to power through the ballot box. Their number and their influence grew exponentially during the 1914–18 war (the Rhondda had five TLCs before the war) as conscription, food rationing, rents, censorship and state infiltration of daily life impacted upon local areas. Nowhere was this more the case than in the central coalfield of South Wales, a strategic region for the wartime economy and an industrial tinderbox for strike action and general disaffection. Until the 1920s and the successful achievement of Labour political victories across South Wales at municipal and parliamentary level, the TLCs reflected the kaleidoscopic variety of what exactly the people-influenced labour movement held to as its core designation for electoral purpose and advance.

Lodge No.	Lodge Name	Average No. of Membersfor 1919.		
		Lodge Basis	District Basis	+ Increase – Decrease
1	Bodringallt	328	328	+ 62
2	Maindy	805	805	+ 263
3	Cilely	592	592	+ 68
4	Maerdy	1933	1933	+ 560
5	Fernhill	1322	1423	+ 214
6	Naval	2213	2213	+ 382
8	Tylorstown	3179	3179	+ 613
10	Coed Ely	1360	1360	+ 230
11	Caerlan	57	57	+ 14
13	Gelli Steam	48	48	+ 48
14	Parc and Dare	680	680	+ 3
15	Parc and Dare	1016	1016	+ 68
16	Gelli House	362	362	+ 97
17	National	1017	1017	+ 186
19	Tynybedw	513	513	+ 91
20	Eastern	516	653	+ 53
21	Mid-Rhondda	275	275	+ 60
22	Penrhiwceiber	644	910	– 61
23	Abergorky	1589	1589	+ 483
24	Ferndale	2742	2475	+ 586
25	Llwynypia	2975	2845	+ 1005
26	Albion	1207	1352	+ 155
27	Ynysfaio	1115	1115	+ 238
28	Standard	1051	1051	+ 195
29	Blaenclydach	393	429	+ 42
30	Cymmer	1726	1999	+ 470
31	Lewis Merthyr	1427	1651	+ 306
32	Cambrian	3500	3500	+ 704
33	Tydraw	644	644	+ 98
34	Lady Lewis	946	967	+ 148
35	Hendrewen	184	219	+ 40
36	Bute Merthyr	689	689	+ 85
37	Nantdyrus	145	145	+ 52
38	Tylcha Fach	289	289	+ 40
	Totals	37,482	39,321	+ 7659
				– 61
			Nett Increase	7598

The minute books of the Treherbert Trades and Labour Council for 1917 to 1925 survive, along with correspondence from 1920 to 1923, to let us see beneath the surface narrative of candidates, elections, and statistics, so as to feel the pulse of what was once a living condition for the politics of community-led activism. Close to the ground and empowered by the local weight of the membership of the SWMF. This TLC, typical of many such, was a veritable and credible Rhondda Soviet.

The Treherbert TLC, established in 1907, had, among its affiliates, the Co-operative Wholesale Society, the Women's Co-operative Guild, the Class Teachers Association, and delegates from the Shopworkers' Union and railway unions, whilst crucially the local miners' lodges in 1919 mustered over 6,000 members among the two Rhondda valleys' cohort of 40,000 miners. This was an army in waiting. At a meeting of the lecture committee of the TLC in October 1917, the secretary reported 'that permission had been given for the holding of the Tom Mann lecture at Libanus Chapel' for the end of the month and resolved that 'the subject of the lecture be industrial organisation: the need of the hour'. By 1919, with the war ended and the post-war settlement within the coal industry erupting with the nationwide strikes of 1919 (with both 1921 and 1926 to follow), the TLC set about considering the general policy it had followed hitherto. On 10 May 1919 the council cogitated at length:

> the motion 'to consider the policy of the trades council' was discussed. This went on for some time, becoming rather heated, as some delegates were very much in favour of leaving political work entirely alone, and making use of industrial means for all purposes, whilst others were in favour of using political means.

That discussion exhausted itself with a late closure so that a special meeting was convened for 'the following Monday' where it was resolved to put back to the lodges a resolution that 'branches keep to the original procedures'. The lodges, in turn, mandated the TLC to carry on its existing policy of both direct industrial action and political empowerment through the council and parliament. This was a balancing act, forerunner of many to come across the coalfield in the interwar years, at which they proved adept as circumstances merited: in 1919 the TLC ordered 100 copies of the Constitution of Soviet Russia at the request of the Russian Information Bureau and strongly supported the Hands Off Russia Committee, but, in 1922, firmly rebuffed the request of the local Communist Party branch to affiliate (individual Labour Party membership was not the norm until the 1920s so individual entry into that party required an attachment to an affiliated body). Nonetheless, as the minutes record, the Treherbert TLC was acutely conscious of its unique umbrella status as a body able to bring offshoots and branches of the (still) protean labour movement together and, thus, in 1922, also decided, in the interests of avoiding clashes of their own proselytising meetings with such as those of the ILP, that they should organise a 'series of social evenings under their auspices' to foster 'a closer intimacy and social relationship between the different Labour sections of the ward'.

What was paramount, as their deliberations reveal, was the exercise of the power derived directly from an amalgam of local trades unions within the TLC to act on behalf of all constituent parts of a wider progressive labour coalition. This action was astonishingly far-reaching. A report to the TLC from Councillor Lloyd, serving on the Rhondda Urban District's Education Committee, sounds like a clash between clericalism and secularism in the French Third Republic. Only there was no clash more a roll over; when three teachers in the local Ynyswen schools had been found, on inspection, to be 'giving scriptural lessons in the time allotted for secular instruction' they were reprimanded and duly apologised whilst another teacher was supported by a delegation of the TLC to the RUDC when threatened with transference from the school for 'doing other than school work'. W. G. Cove remained in place, and went on to become the Labour MP for Aberavon (1929–59), succeeding the first heroic then toxic Ramsay MacDonald.

This panoramic embrace of the interaction of their material strength with a cultural and social purposefulness clearly derives from the intimate connections they intuited between what was to be endured in the present and what was to be aspired for in an imminent future over which they sought control. During the cusp years from 1917 to 1919, the interventions made through resolution and follow-up were as bold as they were persistent. The consistency comes because the TLC was cutting all its patterns from the same cloth: that condition of life of the people out of which their own existence had come.

The minutes for these years focus, cheek by jowl, on the mundane and the contingent alongside the idealistic and the foundational: the war aims of the Labour Party, better street lighting, defence of free speech and support of the No Conscription Fellowship, the price of foodstuffs and the establishment of Food Vigilance Committees in each ward, the provision of public urinals and especially for women, refuse collection in the back streets and the shortage of school books in some schools, agitation against rent increases for tenants and more liaison with the Rhondda Labour Party (founded in 1911), the creation of a women's Labour group and the call for mass meetings to be held on Sundays, links to the national Labour Party and an educational programme of visiting lecturers. The latter was extremely ambitious, listing most of the prominent political and union leaders of the day from Bernard Shaw and Dick Wallhead of the ILP to miners' leader Robert Smillie and Transport Workers' Union secretary, Robert Williams. Ambition paid off when the latter two did come, along with a score of more local miners' agents and ILP activists.

Perhaps, most tellingly, is the tone of indignation and implicit command which the TLC could adopt when its ends were thwarted by the rival means of others. When the police were deemed to have exceeded their authority in the mining disputes of 1919 and 1920, the TLC's secretary wrote to the Chief Constable of Glamorgan to request the removal of a police sergeant and a constable so as to preserve 'peace in the district', citing as the reason their 'officiousness in recent disputes'. To Frank Hodges, the general secretary of the Miners' Federation of Great Britain, they addressed in October 1920 a letter asking for action to be taken against posters being put up at the

Pontypridd General Post Office which bore the message from Lady Milner calling on 'the miners' wives to strike against performing their domestic duties in the miners' homes'. They called this 'private propaganda against the miners [in] a public building' to be an 'unwarranted attack' and 'a serious menace to the public peace of the district.' Solidarity, whether on the streets or within the home, trumped all.

Most startling, perhaps, was the response to any affront to the assumption of hegemonic, and indeed secular, control. On July 26, 1920, the TLC's secretary of the propaganda committee wrote to the manager of the Gaiety Cinema in Treherbert enclosing a list of proposed speakers for alternate Sundays from September to April. The cinema manager had previously demurred at the TLC's presumption of a fixed agreement, so the letter continued:

> I would remind you that you have already gone into this matter with myself and our treasurer two winters ago in your own office, and I quite fail to see the need at this juncture for all the fuss over the renting of your hall to the body of organised workers I represent.
>
> During the two winters we have used your premises no complaint has been made by anyone representing your interests nor have the police so much as hinted at the need for interference.
>
> I would further remind you that it was due to the activities of the Rhondda Trades Councils that the embargo on the Sunday opening of halls was finally removed by the UDC and that since the embargo has been removed the chapels have been the first to take advantage of the increased liberty to the detriment of those bodies who have long worked for this end.
>
> Organised labour was very angry last winter because of the poor facilities afforded for public lectures and they are likely to be still angrier this coming winter if the policy of obstruction is gone on with.
>
> It must be clearly understood that the accompanying list of speakers can only be a provisional list but it is *the* list passed by the Treherbert Trades Council and the local lodges of the SWMF.

The bravado and self-confidence behind these demands, replicated across the coalfield as Labour assumed electoral control at all levels from 1922, was quickly undercut in practice by first sporadic and then the long-term unemployment in the coal industry which depleted membership and funds. Nonetheless, even in the face of such reversal of pre-war boom times, the TLC's response was pragmatic and directed by the populist sensibilities of the ambient community, for which, after all, 'organised labour' was organised. So, for the summer of 1922, the TLC worked to arrange a fete and gala carnival to be held on an annual basis on Labour Day: the newly set up carnival committee were deputed to organise boxing booths and field sports; the variety committee were to busy themselves with all kinds of musical entertainment and dancing; the local Women's Co-operative Guild and Women's Labour Party were to be asked to provide refreshments for the attendees. Policy and propaganda required, as always, participation and popularity if what was to arise was indeed coming out of the people, and crucially to be in place as a bulwark for togetherness. In essence, the loose confederacy of 'Labour' associations from 1911 on within Rhondda knitted together more formally from 1923 with the restructuring of Rhondda Borough Labour Party (and again after 1927 to formally exclude the incursions of the Communist Party) and, more financially and organisationally watertight, TLC functions morphed into the politics of Ward Labour Parties under an overall leadership. They had, in the interim, served a crucial, umbrella purpose.

For all this first 'Labour' generation, and those near to it, we need to unpick another revisionist thread simplification to take our understanding of contemporary complexity further. And that means restoring the cataclysmic effect of the defeat of the 1926 General Strike and Lockout to their lives and in their thinking. Not a binary matter at all. It did not mean either and simplistically a Bevanite abandonment of extra-parliamentary action as useless, for he did not, in the actuality, so distinguish that aspect of political activity before or after 1926; and it did not mean a Hornerite dismissal of reformist politics for it was Horner who was indicted by his own party comrades for dismissing the political adventurism of all-out militancy in the early 1930s and

Horner who built up the 'reformist' NUM of 1944 from the ruins of 1926; and industrial defeats did not mean the sidelining of the Fed as the paramount political force in Welsh life for, after 1926, out of its ranks of officials and leaders came in 1929 the Ebbw Vale MP Nye Bevan, in 1931 the Pontypridd MP D. L. Davies, in 1933 the Rhondda East MP W. H. Mainwaring, in 1934 the Merthyr Tydfil MP S. O. Davies, in 1935 the Pontypool MP Arthur Jenkins, in 1936 the Llanelli MP Jim Griffiths, and in 1939 the Caerphilly MP Ness Edwards. What actually happened after 1926, in a number of ways, was a displacement of the variety of ideas and of avenues for which, in an emblematic sense, that forcing house of ideas and of careers, the Central Labour College had stood since 1912. It was the place, said one of its former students, Ness Edwards, in 1965, 'whence came the ideas that dominated South Wales in the first quarter of this century' and it was, he added, in its closure in 1929, through lack of trades union financial resource 'a victim of the General Strike'.

1926, then, had political fall-out and it ushered in further economic misery as the defence of living standards in the coalfield by collective institutions was overrun for almost a decade. But it was, too, representative or emblematic of a cultural space in which the self-definition of people had become wider and deeper than that contained politically by the Labour Party and its outer reaches. It was, at this moment, and in its subsequent unfolding, the culmination of values lived and expressed not because of any ideas generated or any models set but because, at this point among an industrial and urban working class across Britain there was a firm grasp of the conceptual differences between egalitarianism and liberty, between commonality and individuality, between being 'one of us' and 'one of them'. The solidarity and the sacrifice shown by millions of working-class people in the summer of 1926, most not directly affected by the coal dispute which had led to the nine days' General Strike and lumbered on into the six-months' miners' lockout, was not only unprecedented; it revealed the linkage of daily lives to a social morality that preceded and post-dated mere politics. It remains crucial to our understanding of the politics not of politicians but of people.

The most profound work, of thinking and of practice, done on this vexed question of culture and society and of how one is shaped or influenced by the other – but which by which? – is, of course, that of Raymond Williams. He tried, over many frustrating decades, to make the broader labour movement understand this connection. And not least because the episode of the General Strike was quite central to the whole of his thinking and writing. Towards the end of his pioneering critical study of 1958, *Culture and Society* – in which he had traced the ideas of leading thinkers and writers around the changing concepts of 'industry', 'democracy' and 'culture', terms which had come into British life since the late eighteenth century – he had concluded his study by insisting that the working-class contribution to all this was, by the 1950s, both creative and necessarily collective, social in its achievements more than individuated.

> Class feeling is a mode, rather than a uniform possession of all the individuals who might, objectively, be assigned to that class. When we speak, for instance, of a working-class idea, we do not mean that all working people possess it, or even approve of it. We mean rather that this is the essential idea embodied in the organisations and institutions which that class creates... 'working-class culture'... is not (then) proletarian art, or council homes, or a particular use of language; it is rather the basic collective idea, and the institutions, manners, habits of thought, and intentions which proceed from that.

And in the novel that he was writing through those immediate post-war years – eventually to be published as *Border Country* in 1960 – Raymond Williams graphically, in terms of real, diffused human relationships, depicted the uneasy struggle, from that cultural base, to a kind of consciousness, one that vivifies collective institutions rather than the other way around. Epiphanies flood the future with light; institution worship is invariably backlit.

What Williams brilliantly and movingly shows in his wonderful novel is how social experience, living and fluid and never to-be-incorporated, is of more value than any idea or institution because it is, in its human, passing shape, the purpose behind ideas and institutions, whose own proper function is to fulfil that life. In *Border Country* there is a crucial dialogue between the railway signalmen and friends, Morgan Rosser and Harry Price, as to whether the General Strike is for power and the TUC or, primarily, in support of the miners. Beyond these two men, any such abstraction from immediate work and surroundings remains problematic for the others involved. The issue goes to the heart of any common political endeavour and to that experience of independent working-class politics spreading, in concentric circles across Wales but inevitably deepest in the mass concentration of people in the coalfield. Here, the case of Abergavenny and its offshoots of industrial work in outlying rural areas, such as Williams' Pandy, becomes a paradigm both of that history and of the atomised Welsh working class so plainly visible after the last hurrahs of 1972 and 1974.

Consider that railway workforce in Monmouthshire in the 1920s, their coherence and their fragmented attachment to each other and to a culture held, against all odds, in common. Each railway station had its stationmaster, its booking clerks and porters. There were locomotive men, the drivers and firemen to fuel the boilers. In the locomotive depots there were storemen and shedsmen for the turntables. There were sandmen to dig up the sand from a mountainous pile in one of the sheds to fill the locomotives' sand boxes. The trains had to be coaled by men who shovelled up to thirty tons a day and watered from the great water towers with their swinging funnels. There were workers in the wheel shops and paint shops. There were fire droppers whose hot and gritty work was to rake the fires of the engines and clean out the heavy ash-pans. Behind the locomotive sheds were railway barracks for crews on an overnight stop. This workforce was a small, interdependent army. It could not congregate in one place as other industrial workers could – they all assembled for an annual dinner at the Swan Hotel on Good Fridays, the only time all were on holiday together, and when a football match would be played – but it had a clear notion of itself as a distinct community of interest.

This was the culture, with benefit and sickness societies and sports teams, to which Raymond's father, Harry Williams, belonged. The Labour Party and most other progressive movements in interwar Abergavenny depended upon the organisation and the support of these people. This was what allowed his son to say forty years on: 'as an adolescent I remember looking at these men ... with a certain resentment – they seemed so absolutely confident. I have never seen such self-confident people since.' Undoubtedly, this was the source of that supply of sustained and calm decisiveness with which railwaymen accepted their involvement in the 1926 General Strike. The unity of moral certainty and collective action, self-justifying and self-sustaining even in defeat, was what made that episode such a crucial one for Raymond. He was only five at the time but its implications rolled on into his youth, and its significance, not as event but as epiphany, was one of which he never lost sight. For Abergavenny railwaymen the future would be one of reduced employment in the Depression years of the 1930s as the coal trains rattled through much less often and then redundancies and eventually disappearance as a rail hub in the wake of economic rationalisation, rail closures and regional mergers from the 1960s. In 1926, however, the links with the miners as the principal coservitors of the capitalist world in Britain were very much in place and ready to be memorably expressed in an industrial fashion that was, in essence, a political challenge. To come out in sympathy with the miners in their rumbling dispute of 1925 and 1926 was to act outside the normal or accepted boundaries of industrial relations. It was, as the dialectic in *Border Country* between signalmen Harry Price and Morgan Rosser resolves, an inescapable confrontation with the state.

A popular guidebook to interwar South Wales introduced Abergavenny to its visitors as 'a clean, well-lighted, healthy, flourishing market town, charmingly situated, well-drained, and having a good supply of pure water ... one of the best starting-points for excursions into the Black Mountains.' In the interests of truthful observation, it could not also avoid the wrinkle-nosed observation that the 'prosperity of the town now largely depends upon the collieries and steel works in its vicinity' but quickly added, 'fortunately, the sites of these are concealed by the mountains.' In 1926 to be out of sight was not to be out of mind. For the nine days of the General Strike, supported by the NUR and called by the TUC from 3 May to 12 May, the solidarity shown all over Britain for the miners' cause by industrial workers was astonishing. Abergavenny was no exception. Councils of Action had been established in the South Wales Valleys to control or prevent the movement of essential supplies, from coal to foodstuffs, and to act as authorising body for those wishing or needing to travel. Those going to Abergavenny market to trade or shop were required to have permits issued. In the town, NUR officials scrutinised such permits and questioned those without them to the indignant horror of the town's elite who 'thought that such a thing could not happen outside Russia'.

The feeling that there were alternative sources of power available other than that of those who customarily ran things was exhilarating and made all the more so by the quiet discipline with which strikers maintained their loyalty. The NUR had two branches in the area: Abergavenny No. 1 and Abergavenny No. 2 which covered the Pandy men. The latter were relatively isolated in a small country station with, at first glance, no obvious leadership and their livelihoods put at risk by this tangential action. There were rallies and demonstrations in Abergavenny – even the Borough Band played *The Red Flag* as the NUR and Trades Council celebrated May Day in the castle grounds – and speeches were made under lofted banners. Still, the decisions on the ground, in spots like Pandy, were the hard ones to take. All around them, the government's supporters, long gathered together by local gentry in the name of the Organisation for Maintenance of Supplies (OMS), were quick and ready to volunteer to break the strike. The town clerk acted as emergency food officer and the mayor as assistant road officer to maintain transport links. When it was finished, and the agony of the miners' lockout until the winter just begun, the mayor even thanked 'all sections of the community, strikers, and non-strikers and volunteers for the conduct they exhibited during that time'. Yet this was to mistake the unflinching determination quietly undertaken for quiescence. In *Border Country* the consciousness of the meaning of their action becomes, in defeat, a more vital component of their lives than the sporadic act of rebellion itself.

What had unfolded in Pandy before the child could have any real knowledge of it provided him, as he later absorbed it, with the material that allowed him to show a working-class world, albeit small scale and literally on the fringe, as self-acting and self-aware. He took a long time to write *Border Country* because he had to discover a form which would let him present his parents' lives whole, and from inside their perspective, whilst connecting their lived experience to his own, necessarily uncoupled, existence. The General Strike was the historical catalyst for the discovery of that form. He came to realise that right at the start of his life he had been among people who were caught up in the very epicentre of the triumph *and* the problematic of the twentieth-century working class in Britain.

Fifty years later he told an assembled audience of coal miners, trade unionists and labour historians, in Pontypridd at the heart of the South Wales coalfield, how acknowledgement of *their* centrality to the struggle, then and in the present, should not hide the significance of less heralded moments, since in late-twentieth-century Britain the diffuse, the fragmented, the socially uncertain, the economically diverse and the culturally ambivalent was more and more the norm. The problem of human control over human destiny had also been raised and answered in Pandy in 1926:

> I came down this morning from a village above Abergavenny: travelling the quite short distance to this centre of the mining valleys, and travelling also, in memories, the connections and the distance between one kind of country and another. In 1926, in that village, my father was one of three signalmen in the old Great Western Railway box. He was an ardent participant in the General Strike; so was one of the other two signalmen, and the stationmaster, who was subsequently victimised; so too were the plate layers. One of the signalmen was not. In the discussions and arguments that took place during those critical days, among a small group of men in a very specific social situation, some of the most important themes of the general social significance of 1926 became apparent. They were often recalled, in later years. I heard them throughout my childhood, and I went through them

> again, consciously, with my father, when I was preparing to write the General Strike sequence in *Border Country*...
>
> Consider – that specific situation. These men at that country station were industrial workers, trade unionists, in a small group within a primarily rural and agricultural economy. All of them, like my father, still had close connections with that agricultural life. One of them ran a smallholding in addition to his job on the railway. Most of them had relatives in farm work. All of them had gardens and pigs or bees or ponies which were an important part of their work and income. At the same time, by the very fact of the railway, with the trains passing through from the cities, from the factories, from the ports, from the collieries, and by the fact of the telephone and the telegraph, which was especially important for the signalmen, who through it had a community with other signalmen over a wide social network, talking beyond their work with men they might never actually meet but whom they knew very well through voice and opinion and story, they were part of a modern, industrial working class. It is a special case, of course, but a significant one in the context of the General Strike, which is still too loosely assimilated to strikes of a different kind, with which it, of course, has connections but from which in crucial ways, it has extensions – extensions that raise quite central problems of consciousness... What remains of decisive importance from the events of 1926 is the achievement of that consciousness (where) real men, under difficulty have to struggle to make their own effective choices.

To that, he concluded, had to be added the perspective of complexity or difficulty in a differential, even fragmented society which 'was then and is now, increasingly, our world'. He found first that the perspective of acquired knowledge, of school learning, so ardently desired for him by his father was not one designed to let him see this clearly. At least, not from the start and, thereafter, he would always remain sceptical about the education of any society which could exclude the culture of such as his father.

I am close now to the core of what I want to say: that the common values by which many working-class people lived through most of the last century were the bedrock of Labour's advance and cannot be captured by the forms of conventional explanations of narrative history or by an attenuated political analysis. At the end of Raymond Williams' novel, with the death of Harry Price, the meaning of his existence is not to be paraphrased by eulogy or obituary, it was simply the way he lived his life. Yet this is never to say that living was reflex, automatic, without thoughtful direction. It is, in a different context, what Williams stressed when, specifically accepting a 'parliamentary perspective' as a route, he added that, 'as a matter of practice' there was no point to it, for a socialist purpose, if there was not also 'the most active elements of community politics, local campaigning, specialised interest campaigning' behind it.

From the perspective of the 1945 Labour triumph, and all the internal cultural changes of attitude and personnel within the Labour Party which that entailed and sustained to our own day, a lived and convoluted history was often replaced by a flatter and more circumspect memory. Bevan's rage against institutional trade union support for the leadership of Gaitskell was easy to portray as thwarted, egotistical ambition. But was it just that, in the light of the history Bevan and those he represented in himself, had lived? He could not, in 1955, win against Gaitskell and those, as he wrote to his agent in Ebbw Vale, 'irresponsible groups of trade union bureaucrats ... (who were deciding) ... the policy of the Labour Party' but he would stand, he said, 'because I cannot possibly allow it to be thought that Gaitskell, who's a product of the public school ... is the natural representative of the industrial workers of Great Britain.'

Bevan's iconic significance is incomprehensible without according his words their full connection to the matter in which he saw himself, and was seen as, representative. 'A representative person', he wrote,

> is one who will act in a given situation in much the same way as those he represents would act in the same situation. In short, he must be of their kind [and speak] with the authentic accents of those who elected him. That does not mean he need be provincial. It does mean he should share their values ... be in touch with their realities.

Not, of course, in any mechanistic fashion or through any literal convention of dress or speech but in the shared conviction that the conditions of life of human beings can not only be conditionally improved by municipal lighting, clean water, public parks and decent housing but that such conditions were only the by-product of the possibility for a fully human culture which communities such as the one that nurtured Bevan in Victorian Tredegar valued for itself. These were across late Victorian Wales, but intensified in the Valleys, industrial communities that had rated literacy and literary achievement in both the Welsh language and later in Bevan's English version of that language, as a bedrock of social relations. This is what Ieuan Gwynedd Jones so memorably wrote about such people:

> The eisteddfod, the chapel, the friendly society, the pub were genuinely the creations of a working-class culture providing for itself by itself and with a breathtaking confidence taking over the cultural-literacy role of an aristocracy ... communities such as were these, existing sometimes on the very edges of survival, threatened with the degradation of excessive labour, plagued by endemic sickness, knowing poverty ... need above all self-confidence. Community for them is not some kind of product of conditions – it is the condition of existence.

So, when we remember those people, out of whom Labour also came, let us reject forever the latter-day whine that the curse of Wales has always been a lack of confidence. That is to besmirch the memory of a people who struggled, in hope, against the primary human enemies of exploitation and degradation, with such shining confidence. Bevan's sense of being a people's aristocrat had no immaculate conception. It was the individual flight of a socially given imagination, one grounded and soaring all at the same time with a common impulse. He said that the 'language of priorities is the religion of socialism' not in order to fetishise the practice of prioritising but to hurry on the widening of choice itself.

Bevan's generation had had to choose between any number of political means within a decade or so. The ILP had been founded in 1893, the Labour Representation Committee – forerunner of the Party proper – in 1900, the Communist Party of Great Britain in 1920, the South Wales Miners Federation itself, only in 1898 when Bevan was one year old. It was not so indelibly written in tablets of stone that the way to proceed was so obvious. All of them – the older Noah Ablett, or Arthur Cook, the younger Horner and Bevan – were caught up in the syndicalist fever that tinged parts of their industrial unionism before 1914 and all of them refused, one way or the other, though not on religious or pacifist grounds, to participate in the Great War. They followed, subsequently, diverse political paths. Bevan, parliamentarian and rebel, prophet and cabinet minister, internalised that split *in* his own personality and through his political practice. It is why his condemnatory phrase 'desiccated calculating machine' against Gaitskellism is a moral indictment, not a personal jibe.

After Bevan, that great, angry cry of denunciation he made sound out from within a moral and class consciousness has been replaced by a regretful silence punctuated only by the occasional bleats of complaint. Within a generation of 1960, the resilience of social experience for political action, in the sense of those prior and forming cultural shapes, was substituted, so far as parliamentary Labour was concerned, by the inert configuration of a known, taken-for-granted political landscape in which only the painted scenery was moveable. The people had been moved out: to be, at best, the audience.

No one caught this better, in story after story, than Alun Richards just a decade after Bevan's death.

> How did Barton see it? Like many South Walians who leave home in their teens and never really return except on holiday, Barton retained a warm, myth-inspired image of a tumultuous valley community whose pre-war qualities of shoulder-to-shoulder empathy caused him to think of it with a nostalgic glow as a special world-defeating place. It was true that it had once been unique. Its name was synonymous with lack of deference to privilege. It was the birthplace of working-class folk heroes, and the ghosts of an ancient culture still hovered about it (and) Barton preferred the myth to the (present) reality.

Nothing was more shoulder to shoulder in empathy than the gargantuan demonstrations against the administration of the dole in January and February 1935. Hundreds of thousands marched in an imagistic representation of the crowded valleys which now – we can see from the awestruck thirties novels of Lewis Jones and Gwyn Thomas – even overwhelmed contemporary observers. I say 'now' because the other cultural reality was that that people's protest had been expunged from any mainstream history just thirty years later and was only found again for use in the 1970s. By which time Labour history was more vibrant in Welsh life than Labour politics from which energies and personalities had been drained. There are clues all around as to why this had come about, not least that the Labour Party, and its ancillary branches, had become like the chapels, like the rugby clubs, like that myriad of voluntary cultural organisations that had made up a collective culture, an old, maybe achieved, thing. After 1985 it was, arguably, the last surviving relic. It was, said Merthyr's MP Ted Rowlands around this time, 'a shambles'. Many predicted its death along with that of the society which, in Wales, had spawned it. That that fate, at least, did not overtake Labour is, and it is no accident that it should be so, largely down to Neil Kinnock who, so clearly and maybe so damagingly 'just like one of us', managed in Duncan Tanner's perceptive words an 'indirect contribution to rebuilding the party in Wales ... rational, practical, strongly Welsh in line and sentiment ... (that) has scarcely even been noted'. Kinnock's popularity with people in Wales was strong: perhaps even stronger than with a sizeable proportion of his own party in Wales. Yet the underlying identification with Labour, as a deep cultural formation, has frayed, further electoral successes notwithstanding.

It does not require much thought to conclude that this was because of a combination of ongoing sociological and demographic change allied to a residual sense that New Labour, in Wales anyway, could be just another supermarket brand not a must-have loyalty purchase.

It makes no long-term sense, however, even for self-designated Welsh Labour, to embrace the pubescent love-cult for Owain Glyndwr as if he was a revered Glamorgan County Councillor, now ready for embalming in the Labour Pantheon of Heroes. Bad history makes poor politics. It is understandable that Labour should, with the triumphs of 1945, of 1966 and 1997 behind it, seek to be pan-Wales in message and intent but it makes no sense, at this junction in its own history, to prefer the geographical sound bite of Wales over the electoral interests of its own Welsh supporters where they are most gathered together. As historians, such as Chris Williams in *Democratic Rhondda* (1996) and Daryl Leeworthy in *Labour Country* (2018), have now amply demonstrated, Labour has no reason to be ashamed of its overall administrative performance at any governmental level in Wales, whereas consensus politics – whatever that weak-kneed phrase actually means – attracts professionals more than partisans. The electoral system adopted for Wales has made coalition politics almost inevitable as Labour changes its Lib Dem partner for a Plaid quickstep in a slow slow steady-as-she-goes managerial dance that has not convinced as conviction politics designed for people not places (aka Wales holistically, not the Welsh particularly).

From the perspective of the twenty-first century, Labour would do well, then, to look further back than the 1990s, with all of its shaky constitutional side-stepping, to consider how once it would have made it a priority to tap into the people for fuller democratic participation in government instead of arranging its own internal electoral engineering. It was in the early 1980s that Neil Kinnock, fresh from 1979 and all that, argued that the crisis in politics in Wales was not the lack of devolution but the loss of democratic contact with the people. We know Neil Kinnock, at least publicly, changed his mind over devolution; I suspect he might still harbour misgivings about the deeper crisis that remains an ongoing one almost three decades after 1997.

And so he should, as any cursory stroll through any of the once-great urban citadels of Welsh life would reveal. You cannot escape the gap-toothed shopping streets from Aberaman to Tonypandy, or the neglect of precincts and car parks and public spaces, or the menacing neglect of the human potential sloshing around estates from Wrexham or Pontypridd or Maesteg. I sense no unrelenting obeisance to Labour's past here yet it *is* here, in Llanelli and in the Rhondda and even in the Vale of Glamorgan that Labour's future will eventually turn. Some of the poverty, dirt-infested houses, furniture left to rot in the streets, the taste of deprivation generally, is so primary that it remains a living disgrace, and where it affects, as it does, generations of children, should be there to be dealt with at the head of every policy queue. Yet one-off policies without permeating values are like soufflés without aeration.

Of course Labour will require bread-and-butter policies and of course it will need to be inclusive of all, especially the most materially and spiritually deprived, but it will not hold on let alone take us forward if it does not help generate a sense of aspiration through cultural achievement; if it does not prioritise some things, even against other places and other people, in terms of embracing the poetry of its own historic past and the prose of its present hinterland. What is still required is the contemporary equivalent of what a labour movement once did automatically in Institute Libraries and Welfare Halls – enable minds to grow fat on books, ideas, films, paintings – not as a prescriptive culture but as a descriptive, open-ended design for life. However this is brought up to date in a digital age, the availability of technology without the backfill of a content resource which, in part anyway, locates us, with pride, where we are so that we can soar away, and come back, would be a vapid consumerism bereft of the creative energies that truly makes culture popular. The Kulturkampf that has been waged in Wales has been a reverberating echo because the loudest shouting has all been done in a language the ultimately necessary listeners – or why else speak at all? – do not understand. Or, as many hope and argue, do not *yet* understand. If this linguistic emphasis is the agreed and accepted cultural priority of a whole society, then there can be no argument with the media and educational structures we have wilfully developed. 'If' is a word with implications. Those implications are still being played out.

What is now required is an intellectual agenda within politics as in the past – long term and educational – to inspire the people Labour has been more concerned recently to administer than to represent and lead; what is required, and may now happen, is the skipping of a political generation; what is inevitable is putting an end to the fudged message of where power lies in and for Wales; what follows is an acceptance of how culture in Wales is being redefined and a decision as to which parts, and how, Labour would choose as its own for it can neither be all-embracing or utterly separated in some fastidious manner from those aspects of the culture it might not actually like.

What kind of a Labour movement is it which can emblazon economic and social regeneration on its every banner and yet, still, not insist that the art, in all its forms, which speaks of the culture, out indeed of the very people which it represents, and the culture which created Labour, is not in every library, in every school, on the walls of galleries, on the air in our own accents, on the screen, large and small, on our lips, in our minds, coming through the feelings and our imaginations so that substance can be given to facts and vitality to organisations? When will Labour fully wake up to the cultural struggle it must win to survive as its true self? Certainly, that process, organised from the same roots whence Bevan sprang, will not be about celebrating the past because the culture of *that* Welsh people has changed irredeemably. But nor would a creative political culture for the future willingly relinquish that detailed history which gives contemporary reference to the abstract ideas which could ignite the minds of this different, emerging Welsh people. Certainly in this current phase of identity politics which is upon us, *which* identity is reorganised, *which* identity is privileged, *which* identity is falsified and *which* identity is verified will be what forms the culture that creates the rest of twenty-first-century Welsh politics and life.

FIXING THINGS

The reporter had arrived late. He stood at the back of the rectangular expanse of the lounge bar of the workmen's club. It was a packed meeting. Wood-grained Formica-topped tables were aligned like rows of dominoes across the burgundy red wall-to-wall carpet. The party's ward members sat upright and intent on the plush-bottomed seats of chairs whose tubular steel legs sank into the pile of the carpet. The reporter was impressed at the turnout of maybe 200 or more paid-up party members from up and down the valley, and, he noted, there was more than a smattering of younger faces, women as well as men and way beyond the expectation of the membership of what was now generally perceived as a geriatric and moribund organisation, one slowly rotting away in a mulch of complacency and corruption. The reporter took out his notepad and scrawled a line or two to use in his piece.

On the raised stage at the far end of the lounge, the party's district secretary was rounding things off. Conclusion had been concluded he was saying in a voice that solicited attention and brooked no counter remarks from anyone on the platform. He looked in particular at two men in their late middle age, younger than him then, who sat on his right with peeved expressions. On his left was a woman in her late thirties who glanced at him in a puzzled and somehow apprehensive manner, almost as if she wanted to intervene. If she dared to do so, that is. Instead she sat still, her hands fiddling with some order papers she kept rearranging on the lap of her floral patterned, specially bought dress.

The district secretary made a show of clearing his

throat. He had no need of the microphone. His voice would carry across the lounge, over the heads of all the ward members to reach into the furthest corners and right to the back of the room as if he was speaking directly to and for the benefit of the reporter whose presence he had immediately clocked. After the preamble he came, quietly triumphant, to the point and purpose of the meeting.

'As I said then, comrades, and by a clear overall majority and with twelve ward votes to ten, our new chairperson - note the up-to-date jargon, friends! - will be Cynthia Evans of the Town Ward, to serve for the forthcoming year. Congrats Cyn. You are our first-ever woman in the chair, so double congrats I suppose are in order, as is, comrades and friends, a clap all round. Applause, please.'

There was a brief but intense bout of handclapping and then the chairs were shuffled to the side as the members heard the shutters go up at the hitherto closed bar. The district secretary stepped down off the platform and weaved a way through the thirsty crowd of members making for the bar. He skirted around the tables and chairs, avoiding any chit-chat, to reach the reporter before he had a chance to leave.

'Glad you could make it, boy,' he said and simultaneously held the reporter tight by his elbow so that he could be half-swivelled around to survey the scene.

'See?' he said. 'See, boy. Told you over the phone, didn't I? What did I say you'd see? Well, here it is. A party refreshed. A party in progress. Young. Youthful. And a woman newly elected as chair, mind you. So, let's have less of your media slurs. Less of your press propaganda decrying a century of our control. Because, and you can feel it can't you, this, boy, is the people's democracy in action. Here, on our patch.'

Behind the district secretary, Cynthia Evans was trying to attract his attention. She muttered his name, Glan, quietly, but insistently. Glan. Glan. 'In a sec, Cyn,' he said. 'In a sec.' The reporter smiled at her over the shoulder of the district secretary, who, annoyed that his own buttonholing had had to pause, turned to Cynthia Evans and said, 'Not now, Cyn, not now. Business to do and this young man, former pupil of mine, is Royston Williams. See,' and turned away again. Only she was not put off and started over to say, 'Glan, Glan' until the latter, visibly aggrieved now, snapped out a 'What is it then, Cyn? What do you want?'

Cynthia Evans said that she was puzzled and wanted to be sure about the numbers which, surely, could not be right could they, that they didn't, so to speak, add up. People were bound to ask. There were already some murmurings. Not least from her defeated and disgruntled rivals. So, she said, sotto voce, in the near presence of Royston Williams, 'I was told we only had ten wards in the bag and that both the Central and Riverside wards, and with their heavy membership rolls, were going elsewhere. And they more or less told me that directly, just an hour ago, so, Glan, has there been a miscount, an error to include those two particular wards on our side?'

The district secretary, with the press unusually for once at his beck and call, lost patience with his new chairperson. 'Oh, that,' he said, 'don't worry about any of that, Cyn. I fixed those two before the meeting began.' And, with that, he turned back to the reporter to underline the good news that was, wasn't it, plain to see.

BORDERLINES

ENCOUNTERING ERIC

Towards the close of the sixties, the paths of a pre-war intellectual Left and a post-Suez New Left occasionally crossed thanks to the common and swelling interest evoked by the practice of history from below. And none more so to astonishing effect than the Ruskin College History Workshops which were orchestrated over autumnal weekends at Oxford by the saturnine genius of Raphael Samuel. Hundreds would be in attendance for the main lectures as the pinnacles of the associated and intense workshop seminars. The atmosphere was akin to a revivalist tent meeting but one wreathed in the sweetly acrid smoke of marijuana and lubricated beforehand by flat-topped straight pint glasses of real ale. Standing room only at the back for Welsh firecrackers like Gwyn A. Williams on Prince Madoc's 'discovery' of America, or for that cerebral historical visionary the Savonarola-esque Edward Thompson.

In 1969 I had travelled down from the University of Lancaster to experience a vicarious pride in the dramatic stage presence of Gwyn Alf and the admiration his staccato eloquence aroused in the largely Saxon audience; and that same weekend also to hear a different kind of academic stagecraft in the measured yet startling comparisons which E. J. Hobsbawm (1917–2012) could bring to bear on mechanics institutes and Lancashire's spinning mills, on the main purpose of front room pianos by the late-Victorian working class, and the advent of the first commercial fryers for fish and chips at that proletarian Las Vegas, Blackpool.

I would come to know Eric at various levels in the years that followed. To be examined by him in 1976 for my PhD; to share platforms with him at Llafur conferences in Swansea; to interview him privately for his memories of his Cambridge contemporary Raymond Williams; to be chaired by him at Birkbeck when my biography of Raymond appeared in 2008; to be introduced by him at Hay when I subsequently gave the annual Raymond Williams Lecture at the Festival; and when in 1995 I was his chosen interviewer at Hay when his volume, *The Age of Extremes* (1994) was published. What he said then stands, I believe, the test of time for its bite and its projections.

It was at Hay, too, that in 2000 I introduced Eric at his almost star-struck request to Gore Vidal (1925–2012), who was holding expansive court at a grand party in his honour. He had sat, large and wide, on a red velvet armchair, greeting well-wishers and groupies after the panel discussion for Radio Wales which I had earlier chaired; he invited my wife, Norette, to sit on his extended knee and when she demurred by saying she was not as light as she seemed, he quipped that he was not as heavy as he looked. Oh, yes, he was. He and Eric were quickly and intimately deep in a discussion of personal and mutual admiration. Gore Vidal, widening the circle, mentioned that I was to interview Norman Mailer at the end of that rainy and stormy Border week. 'I have told him 'Good luck with that',' said Gore to Eric.

* * *

Dai Smith (DS): What I've always liked about Eric Hobsbawm, as a historian ever since I was reading him in the 1960s, was that he shared the ability with some of us who were not English – if I may put it that way – not to be myopic or Anglocentric. All of his work has managed to be specific about events, nations, identities. He's always managed, too, to bring *that* gift to his other great gift which is to give us an explanation of why things have happened and it is in those terrific surveys, not just the very specific books such as *Bandits* and *Labouring Men*, but the *Age of Revolution* in 1962, the *Age of Capital* in 1975, the *Age of Empire* in 1987, and now the *Age of Extremes*, his current history, that Eric has always managed to hold these two things together. I think that it makes him, among a generation of historians who have reshaped the intellectual life of the British Isles since 1945, pre-eminent. So, Eric, you stress in the book, right at the beginning, that it isn't anecdotal, impressionistic, but, and if only by virtue of the fact that the dates of the book, 1914 to 1991, almost coincide with your own birthdate and your subsequent life, it is of course touched all the way through by autobiography. Was that difficult for you as a historian to come to terms with?

Eric Hobsbawm (EH): It's always difficult to come to terms with. There are really three kinds of history. There's the ones where you deal with periods in which you have no direct contact at all – you get at them through secondary literature, through primary literature, and so on, but you come there as a stranger – there's the ones where you write about your own lifetime and there's also the in-between ones, which I also tried to come to terms with in an earlier book, which is just before you can start remembering yourself but nevertheless which isn't completely strange to you because it goes back to the earliest kind of family photos that anybody in the family can still explicate. In some ways that's more difficult than actually dealing with your own lifetime because in your own lifetime, at least in the first place, you know what your bias is, you know what possibly you have to check your experience against. Of course, as a historian, you've got to check it against the recorded facts as research gets them. And yet, in a way, the first thing you've got to try and do is find out, see, how far what you can remember fits and how far it doesn't because sometimes it does fit and sometimes it doesn't. When I was young in the 1930s, for instance, we all thought that what was happening was a great mobilisation of forces, of all anti-fascists and democrats against fascism and Nazism. Looking back while I was writing the book and looking at the actual records, I can see that it wasn't like that at all. There was very little extra mobilisation against fascism until Hitler poked – you know, forced everybody into a common cause. The only parts of the world which turned left in the 1930s in any significant way were Scandinavia and the United States. There was nothing in Europe comparable to the huge shift from Republicans to Roosevelt and Democrats. Now, on the other hand you sometimes find that your own contemporary period impressions are correct. Say somewhere in the late fifties I began to notice that I was reacting differently to life from what I had been doing for the past twenty years. Coming from Central Europe, one had always got used to the idea that the only thing that you had to be absolutely certain of was to have a valid passport, if necessary with a visa, and enough money in the bank to buy a ticket to wherever you could go if things got bad and you never thought further ahead than six months or twelve months. Then suddenly towards the middle to late fifties you began to notice that you were actually starting to plan ahead. I said to myself things have changed, we're in a different historical period, we're out of the period of crisis, life can move on. Well, that happened to have been a correct impression. So, there's that. It seems to me one's got to tie one's autobiography, if you like, and of course there's the other even more important emotional issue, you've got to find out, you've got to explain, why you felt what you did, you thought what you did, you acted the way you did and, whether it was correct or not, exactly how it came about that you yourself [did these things] – because you've got to treat yourself, to some extent, as an object of research as well as a subject acting within.

DS: This is what gives some parts of the book a special frisson. You feel that you're reading not only the words of a historian who has been practising over those sixty years or whatever but also that there is a sense that you are telling, you're accounting for, your own life in a public and a professional sense. But let me take you one step further before we get into the content of the book because towards the end of the book you start saying that this current generation have no interest in history, that this current generation live in a 'permanent present'. Do historians, Eric, still matter?

EH: I think historians matter more than ever because of that very fact. We are, if you like, the remembrancers, whose business it is to remember what other people don't remember or what the mechanism of media society remembers for a day and then puts in the dustbin. [...] People may not want to listen but if they were to listen, they have to go and listen to historians because there's nobody else to listen to.

DS: Can we talk about a twentieth century, or are we talking about fragments?

EH: No, I think what we're talking about and what gives a unity to the history of this period from 1914 until the present is, in the first place, the breakdown of nineteenth-century civilisation. You can call it different things – you can call it bourgeois Liberal; you can call it Liberal capitalism – but to all intents that kind of civilisation broke and for thirty-odd years it was by no means clear that it would survive. A lot of people did not believe it survived and you can't understand the period unless you recall that it appeared to be in a possibly final crisis. Then it recovered. It was restructured. Then for twenty-five years you get what was a mysterious but unquestionably extraordinary age, roughly the third quarter of the twentieth century, in which all the problems which previously appeared to have existed disappeared. That's what it looked like. All you have to do is remember the way in which the late Tony Crosland or the various great people in the late fifties talked as though the great problems had been solved and similarly, of course, on the other side, the socialist side, people thought things were okay, the way forward had been found, everything was going great. And then it happens that from the early seventies on this was no longer the case. So, in a sense what gives, in my view, the history of this short twentieth century, 1914 to the 1990s, its shape, is, if you like, a breakdown, a reconstitution, and then once again if not a breakdown but a slide into an uncertain future. It's a sort of historical triptych.

DS: Arguably, Eric, this is a very Eurocentric view. Some of your critics have said that although you've taken the world as your oyster in this book, it also takes you back into Europe. But you yourself attack that head on, don't you, by saying that if you look at the great changes in what we've come to call the Third World, whether they're economic modernisation or whether they're revolutions or coups d'état, or whatever, that all of these 'have derived their dynamics from somewhere outside themselves'.

EH: Yes, I certainly reject the accusation that this is a Eurocentric book. In fact, it spends a good deal of its time actually trying to come to terms, analyse, with what has been happening in the Third World. One would have liked to have spent more time on it but in fact you've got to try and plan in such a way, and I thought three chapters would be about as much as I could put in. Similarly, I think one can't measure these things in terms of column inches. What I say about China, which is clearly one of the most important countries in the world, is comparatively brief. Yet that doesn't indicate, you can't get the impression that I underestimate this. So, I would not accept this [complaint] at all. I think this is true because, as you rightly say, so far the development of the non-European world has been essentially, in terms of first reacting to or second imitating, the kind of dynamics which were developed in the Western world and nowhere else. We may be getting to the stage where this is no longer the case. We may be getting to the stage in the late twentieth century where the centre, at any rate technologically or economically, may be found, let us say, in East Asia and South-East Asia, at any rate in the Pacific area. Although even then we may still probably have to ask ourselves something that a Swedish professor once asked me when we were discussing this. He was saying, 'Just supposing Japan is going to become what America was for the twentieth century, does this mean that Japan will influence our culture in the way in which the United States has influenced our culture in the twentieth century, and if not why not, and what are the signs?' These are questions which I don't propose to answer but at least they have to be posed. So, until the end of the twentieth century, it seems to me, we must still regard the dynamics of historical change as coming from a particular region of the world, which happens to be the Atlantic region.

DS: Eric, I suppose in a sense, both in the book and your own life, 1917, the October Revolution, the coming of the Soviet Union, was all through this period, not just for many committed people but actually in a wider reality, a way of offering an alternative to Liberal society.

EH: It was. It was the offering of an alternative. I think it was the offering an alternative because people felt that there was no future the way things were going, so consequently anything that looked even faintly like an alternative was something which offered hope. I think, myself, both the October Revolution, the emergence of a Soviet Russia or the planned economy as something which was considered a global alternative to the Western economy, to Western society, was in some sense a function of the crisis, the catastrophes in which this old society found itself. Everything was going wrong. After a hundred years in which the biggest war in Europe – not in the United States, since the American Civil War was really rather big, but in Europe – was smaller than the Bolivia-Paraguay Chaco War of 1932. Then we find ourselves in these thirty-one years of world total war in which the number of people killed, scattered, murdered, and all the rest of it, runs into the tens of millions. The institutions, liberal institutions, parliamentary institutions, appear to have been advancing, then constitutional government, from World War I on, from 1918 on, until the middle of World War II, kept going back. There were perhaps only sixty-odd independent states in the world in those days and in 1918 probably only about thirty-five of these, give or take one or two extras in South America, could be regarded as parliamentary republics of one kind or another. By 1942, there were twelve in the entire world which could be regarded so in some sense. The thing was going down, down, down. And finally, and this is the thing which really was most extraordinary because it affected even the United States, which was immune to wars because nobody fought on its soil and which was immune to political subversion and so on, the economy went bust. The United States going up and really on the verge, say in the 1920s, already about to occupy the sort of position it occupied after 1946, and then came the 1929 slump. Bang. It's tremendous, quite dramatic.

Under these circumstances, this is the background against which the new hopes, or if you like the fears and the hopes, were formulated. For people of my generation, the choice wasn't between different options for the future but between no future and some future. Of course, the great revolution, which had inspired enormous numbers of people, most extraordinary numbers of people, people whom one wouldn't associate with it, that seemed to be at least a hope.

DS: Let's switch tack slightly. I'm very anxious that we turn, Eric, to one of the aspects which forcibly struck me as I was reading the book and that is to the question of the arts, which you deal with in general terms, but which also runs in a filament sense throughout the book. There's a lovely bit in which you talk about seeing the Odessa Steps sequence in the film *Battleship Potemkin* (1925) in a cinema in Charing Cross in the 1930s and then later on in a footnote, and only in a footnote, you say that people who watch the gangster film *The Untouchables* (1987) if they don't get the message of the parodied sequence in the movie then they didn't see the original. Now, through this medium, ordinary people throughout this century have begun to see and look and deal with their lives, and have the connected opportunities to deal with their lives particularly through moving images, through cinema and now television, in ways that were unimaginable before this century began.

EH: Absolutely. The interesting thing is that while, technically speaking, these ways of seeing, or ways of communicating, were already available before 1914, they really didn't come into their own until the short twentieth century. The movies had just about got to the verge of doing so by 1914 but even so, the logic, that is to say the logic of an art which is produced in a completely different way to the traditional high arts, took a long time in establishing itself and in working its way through.

DS: You talk about populist French cinema as being one of the few art forms in the twentieth century, in the thirties, which actually hit the interests of the intellectual, that is, they followed it, and still entertained, it still told a story. Are you hinting to us that somewhere along the line, along with avant-gardisms and post-modernisms, we've missed the way here?

EH: I don't think we've missed the way; the way has been found. It seems to me very largely avant-garde and high art have been marginalised and pushed into a dead end. For instance, all attempts by avant-garde music to introduce electronic music have been absolute poison at the box office. And yet electronic music via rock music has been absolutely the standard medium through which people do it. It seems to me that the major dynamos of cultural change have in fact been the mass media during this twentieth century or have been the technologically dominated mass media starting from the press, films, radio, television, and that these have in some ways, I won't say emancipated themselves from the arts but transformed culture in ways which people previously wouldn't have regarded as possible.

DS: But not just culture. You mention radio there. You talk in the book about radio liberating and particularly liberating women and housebound women, working-class women, in the 1930s. You say it isn't the medium that is so important, i.e. radio, but the message, i.e. that they're suddenly plugged into other things.

EH: Radio is, in some ways, the most revolutionary because it became so universally accessible in the west and later on – thanks to this extraordinary, and I believe decisive, innovation of the small portable long-life battery and the small portable radio, the transistor – everywhere. [...] In two ways culture had become I won't say democratised but universalised. In the sense that everybody is within access and particularly, of course, it has been the fundamental cultural change for married women in the twentieth century, at least in this country. Housebound married women. There aren't all that many of them around now but there were for large parts of the twentieth century. And in the other sense, it's that in most parts of the world, thanks to radio, it has become possible to transform local languages, local idioms, and local dialects, into something through which the world can be brought to people who were previously completely isolated from it. It is technically cheap to produce, and it is financially viable for people to set up a little radio station talking to people in their own language. So for people who were previously cut off from the wider culture, it can be brought to them. That's new. That's an absolutely novel situation.

DS: John Davies in his history of the BBC in Wales suggests that Wales since the 1920s has, in some sense, been an artefact created by the BBC.

EH: I think there's a good deal to that.

DS: I think there's a good deal to that! As always, the historian speaks the truth.

SPARRING WITH NORMAN

Historical understanding, through the objective assessment of evidence and the analysis of judgement, is the paramount investigative means we have to consider in place and over time our human significance. Such has anyway been the guiding belief of my own intellectual life. That, of course, is not to say that what 'history' looks like as an unfolded experience or unscrolled writing, is ever one single thing. Narrative can trump analysis if the latter desiccates overmuch the fluidity of lives as they were lived. Analysis can eclipse the telling of stories when a shadow complexity is more revelatory of why things occurred than a spirited retailing of the how of it. For me, for sure, the literary properties of history, the shaping of its telling, are as vital as any painstaking accumulation of documented material. Yet the latter is the dross out of which the gold is spun. Facts become fictions we inhabit or interpret just as our fiction of being is framed and bound by the primacy of its material fact.

There is, too, in all of this, an implicit disdain for the deceit of lies and an explicit spurning of any mythical fantasies. The former can, indeed, be effective, even if it is malignant, whether socially or politically; the latter is a form of opiate herd immunisation acceptable to those who cannot deal with the burden of any actual history, or it is the proactive wish fulfilment of those who would shortcut history by elevating personal or national identities above the consciousness of what is held in common by all humankind. History, as an interpretative tool, is always a secular art and never a sacral remembrance. The politics and the civic forms of social democracy which it entails are, as Tony Judt stressed in his *Ill Fares the Land* (2010), of universal need and application.

The boundaries within which the Welsh have lived in all our changing complexity, since the twinned vortices of industrialisation and urbanisation spun Wales into modernity have proved an exemplar for Judt's dicta, both as a lived experience and a study for values. When I was younger and the lineaments of that world were still within touching distance, I believed that if historical understanding could be communicated widely that the obfuscation of tribal and emotive breast beating could be overcome by rational argument alone. Another mistake on my part. Commitment entails the taking of sides and which side are you on, that great rallying call to collective action from the 1930s, remains the crux of the continuous existential struggle with which we are confronted.

All of which may seem a circuitous route into the public conversation in Hay which I had with Norman Mailer in June 2000 but therein lies the motif of this present book. That any interpretative engagement with a lived history requires appropriate form if it is to have a resonance of meaningfulness for a wider audience than the local one from which comes specificity and particularity. All history is shaped in this sense but not all of it will be told in a fictive manner. Norman Mailer (1923–2007) had, so far as I was admiringly concerned, been so personally engaged across all of his multi-vocal writing career, making *Advertisements for Myself* (1959), a crossover daredevil predecessor of *Armies of the Night: The Novel as History: History as a Novel* (1968). As a society, we could not do much better, historically and collectively, than to make *Advertisements for Ourselves* a priority. After all, American Wales had decreed what was, individually and collectively, to be the side we were on and how to tell that tale.

* * *

Dai Smith (DS): Let me start by saying that in *The Time Of Our Time* (1998), your new compilation, that's more than an anthology isn't it, there's a kind of a reflection on your writings by yourself as well as a pulling them together. Something you call a looking at the cultural and social history of the last fifty years. At the beginning of the book, Hemingway comes in, as you'd expect, there's a fragment about Hemingway and boxing, but at the end it's Dos Passos you defer to, a writer with whom you're not normally associated but what I thought was – though you do write about Dos Passos in your 1959 compilation *Advertisements for Myself* – that this was some kind of way in which you bridge the individual vision of Hemingway and the collective documentation of Dos Passos. That what you've been doing over the last fifty years, is pulling that together?

Norman Mailer (NM): Not consciously, you know. Writers are really simpler than critics, as you know. We're very simple people at one side of ourselves, which is if something works well for us, we'll do it. If we read someone and we know that that writer is going to mean an awful lot to us, in other words is going to make us a better writer, then we love that writer. We're primitive that way. So at a certain point in my life, I loved Hemingway, at another point I really revered Dos Passos because it seemed to me that he was trying to do the thing that all American writers fifty years ago wanted to do, which was to write the Great American Novel. You never hear that anymore because it's impossible. Not only America but the entire world – each nation in the world is separated into enclaves. The job of the novelist has become so overwhelming that, generally speaking, there's a tendency now in the novel to write more and more about less and less, to refine the nuances of an enclave somewhere. But I've been around so long that I come from a totally different tradition which was you try to do the whole thing. So Dos Passos was immense for that. No other American writer, to my knowledge, ever tried to encompass America the way he did, and no one since has come close. A few of us have tried but Dos Passos did that.

DS: But you've kind of strained him, sieved him through what you got from Hemingway as well, when you came to do it.

NM: Well, from Hemingway I got a notion that went deep into me – I won't evade the imagery, it went *deep* into me, I was penetrated by Hemingway's ethos and looking back on it, now, it was the most expensive influence I've ever had. My loyalty to Hemingway got me into ridiculous situations, you know, because I ended up buying his notion of women. I really believed in the firm notion of his that men should be strong and brave and good and loyal and should tell the truth, and that the reward would be that they would have lovely women.

DS: Has it worked out?

NM: It works out, in part, it works out in such a way that you could write a wonderful novel about the ways in which it works and doesn't work. But, in fact, as a practical matter, no, it doesn't work out at all – politically speaking.

DS: But you're being a little unfair on yourself because you also were the first, I'd say, to talk about the anguish that Hemingway had, even during his lifetime. This guy was not quite the big macho bull character that maybe he was presenting himself as.

NM: No, he wasn't. He couldn't be. Nobody could be. Essentially anyone who is macho is saying I'm a gambler, and I'm going into this casino, which in this case the casino is open life, life out on the street, life out in the amatory wars, life out there doing the best you can do under every circumstance, and it means that I'm gonna gamble all my funds and either walk out a billionaire or absolutely flat. Anyone who is truly macho has to lose sooner or later – just as you have to lose if you kept betting in a gambling casino night after night after night. So it's a practical matter. Guys who are macho generally are excellent actors and nobody can be as tough as they pretend to be. I remember that even a tremendously terrifying and macho character like Sonny Liston used to be afraid to walk into the ring because, no matter how tough he was, he couldn't stop a bullet, the bullet would stop him. So, he had fear of going into the ring. And macho people live in this fear, this deep fear that Hemingway had.

DS: You've brought boxing up a bit earlier in the conversation than I was going to but since we've gone there – when did you become aware of boxers as such. Was that late for you?

NM: Relatively late. In college, I didn't do any boxing.

DS: Following fighters, in Long Branch, New Jersey, when you were growing up a Welsh fighter came, didn't he?

NM: Yeah, Tommy Farr. And all the Jewish people in Long Branch loved him.

DS: Why?

NM: And all the Italians.

DS: Why?

NM: And all the Irish.

DS: Why?

NM: Because he was available and he was easy and he wasn't terrified of Joe Louis, which impressed us immensely. Max Baer was the man he was fighting then. Max Baer had this tremendous reputation, and everybody thought he was going to be a great champion – he'd just become champion, I think a fight or two before, and Farr was not afraid of him. Then he went in there and ended up going fifteen rounds with Baer, losing the decision.

DS: We all think he beat Joe Louis as well.

NM: He was gutsy, he was a gutsy fighter.

DS: But then when you came to write about boxers, Norman, and obviously I'm thinking of the early work about Liston and maybe particularly the essay on Benny Paret. At the end of the essay, you say something like that this could no longer be a sport for you, or that it would always be more than a sport, and I'm thinking of what we see now about Mohammad Ali and his health.

NM: It could never be a simple sport for me anymore. That you had to recognise that there were tragic elements in it and there were very dangerous elements in it, and if you loved it you had to recognise that you had to recognise that you loved it in the same way that people who love meat can still eat it after they've seen a hundred or a thousand cows strung up on the line going to the slaughter.

DS: So, is it okay in the end?

NM: Boxing? Yeah. I would argue that boxing is okay, finally, because what would some of these kids be doing if they weren't boxing? They'd be mugging people on the street, they'd be in prison, they'd be having worse lives. Their basic attitude from the beginning is that I'm gonna take a lot of punishment in my life and I wanna have some rewards for that punishment.

DS: And Ali would have known that up front?

NM: Ali I think was *sui generis*. Ali was a genius. He was out of measure. Apart from the conventional stuff – he broke all the rules in boxing, he boxed with his head back and he fought with his hands low, and he'd invite people to come to him on the ropes – he understood the fundamental principle of history, which is that history moves by the overcoming of a tradition. Discovering the weakness in a given tradition and transcending it, and Ali did that. He was an absolute genius.

DS: You've said that the way you approach fiction has informed all your writing.

NM: It's the way I approach nonfiction, as if it were fiction.

DS: Explain that to me.

NM: Well, I've now come to a nice, glorified theory that all history is fiction. This is my reasoning on it. If you're writing a history of the French Revolution, a good history, and in a particular chapter of it, let's say a chapter that would cover the origins of the Terror, a good historian – let's say there are a hundred essential facts that have to be traced – a good historian would come up with twelve of them, given the limits of human research, and a good novelist will come up with four. So, the novelist builds his chapter on only four facts out of a hundred, the historian builds it on twelve out of a hundred, and they're both writing fiction because they're each giving you a portrait of how they lived at that point and what they were up to and what they thought.

DS: So, why's the novelist better at it?

NM: Well, the thing is fiction is usually, err...

DS: I meant you! Why are *you* better at it? If you take *Armies of the Night*, you call it the novel as history/the history as novel, you enter as a protagonist, in the time, I don't know how or why, but you just broke the form.

NM: Well, I was trying to break the form and I didn't even know why. Years later I'm now saying that all history is fiction, but the point is that there's such a thing as good history, excellent history, which is a fairly high form of fiction and there is occasionally fiction that is excellent as history because even though it has fewer real facts in it and less research than the conventional historian, nonetheless there may be more feeling for the moment of the period and what the emotions were that shaped it. But all history is approximation, and fiction is an approximation, and what you try to do in fiction is try to create some crystal of experience, which different readers can come through and shine their imaginative light through in different directions and come up with different verities for themselves. The wonderful thing about fiction for me is that it's separate from all the other disciplines. By now, people only trust disciplines, given our technological age. They will trust a sociologist or a psychotherapist or an anthropologist long before they'll trust a good novelist. And yet the novelist is the only one who deals with the question no one else deals with. I wrote something for the beginning of *The Time of Our Time* where I said the novelist is the only one who says to himself, 'What the hell is love?' 'Do I love my wife?' 'Do I really love my wife?' 'Does my wife really love me?' 'Do I love my children?' And then comes the real question: 'Do we love our children so much that we're willing to die for the children, or will we let the children die for us?' These are the kinds of questions that novelists get into, they're intense and they're immense, and no one else tries to get near that. They can't. They'd be destroyed by their fellow academicians.

DS: So, *The Executioner's Song* is truth because it is fiction?

NM: It isn't truth. There's no such thing as *truth*. Jean Malaquais once had a wonderful remark, 'The only time I know the truth is at the point of my pen when I'm writing it.' And I thought he's absolutely right. This is it – a peculiar thing that happens when you're writing, which is occasionally, when you're writing well, you'll write something, and you didn't know you knew it and you're saying something and it's true. That's the closest you ever get as a writer to truth. But it's not *the truth*.

DS: When you were writing *Armies of the Night*, which you write from different perspectives, but you were writing against deadlines weren't you, you were writing almost in a fury, did you realise when you finished the impact that particular book was going to make?

NM: I probably had hopes. I was so close to it. It was such a peculiar book because I suddenly discovered I was a very good nineteenth-century character. I say nineteenth-century character because I knew from the beginning there'd be no sex in the book. But, you know, a good character in the sense that he was half serious, half comic, had a view of himself that was on one hand too modest and the other hand too large, and kept putting square pegs into round holes, and having dowls rattle around in cut-out squares, and so on, and it worked. And suddenly I was writing about myself in the third person and had the most extraordinary experience because it was no longer a literary form, as such. It obviously wasn't a novel, but it read like a novel in which there was a character called Norman Mailer. It wasn't fact, as such. But it was fact. It was in between. It was something that had never quite been there before, at least for me. And I so wrote, for me, with enormous energy and incredible recall.

DS: Tell me about your own politics, are you still a Left Conservative?

NM: Yes, yes. Let me name drop. I had the pleasure of meeting Che Guevara one time in a party in New York. He was in for a day or two and someone gave a party for him. There were not too many of us there. I had a favourite question in those days, which was, 'If you as a leader come across a situation where it's a question of cutting down five trees or shooting five people, which would you do?' And I had an answer in my own mind. The answer that I thought would be, for me, the politically correct answer, would have been that I would look at them. Not 'Oh every human life must be saved at all costs', or 'I would never cut down a tree', instead 'I would look at them.' Instead, what Guevara did was he gave a sly grin and he said: 'Oh, signor, we do not really have trees in Cuba.' That to me is Left Conservatism: do you cut down the trees or do you shoot the people.

DS: You used to judge yourself against your contemporaries, whether it was James Jones, Styron...

NM: Always, always, all of them.

DS: ... who is any good now?

NM: Too many that are good. Way too many. DeLillo's good. Roth is very good. Updike is very good. Bellow is very good. Joyce Carol Oates is like a dark horse in the Kentucky Derby. What I would say is that I've come to realise that novelists, particularly, I can't speak for poets or short-story writers, but for novelists, good novelists are as competitive as good athletes. So in other words, we never read each other just for pure pleasure, that's the rarest thing in the world. Maybe if your child wrote a wonderful novel, then you might read it for pure pleasure but short of that when we read, I'm always reading very critically on the one hand and very competitively on the other, I'm saying, 'Oh this is real good what he's doing here or what she's doing here, can I do it better.' The same way an athlete. This sort of profound competitiveness exists in novelists, we never talk about it.

DS: We began by talking about *The Time of Our Time* and the way in which it brings together your work, last question from me, and again it's something from you, I think in *Advertisements For Myself*, where you talk about 'setting out to create a revolution in the consciousness of our time'. Did you do it?

NM: No, I failed, abysmally, utterly. Everything that I was for has failed. Everything that I hated, detested and scorned has succeeded.

DS: Well, I think you succeeded.

OUR MAN INSIDE

The Saturday night I quizzed Norman Mailer at Hay in the wet summer of 2000, my old friend Alun Richards was in the audience. He had urged me to ask Mailer about Hemingway. So I did. I usually ended up following Al's lead, certainly leaning on his instincts. I thought him to be the only writer of his post-war generation who had managed to peel away the social layers and mores of a South Wales too readily clichéd and confined by the monotone working-class decibel of that proletariat's overwhelming presence.

Alun's short stories especially, and sporadically in his novels and plays, were the real grift on that world's concomitant snobbery, exploitation, aspiration and hypocrisy. The women he wrote about were never ciphers in this male-orientated society: they told deeper truths and exacted subtle revenge. Some of this gimlet-eyed poking, at the very least, came from his upbringing: a single, abandoned mother and a firm but doting grandmother were his early lodestars and the family, supported by the shop of his grandfather, the Pontypridd grocer, Tom Jeremy, were, for those days and in those interwar places, well-to-do. Alun flourished there, at home, and, perhaps in tandem, for being 'different' from his school and street friends, nosedived elsewhere.

Alun was a writer because, as he grew up in the 1930s and 1940s, his genius was given rich material to squirrel away and use through his lifetime. Pontypridd was the key to that, and it was his imaginative kingdom as surely as Yoknapatawpha was Faulkner's or Pottsville, Pennsylvania was John O'Hara's. With the latter he felt an intense unity of purpose in exploring the social intricacies of rough, tough coalfields which insider/outsiders knew were *not* homogenous, where clichés could betray intensely localised gradations of social class, education and accent, and where the force of terrible events was acutely felt. Depression, war, constant death of the young in poverty or battle. Like no one else Alun understood all this close up: three uncles dead as a direct result of the First World War and his mother's much-loved youngest brother, Ithel, a decorated hero, shot down over Le Havre in the Second World War. Streets of extreme deprivation in his youth were a spit away from tree-lined avenues, Tyfica and Gelliwastad, where maids worked, where croquet was played on tree-shaded lawns from whence the collieries could not be seen and creamy long-legged women with Craven A cigarettes on their lipsticked mouths went weekly to shop 'in town' but meant London. This was the intricate, fascinating stuff of *real* life, not a sociological treatise.

Sociology? He could barely contain himself at the fudge of academic generalities when the specifics of lived lives were so dramatic and so full of meaning. He would take my compliment to him as the true master historian of that vanished South Welsh experience as well meant. Though he would not think it the best compliment he could garner. And that would be for his deeply sensitive and compassionate plumbing of the life relationships – especially between men and men, and then women and men – which all this freighted history engendered. And for its representation through his hard-earned craft into the narrative of a fiction more revealing than the passage of life itself. He was a writer because he cared passionately about all that and wanted, more than anything, to get it right. He did so, triumphantly.

Alun was a writer who grew, nurturing this terrific gift through the rocky road of alternative, never quite convincing, careers as secondary school teacher, naval lieutenant, probation officer, and a very close brush with early death as a tuberculosis patient. Those less-than-cosy experiences equipped him up front with a resolute attitude to what and whom and whatever lay in his path – 'I was never blameless,' he later confessed – and what could be defined as an enemy among the latter – what was petty, what was snobbish, what was self-serving and self-defining, who was mean and who was cruel, who denied the outside world and the significance of *his* South Wales in favour of what was an inward-regarding and lesser Wales – all these, and more, fell before his scathing wit, his comic timing and his moralist's wrath. In print and in person, he was all wrapped up in one persona, both Rabelais and Savonarola.

There was always a paradoxical field force around Alun Morgan Richards. To begin with, he was, in his prime, a big man: tall and broad and somewhat all enveloping as a presence in a room. You sensed he could smash something up at any minute. This was a function, maybe, of an innate clumsiness; all hands and large well-shod feet and myopic eyesight, the milk-bottled lenses of the spectacles that were a legacy of the TB he suffered from and overcame in his twenties. But there was more than that, too: a short fuse and a willingness to scorn the conventional. That was, in essence, why he admired Aneurin Bevan so much: there is a glimpse of Al in the crowd at Sophia Gardens, Cardiff, at the South Wales Miners' Gala in 1959, there to listen to Nye's finger-jabbing dissection of the stupidity of his class enemies. It was a dismissive brand of wit, a scornful magician's wand waved to banish the false assumptions which sustained the overlordship imposed on his, and Al's, chosen people.

Beneath a patina of sophistication and the intellectual distancing of talent – from sixteen onwards the publication of poems and stories in the Pontypridd Grammar School magazine and an ambition to write that was, subsequently, unremitting – there was a desire to belong to that collective experience he was also witnessing. Literally, I think, to be 'one of the boys', accepted without any distinction of difference.

His contemporary Russell Robbins, future rugby legend for Wales and the British Lions from the mid-1950s, told me that once the school had organised in the immediate post-war years a trip by train to Bristol Zoo for the hormone-popping adolescents of the fifth form. They returned on a stifling hot summer's day through the Severn Tunnel after hours of raucous mayhem. The train was stalled outside Newport. It was a train of enclosed carriages for six or so people and no corridor. The doors were locked. In one compartment sat Russ and Al; the central sliding window with its leather strap to open and close would not work. Stuck fast. A boy fainted from the heat. Al stood up and threw himself, hob-nailed boots first, at the window. It shattered and air broke in. Russ's complaint was that they all had to pay for the damage and not everyone had the money at home to do that with any ease.

By the time I knew Alun Richards, from 1976 on, his own

anecdotes were polished and devastating. Generally they pincered BBC Wales programme commissioners and University of Wales academics for their self-inflation in office and skewered anyone who belittled others in any way whatsoever. The paradox, again, was that on the other side of his dismissive rage against those in positions of power, administrative or pedagogic, and promoted by cultural entitlement instead of talent or creativity, lay a deep well of compassion. In an odd way he used his physical size, his imposing standards of dress and his commercial success as a professional in the writing game, to open roads of encouragement and avenues of respect for others who may have felt lesser.

One story with which to end. After a weekend of international rugby watching, and quite a few drinks to accompany a Welsh victory, Alun stayed over in our home on Barry Island. He had arrived from Swansea by motorbike, a solid, black and gleaming hulk of a bike: his beloved Suzuki. He parked it in the garage and came into the house like Darth Vader: black leather leggings, motorcycle boots, a black leather, zipped and buckled jacket and thick motorcycle gloves, and all topped off by a visored and bulky motorcycle helmet. He seemed to be almost seven feet tall. Wow, we said, and he had removed the helmet to give us his wide-mouthed grin. On the Sunday morning after an early and restorative breakfast, he had dressed up once more and wheeled out his behemoth of a bike for the easy Sunday run down the M4 to home with Helen in West Cross.

The way Al subsequently told it, he was on an empty stretch of motorway above the Port Talbot steelworks when he heard the police siren. A patrol car. Flashing lights. He pulled over on the hard shoulder and waited. He saw the policeman approach on foot. A young copper, notebook at the ready.

'Do you realise the speed you were doing back there? Sir.' said the policeman.

'No officer,' said Al. 'Sorry.'

'Well it was a ton, mate. A ton.'

'Oh dear,' said Al. 'I hadn't realised. No traffic about. See.'

'That's nothing to do with it,' said the man in charge of the incident.

Alun now took off his helmet and revealed a contrite, sheepish face, one grizzled with iron-grey bristle, thin, his hair flattened above the lines and creases of age. Darth Vader unmasked.

'Christ!' said the policeman. 'How old are you?'

'Sixty-five,' said Al, with all due pride and propriety.

'Jesus,' said the policeman. 'You were doing one hundred miles an hour. At your age. What do you do? Retired?'

'No,' said Al, thinking of what might, just might, impress and so avoid a big ticket. 'I'm an author.'

'Orthaw?' said the young copper. 'Orth-or?' and opened his notebook, pencil hovering above the page, hesitating for the initial vowel. 'How do you spell that? Is it OK if I put down 'writer'?'

'Oh, yes,' said Al, very pleased now. 'Writer will be fine by me.'

He rarely committed to paper any abstruse thoughts on the nature of writing and, specifically, of being a writer. He just, as he saw it, did it. But, over numerous conversations and conviviality, over the years since we met, he did talk obsessively and compellingly about the essential characteristics of the writing he admired most, and not necessarily the very best of it except in the sense of writing that strove for sincerity of intent more than the authenticity of simulacra. I listened intently as he roamed over what he had taken from Conrad or Mann or Silone or Scott Fitzgerald and how his passion for biographical writing never extended to any trust in the biography of a writer being able to deliver any insight to the work more profoundly than the original text itself delivered to the attentive reader. Yes, he was a reader of purposefulness as much as a writer of intent. He was never confined by the industrial valleys or the maritime experience of Glamorgan, his home patch in his novel of that name in 1966, or across the four novels and the two short-story collections which should emblazon his name across any serious cultural capture of twentieth-century Wales, but he readily accepted that it was this defining history which gave him the precise particularity which he would seek to fashion and shape into the essential if implicit comparisons which give his best work its universal patterning.

When I became pro-vice-chancellor at the University of Glamorgan in Pontypridd, it was all of this that I wanted him to distil by giving the Rhys Davies Memorial Lecture at the university in his home town. It has never been published before. Here it is, in a slightly redacted form, as he delivered it on 9 November 2001.

THE WRITERS AT MY ELBOW
BY
ALUN RICHARDS
(1929-2004)

In a sense, I have been waiting sixty-five years for this moment, the chance to present myself in public as THE MAN FROM OUT OF TOWN. At the age of seven I was first taken to the Town Hall in Pontypridd where there was an amateur dramatic week, when various societies from all over the Valleys competed for a drama cup, and for the entire week a man from out of town – from London – was specially invited to adjudicate and decide the winner. Each night he would also comment and finally sum up. I remember he sat in the front seat of the dress circle in a dinner jacket, and he had that most unheard-of things, a clip-board with a pad *and* a light. He also was seen once with a cloak and was very much a grand seigneur, and on the last night, he appeared on stage, after waiting for the assembled players to re-assemble themselves. Then he spoke to all of us with perfect articulation in stentorian tones, sometimes naming names in individual performances.

> *'Mrs Beatie Davies playing Maud. 7 for Deportment, 3 for Interpretation, 10 for posture, Movement on stage – 5!'*

And we were spellbound! We wouldn't have taken it from anybody else. But the man from out of town was special and with such an aura.

However, it's a difficult pose to keep up, especially without a cloak, and I haven't forgotten how grateful I was to see all those plays performed and interpreted. Nor could I for a moment really be an outsider, for I recall an immense amount of gratitude to certain of my schoolmasters in those years when I grew up here and it would be very ungrateful of me to come home without naming them; in my primary school in Lan Wood to Stan Williams who read to us on those lovely Friday afternoons when the extra bottle of free milk had been distributed, the sodden daps were dry on the steaming radiators, and those who were going to faint because of exhaustion or malnutrition had already done so, and there was a warm expectation of pleasure and the home-time bell not too far off. A gentle man, Stan Williams encouraged us daily for three years. There were only three of us out of forty-five who could afford the County School where I had an even bigger debt to Ken Railton, my English master, who set a tone for me that was exactly mirrored, I discovered later, by many writers' mentors, in particular for J. B. Priestley, who wrote of his English master:

> I can see and hear him again, quite clearly across the years that changed all human history, and if his influence on me was far greater, as indeed it was, than that of all the professors and lecturers I heard later in Cambridge and the critics I met in London, that was because I sat in a classroom at the right time with a teacher who loved good writing.
>
> (*Margin Released*, Heinemann, 1962)

It is this quality further defined by Priestley as 'the essence of literary sensibility which lacked the precision of those finer minds who could write PhD theses on the use of the semicolon in the later works of George Elliot!' Like many writers, he couldn't resist a barb at those who would later dismiss him. I think he was also saying that the problem with most criticism is that there is not enough cheering. Even when the criticism is adverse, it is not so much that the knives are out, but the manicure set, nice scissors snipping away. Again, most writing and talking about writing often seems to me to be too neat. There is no untidiness, more often than not, ideas are slotted away like instruments in a chiropodist's tray. It is not so much the cutting apparatus we need, but understanding and less of the presumptions of omniscience in well-tailored journalistic pieces. It's as well to remember that most creativity comes from some kind of heat, currents of feeling in response to direct experience which ultimately finds some kind of shape in one form or another. But having said that, there is no reason why we should not look a little closer and try to formulate opinions about what is useful to us. For my own part, I propose to cheer and utter a few huzzahs. By the way, I should hasten to say though, that I do not regard myself as a critic, and do not like making broad surveys or literary comparisons, although from time to time when I have been asked as a professional writer to undertake some task or other, I have in the main, followed my nose. Very valuable instrument the nose, editors edit with it, sniff things out. Questions I ask myself about any given topic tend to be haphazard, but the most important is, does this or that proposition offend my common sense? I am suspicious of received ideas, not least my own, when they are perforce collected for a lecture like this, but whatever I am or am not, I have always been a reader, and haphazard as my reading has been, all my life I have always been grateful to writers, short-story writers in particular, for the glimpses they have given me into the lives of others, to other worlds, to an experience of life outside my own.

This began with the short-story collections and pocketbooks issued in the war, some of them cheaply printed for the US Army, which soon became available and on sale in Pontypridd market for many years. I should say that, like many people who grew up in a small town, I have always had a sense of the road by which the circus arrived, and left, with all the magic of its riches and illusions, its baubles and its princesses, so that the short story took on a special glamour for me. It was the Big Top!

My hope now, all these years later, is that I can better understand the stance taken by the writer, the way of looking which, it seems to me, underlies the success of any memorable story. The problem is to define a universal attribute, a way of looking that is constant and defines the writer's stance, which is the key to it all.

The writer Cecil Lewis saw an analogy in nature and identified a fish, *Anableps anableps* which inhabits the swamps of South America. (I call it the writer fish.) It feeds on the weeds and small creatures which lie on or just below the surface of the water. To do this, it has to swim snake-like on the surface. But this leaves it exposed to sea birds that prey upon it. To meet this perpetual crisis – life from one element, a death from another – nature has endowed it with special equipment. It has double vision. In two rather protuberant sockets in its head, lie four eyes: the upper pair look up into the air, the lower down into the water.

This provision to meet two opposing sets of conditions is, according to Lewis, not only unique in nature, but a striking parallel to the human condition. Man can look up and down, look out and look in. Of course, no one but a saint 'can see life steadily and see it whole', but it is the challenge which the writer faces before he can create and then it is his task through his knowledge of the particular to find the universal, to see with all four eyes as it were. It is this matter of stance and seeing to which I wish to draw your attention. It is a matter of the whole of oneself being directed – focussed is the in-word now – at the moment of writing. From the set off, to use a phrase of Elizabeth Bowen's who says the most important characteristic of the short story is its necessariness to the writer so that it must spring from a perception pressing enough, acute enough, to have made the writer write.

Defining this stance in its entirety is a problem. Only recently, Alan Sillitoe, for example, talks of himself as being two people. He has remained close to his roots – he wants to give voice to the people of Nottingham, and yet apparently, at the same time he has severed them from his own life without much sense of pain. Just to confuse us, he calls this bilingualism, the balance between involvement and detachment, so perhaps what we are really looking at is the decision on the writer's part to go outside his milieu and look in at it, or look back on it, to understand his involvement and detachment from it.

It is a stance, for example, which allows the writer to observe, that opens gates for him or her, that draws back curtains and makes him party to knowledge that you would never expect. Part of it might be a capacity for sponge-like absorption, but then there must be selection. The writer, of course, is also editor, and perhaps the best way of understanding this is to examine texts, and my plan is to start with an away fixture and work home, as it were.

I have chosen Alun Lewis's short story *Ward O 3 (b)*, a wartime hospital story set in India in 1941. Lewis, an Aberdare boy, as they say locally, is writing about a Captain Brownlow Grace, a regular officer who has lost an arm in Burma and who hates a junior officer called Moncrieff in the next bed.

> This is not unnatural. Moncrieff is a university student, Oxford or some bloody place as far as Brownlow Grace knows. He whistles classical music, wears his hair long, which is impermissible in a civilian officer and tolerated only in a cavalry officer with at least five years' service in India behind him. Brownlow Grace has done eight. Moncrieff says a thing is too wearing, dreadfully tedious, simply marvellous, wizard. He indulges his moods and casts himself on his bed in ecstasies of despair. ... He has thirty photographs of himself, mounted enlargements, in Service Dress and Service cap, which he is sending off gradually to a network of young ladies in Greater London, Cape Town, where he stayed on the way out, and the chain of hospitals he passed through on his return from Burma.

Alun Lewis (1915–1944), I have always felt, had the ability, not just to get into the minds of his characters, but to place them perfectly. More than any of his Welsh contemporaries, he creates a varied world, a world which must have been strange to him for so long.

It is not just the ironies and special knowledge of the military that he notes here. Harold Macmillan, for example, as a young Guards officer, was instructed to go through manuals of war and picked out the following idiocy: 'Officers of field rank on entering balloons, are not expected to wear spurs!' He has adopted an ironic stance, but Lewis has all four eyes working in the sense I mean. He can step aside, step right back. Previously, he was the character. Now he is himself. As the story moves on:

> The sick have their own slightly different world, their jokes are as necessary and peculiar to them as their medicines; they can't afford to be morbid like the healthy, nor to be indifferent to their environment like the Arab. The outside world has been washed

> out: between them and the encircling mysteries there is only the spotlight of their obsessions holding the small backcloth of ward and garden before them. Anyone appearing before this backcloth has the heightened emphasis and significance of a character upon the stage.

Who can't see life steadily and see it whole! Lewis also knows about visitors being greedily absorbed and examined by every patient, 'with the intenser acumen of disease'. (The insight of illness, I shall come to presently.) Here Lewis approaches it, again from a distance, a distant observer for the moment.

Brownlow Grace had a visitor. This increased his prestige, like having a lot of mail.

> She was by any standards a beautiful woman. One afternoon a young unsophisticated English Miss in a fresh little frock and long hair; the next day French and exotic with the pallor of an undertaker's lily and hair like a statuary: the third day exquisitely Japanese, carmined and beringed with huge amber stones, her hair in a high bun that only a great lover would dare unloose. When she left each evening Sister Normanby came in with a great bustle of fresh air and practicality to tidy his bed and put up his mosquito net.

Finally, in the same story, there's another completely different patient who says to Brownlow Grace:

> Look, I didn't start with the same things as you. You had a pram and a private school and you saw the sea, maybe. My father was a collier and he worked in a wet pit. He got rheumatism and nystagmus and then the dole and parish relief. I'm not telling you a sob story. It's just I was used to different sounds. I used to watch the wheel of the pit spin round year after year after school and Saturdays and Sundays, and then from 1926 on, I watched it not turning round at all, and I can't ever get that wheel out of my mind. It still spins and idles and there's money and nystagmus coming into the house and worse than nystagmus. I just missed the wheel sucking me down the shaft. I got a scholarship to the county school.

Note he is not hammering the Valleys here, but has reflected the universal condition, and in one story, it seems to me, we have a complete picture, a whole, and we have it because Alun Lewis is able to adopt the stance most useful in completing his picture. All four eyes are working and when you come to study it, his knowledge is encyclopaedic. He can do the same in dialogue with every nuance accurate and he has a perfect ear. From his very early apprentice efforts his observations were acute, like the Bracchi's café in his home town which he called Cardinelli's, of which, he noted, that chapel deacons disapproved and did not allow their children to go there because it opened on Sunday. It was, however, acceptable to buy a cornet from the cart!

I should point out that all the four officers in this story are awaiting a medical board determining the date of their discharge. This single thread holds it together and so the detailed and intimate observation is necessary to draw us into it. It does not have the thrust and spine of some of his other stories. What is going to happen next is not a pronounced draw to us as it is in many stories, but it is this ability to see life in that ward clearly and as a whole that holds us, his creation of worlds within a world. He gives you the impression that he has total knowledge and is not in any sense a local boy.

My own life touched upon his in small ways. At the end of the war as a schoolboy with a cricket team in Mountain Ash, I sat on a roller by the sight screens and talked to a teacher who had taught Lewis, and he told me he had cried when the news came through of his death in India. There was always a mystery about it. Later as a student in Newport, I met the sergeant of the burial party by chance in a pub. Lewis had committed suicide, which was not generally known then. He was at odds with his CO and the men knew. I told that story years later to Ron Berry who wrote an indignant letter to Lord Chalfont who was an officer in the same regiment, demanding to know details, but he got a frosty uninformative reply on House of Lords notepaper. Later I gave a lecture in the Cowbridge school which Lewis attended and there was a charming little exhibition in the corridor in a glass case, his photograph, his contributions to the school magazine, some manuscripts and memorabilia, all his books. I hope it is still there.

When I read a story, I generally need a sense that I have been introduced to a place and a person. I also think of the two most important questions you can ask of a writer. Has he, has she, got a voice of his or her own? Can he, can she, create a world? These are very general questions, and the best way to understand them is always to examine texts. I should also say that, like many writers, I have supplemented my income talking to would-be writers when method is all important, the problems of narrative and narrative skills, the nuts and bolts of the business so far as one can divine them, but this carries the risk with it of ignoring the story as a whole as a total experience, which is what it must be. I also like the idea that at the end we should get the impression that a light has been focussed on unsuspecting characters in an untouched moment of life without any obvious artifice. The important word, then, is light, a sense of discovery – and of course, the experience.

A feeling of difference from other people stamps the early path of almost every writer, the idea of separateness, of being distant, hurt or vulnerable, perhaps the fear of being exposed, essentially of being outside the prevailing group and forced into adopting a disguise which is also eventually the path of learning and sometimes provides the enlightenment of unique insights from unexpected and untypical angles. Trauma, tragedy, inadequacy sets him or her apart.

It is no accident, it seems to me, that Rhys Davies (1901–1978) wrote such an early story about an almost precisely similar situation. It is called *Arfon*.

> Mr and Mrs Edwards did not deserve such a child. There was nothing peculiar about them, they were chapel people and a respected business couple, he selling oil, soap, candles, and oddments from a cart in the streets, and she, a thin, staid woman, making savoury pastries on Tuesdays and Fridays, eight for sixpence and very delicious. So no one could understand why such a funny little boy was born to them.
>
> Odd he was to look at, too. He never grew beyond the stature

of a small boy of ten, but his head was ridiculously large, and the expression on his heavy grey face was of such gravity that no one felt at ease in his presence. He would stare at things and people with a prolonged intensity, falling into such depths of brooding meditation, it was not to be wondered at that he had the reputation of being an idiot. They named him Arfon.

His mother and father were convinced he was of idiotic tendencies. Mrs Edwards never forgave him for appearing in a deformed state. So silly he looked, her only child, with his paltry thin body and massive head, she shut herself away from him in resentment and became angry at the continual ache in her heart when she looked at him. His father roared at him, protruding his thick lips and rolling his violent eyes, beating him for the sulky gravity of his face. Mrs Edwards blamed her husband for their son's oddness.

Arfon suffered a great deal. Except for a habit of dreaming visionary dreams and his unusual stature, he was like most other children. Especially when he was born. But as he grew, he found that the world was an ugly place. From the beginning he was aware of contempt and disgust. His mother's resentful rejection of him and his father's bad temper and anger that he would be a burden entered his heart without his being aware what they meant. And the mockery and jeering of the other young people in the place made him quiver with suffering. He had to attend the school on the hillside, and because he hated going among the other children, who poked fun at him mercilessly, he was a fool at the lessons. He would be numb with silent anger and pain. Once, after a particular bout of teasing from the other boys, and fury from the teacher, he had to be sent home with his knickerbockers dirtied. The boys never forgot that.

Arfon is greatly punished in a bleaker place. He is vilely beaten, his skill at drawing is interpreted. His isolation is minutely detailed.

groups of girls tittered as he passed; and the uncouth gangs of youths that go about the lanes tried to tear his trousers down. Often the world seemed to be nothing but malice and meanness and shame.

He is made to work on his father's tradesman's cart.

> At last, late, he began to long for girls, being seventeen. He forced himself to court one or two in the traditional manner: winking at the favoured across the gallery of the chapel and approaching them after the service for a walk. Some went with him. But he did not like their amusement. They seemed to treat him as a joke and he suffered deeply when they tittered at his high, romantic love-making, that was courteous and poetic. They were strong, well-fleshed girls and sometimes he had an impulse to maul them. But he was too proud, and so the girls laughed at him, getting their own back in dissatisfaction.
>
> Then he became passionately enamoured of Dilys Roberts. He had seen her accidentally one warm summer day coming down the garden from the back door of her aunt's cottage. She was wearing nothing but a gay pale green undergarment and, unconscious that he stood behind a lilac bush, she half-waltzed down the path, with beautiful young movements, her heavy gold hair dripping in the shine of the sun. She uttered a little scream when she saw him, but stood her ground and began to abuse him.
>
> 'A Peeping Tom, that's what you are,' she said indignantly.
>
> 'I come here,' he protested, 'every day to see if there's any oil wanted. Look you at my cart outside.'
>
> His face was gleaming with homage.
>
> 'Fine you looked coming down the path. I couldn't turn away or do anything.' And a slight breeze rippled the silk of her garment. His eyes were warm and full of light. She looked at him and recognised his homage. Now she was very self- possessed and haughty in her undergarment.
>
> 'You knock the door first next time,' she told him. 'You got no right to come in people's private property.'

However, a relationship develops. He is able to buy her little trinkets. He becomes obsessed. Within a month she had received from him amber beads, a gold-plated watch and some earrings. He cunningly cheated his customers and stole out of the takings and lied to his father about the value of the stock. She is, however, also seeing a young collier and makes no secret of it.

Arfon responds with more and more gifts which he can ill afford. Now it is a set of beads.

> He drew the beads out of his pocket. The shiny yellow marbles gleamed in the evening dimness. She was silenced and, loosening his arm, she held out her hands excitedly.
>
> 'Oh, aren't they lovely! Are they for me? Oh, I shan't take them. I never meant you to buy me things.' She flushed in gratification and eagerness. He dropped the beads on the tissue paper and gave them to her. He felt the eager warmth of her blood and the gift was nothing as payment. His veins began to burn.
>
> 'I shall wear them!' she cried proudly. She turned to him and said generously, 'You must put them on me the first time.'
>
> They stopped, and he took the beads. But his fingers trembled so much at her nearness that he couldn't fix the clasp properly. His fingers at her neck, while she laughed at him, he felt a sudden strange impulse to handle her slim throat in a rough, passionate grip. His heart beat like a hammer as the dark impulse leapt out of the unknown, his fingers at her slim, fine neck, her unbearably beautiful body so near to his own. He drew away, his chest as though filled with breath that couldn't be released, his face rigid. His fingers had mechanically fastened the clasp.
>
> 'There!' she cried, still quite absorbed in the gift, 'aren't they lovely! Oh, I'm proud of them, I am really.'

There is an inevitability now. Before long, it is a fox fur, the last gift. When she taunts him, eventually he strangles her.

It is a strange ending. After the murder, he falls asleep in a remote mountain hollow in a terrible silence. Then:

> He began to crawl down the steep hillside, not wanting to find the path. He saw the dim rows of dwellings far below in the valley. He did not think of the consequences his tale would have for him. He could be hurt no more, only he must escape and tell what lay stretched in death up in the hills. She must not be there with her awful staring.

Later, Davies says, 'He did not want to live anymore. He had had enough of all that was done under the sky.'

For Rhys Davies, perception of difference was a spur. It wasn't just his own sexual orientation. There were other equally telling factors. Magnificent stories like *The Fashion Plate* and *The Public House* are superbly observed, and he is right on top of his form in them because there is a sense of discovery and revelation which passes itself on to the reader with rare feeling, for he is in many senses a cold writer. In *The Fashion Plate*, this sense of discovery takes place on the page as if the writer is experiencing it at the same time as the reader and there is an underlying excitement to it, encountering this extraordinary woman with the magnificent hats. Here she comes!

> 'The Fashion Plate's coming.' Quickly the news would pass down the main road. Curtains twitched in the front parlour windows, potted shrubs were moved or watered; some colliers' wives, hard worked and canvas-aproned, came boldly to the front doorsteps to stare. In the dingy little shops, wedged here and there among the smart dwellings, customers craned together for a treat... Cleopatra setting out in the golden barge to meet Anthony did not create more interest. There was no one else in the valley quite like her. Her hats! The fancy high-heeled shoes, the brilliantly elegant dresses in the summer, the tweeds and swirl of furs for the bitter days of that mountainous district! The different handbags, gay and sumptuous, the lacy gloves, the parasols and tasselled umbrellas! And how she knew how to wear these things! Graceful as a swan, clean as a flower, she dazzled the eye.

She is encountered through the eyes of a young boy and her uniqueness communicates itself. He is struck as Rhys Davies is. Perhaps something of the same thing occurs in poetry and I am fond of the quotation of Randall Jarrell's: 'A good poet is someone who manages in a lifetime of standing out in thunderstorms, to be struck by lightning five or six times; a dozen or two dozen times and he is great.' This idea of being 'struck' seems to me to be an important one and here Davies is on top of his form. He sees. It is a total all-encompassing view. Like Alun Lewis's of that hospital ward.

Importantly, there is no sense of these stories being written by Davies because there was a ready market for quaint stories of odious Welsh people in New York or London, thus providing a temptation to repeat oneself and to follow success with success in the same vein, always a problem for the professional writer. There is now, it seems to me, to be a ready market for a psychoanalytical approach with a special – to be learned – clinical vocabulary, but I am wary of it. If I am told Rhys Davies lay with a Guardsman – 'Thank you, sir, for leave to whatever!' – it does not alter the strength of the text or the sheer skill of his craft. This is a general principle. If I marvel at the prose of *The Great Gatsby*, my admiration is not increased if someone tells me F. Scott Fitzgerald's mother had the fingernails of her right hand manicured every Thursday *refusing treatment for the left hand because she could do it herself! So what?*

There are other avenues of study more appropriate and less dangerous. These go with the terrain, the time and the place, the attitudes submerged in the community that are often hidden, but are yet powerful. Sometimes they are difficult to isolate. Sometimes it is politic not to do so. For the elderly individual like myself it is a matter of not finding one's own life experience satisfactorily represented in commentaries. All things have an effect on a writer's stance. Few people, for example, touch on the attitudes that prevailed in the coalfield at the outset of industrialisation, attitudes that continued into the next century when immigration increased. I mean the attitudes towards incomers, coal miners, navvies, the impoverished, attitudes that may well have influenced Rhys Davies' mother, bending and worrying over the ledgers of debt in the grocer's shop each night. They affected everybody in the indigenous population, I'm sure, and sometimes they do not reflect credit on our forebears. Perhaps we can learn from elsewhere.

Consider this paragraph from a Sunday School Union Report in 1856.

> On the refuse population of Europe, rolling in vast waves upon our shores, as it passes westward, deposits its dregs upon our seaboard. These congregate in our great cities and send forth their children – a wretched progeny-degraded in the deep degradation of their parents – to the scavengers, physical and moral, of our streets. Mingled with these are also the offcast children of American debauchery, drunkenness and vice. A class more dangerous to the community can hardly be imagined. And how are they to be reached? The public school and the church are of no avail.
>
> (*Secrecy and Power: The Life of Edgar Hoover*, Richard Powers, 1987)

This is from a study of the background in Washington of J. Edgar Hoover and I quote it because its savagery is so surprising. Its author is describing a central vision of America

> as a small community of like-minded neighbours proud of their achievements, resentful of criticism, fiercely opposed to change as the twentieth-century standards of the mass society swept over traditional America, subverting old values, disrupting old customs and dislodging old leaders.

As soon as I read that I thought of Mabon, the old Welsh miners' leader who was displaced by a different breed of man, and now and again, I have had personal glimpses through the eyes of old people in my youth whose attitude, say, to people like the British miners' leader in 1926, Arthur Cook, and pamphlets like *The Miner's Next Step* (1912) drove them to apoplexy. I had an uncle, a headmaster who lived to be over a hundred and his attitudes in some way reflected the animosity to incomers above. He was a headmaster of Maesycoed School and was known for his strictness. Nowadays we would call it brutality but, importantly, his view of most of his charges was as of cannon fodder for the pits. He regarded my grandfather, a blacksmith's son from Conwil Elvet who left school at eleven to work as a sawdust boy in Lipton's in Carmarthen, as ill-educated and inferior, almost muscling into the family, unlike himself who brought with him learning, regular employment and scholarship and The

Stick. He once cautioned me when I was teaching in Ely to take pride in the appearance of my register and its red ticks, for he had begun to teach in the age when he was paid by numbers attending. This scornful phrase 'collier boy' on his lips was echoed by other old men to whom I listened as a young man. One incredible Rhondda man who had been in America for years, a deputy sheriff in Montana, who had sold a mouthful of gold teeth to raise the fare to return home, told me as a twelve-year-old that he had gone from Porth at the turn of the century, walking on New Year's day to Cowbridge where the vicar gave out new pennies to the children of the parish. He joined the queue but the vicar spotted something, refused him, and said, 'You're just a little collier boy, aren't you?'

One man's memory, of course, is not enough to formulate a general theory but it seems to me that Rhys Davies's mother, who hailed from Ynysybwl, may well have caught the attitudes which, say, characterised The Board of Guardians and which, passed on to Rhys, made for many complex feelings which remained as he looked back.

It sometimes seems to me that the real influences of a writer's life are often shadowy, buried away and recalled in casual memories, of feelings that come and go, warnings that were once heeded, prohibitions once thought sovereign. Few people, other than the aged, now react to the word workhouse. But there was a time when it fell like a black shadow upon people's inner thoughts. Mrs Davies, working nightly at the ledger on the grocer's accounts at the back of the shop, lay very much at the back of Rhys Davies's mind, I'm sure. (You can imagine the rows he got into when his clothes got dirty!)

* * *

There are two other factors I want to consider in this matter of stance. The first is expertise, sheer knowledge. Ron Berry's stories, for example, have a greyness that very often reflects attitudes formed by long years of hardship. He is witness of disintegration and his concern for a way of saying and use of language sometimes makes him difficult to read, but there is always a reward, and nowhere is this more evident than when his characters are doing things. *November Kill* is about two men, lonely, deprived, deserted by their mothers as children who find a kind of friendship in exercising and hunting with their dogs in a sparse terrain. Ron Berry (1920–1997) was a naturalist and his eye never seems to miss anything.

> Eight o'clock Sunday morning, quietness everywhere, two milkmen by-passing each other in whining electrical floats, the village main street otherwise deserted. On ahead Pen Arglwydd mountain jutted up at the November sky, a stillness of dark, bare cliffs intergullied with heathered ledges. Scree slopes gave way to invading bracken. Below the rusting bracken, patches of marshland, mole-tumped pasture, scatters of gnarled oaks, relict oaks older than the village, older than the national anthems of mighty Albion. Alders lined feeder streams running into Nant Myrddin. Silver birches were spreading eastward seedspill from a large stand of blackening dying trees.
>
> They rested above the craggy amphitheatre of Dunraven Basin. A frizzled silhouette of conifers curved the Basin summit from end to end. Far distant behind them, the flat crown of Pen Arglwydd clung as if suckered to cold blue sky.
>
> Miskin said: 'Lend me your glasses.'
>
> A hidden grounded raven sounded triple honk calls. Another came peeling over the conifers, swung down, rolled anti-clockwise, flapped straight out, hard primaries coughing like billows, out and out, followed by its honking mate. The big black corvids left the Basin. Down below, acres of glacial bog shone deceptively green.
>
> 'See anything?' Beynon said.
>
> Elbows on his knees, binoculars steadied, Miskin breathed 'Naah', from between his palms.

One of the dogs, a Bedlington bitch, becomes trapped deep below ground in a foxhole. They will have to return on the following morning.

> 'Listen, Beynon, tomorrow morning: mandrel, round nosed

> shovel, hatchet. We'll need a hatchet to make the place safe.' Beynon said, 'I'll bring a crowbar and a bowsaw. There's plenty of timber on top. Those bloody Christmas trees.'
>
> Miskin nodded grunts.
>
> The following day, they felled three sitka spruces, trimmed the six-inch boles and chuted them down grassed gullies to the fox bury.
>
> Miskin organised the work, his authority from five years at the coal face. Taking turns, they hacked and shovelled surface debris, starting a vertical dig above the trapped fox – Miskin's calculation. By late afternoon they were prising out big stones with the crowbar, from the jumbled bulk of the old rockfall. Inter-locked layers of blue pennant sandstone governed the shape and size of their hole. When they were a yard down, a massive inclined slabstone. Miskin stamped on it. He flung curses. It will take another day, perhaps two, to complete the dig, a dogged task.

But who are these men?

> Hospital charity dance in the Social Club on Wednesday night. Beynon and Miskin sat in the snooker room. Very soon, as usual, they speculated about their runaway mothers.
>
> Miskin: 'She never felt anything about me when I was a kid. As for my old man, he was on a loser for a start.'
>
> Beynon: 'Before my old lady went off, she treated my sister and me as if we were nuisances in the house. What do they call it? Maternal instinct? It's a load of bull.'
>
> Miskin: 'D'you think all women are the same, I mean selfish?'
>
> Beynon: 'Christ knows. They go their own way like cats.'

Now, very rarely for Ron Berry, he comments:

> On and on, the same unforgiving rancour, the same helpless groping for motive, a reason to shed guilt, absolve themselves and their mothers.

But then, back to the matter in hand.

> Beynon said, 'My old man's a worrier, he's a clock watcher taking tablets. Duodenal ulcer according to the quack. Knock it back, Miskin, my turn.' He crossed over to the serving hatch with their empties. Happening to glance above the hooded glare on a snooker table, he saw Miskin brooding, his powerful shoulders humped forward, chin pressed to his chest. Beynon thought, she's been four days without food and water. It'll break Miskin's heart if Lady dies underground in Dunraven Basin. He'll quit, sell the dogs. No more weekend fox-hunting. By the Jesus, we'll have to dig her out tomorrow.

Well, they do. And they succeed. Finally, the dog is freed.

> Miskin mumbled, cradled the Bedlington in his arms, 'You daft bloody thing, bloody daft, daft.
>
> Beynon let the shakes drain from his limbs. 'She's stinking of fox,' he said, probing the cavity with a crowbar. 'Aye, he's in there. Lady killed him.' He picked the shreds of fox fur off the chisel tip of the crowbar. 'Definitely, she finished him!' He slumped down again. 'I'm knackered.'
>
> Miskin said, 'Thanks, butty.'
>
> They climbed out. Lady lapped the lukewarm tea, then Miskin carried her all the way home, shovel mandrel and hatchet roped across his back. Beynon carried the bowsaw, crowbar and bucket, a steady plod in cold drizzle, trailed by the brindle lurchers and the long-jawed terrier.

It's not just the expert knowledge and the exact eye that makes that story unique, the how-to characteristic that moves it forward, but the contrasts – the deep concern and courage of the men involved. *A Hero of 1938* where a trapped horse has to be backed out of a flooding stall in great danger is another example. Wherever he is, Berry's characters know what to do in familiar territory as he does. He never makes a mistake. The men, of course, are refugees from society, the society of women in particular, and find themselves only in the company of the dogs and the task in hand. I've said there is a greyness in his work because he often deals with shattered relationships, and now and again, you feel you can hear the crack of doom as in short stories like *Time Spent*, a terrifying portrait of a loveless marriage and a miner with 100 per cent dust who takes his own life, his pigeons substituting for human beings in his relationships.

In many ways, Ron, who was a close friend of mine for over forty years, was the most courageous of all of us. He kept on and on writing with little success, almost no real financial success for years and years, and few people valued his work. In fact, he did not get much recognition until the very end of his life. He would not compromise. His stance was made up from the huge variety of blue-collar jobs which he did, of many blows suffered and many insights gained, but his work remains ironclad and unique. Importantly, his confidence was never challenged by all the vicissitudes of fate.

This confidence is an important aspect of stance, which many academics neglect. Failure of confidence is seldom analysed or even mentioned. We have examined two writers whose lives were cut short; one who, in a sense, cut his own life as writer short was John Morgan, well known as a journalist, BBC pundit and one of the founders of HTV. He, D. B. Rees, a historian who later published the definitive military history of the Korean War, and myself, were very much encouraged by Keidrych Rhys who allowed us the freedom of his magazine *Wales* as short-story writers. This was important to us at the time and I never cease to be grateful to Keidrych who was an Arts Council on his own. Later, John Morgan (1929–1988) wrote some brilliant short stories for the *New Statesman*, one of which I included in the first *Penguin Book of Short Stories* because it reflected an aspect of our humour only rarely recorded. Let me quote the opening:

A Writer Came to Our Place

There was a note on the desk informing me that Mr Sumner, a journalist, would be arriving during the night. I was to show him around the factory, allowing him to see anything and anyone.

'You'd think,' I said to Sid who shared the room with me, and who was resting his feet on the desk, 'that I had nothing better to do.'

He turned out to be plump, Mr Sumner, and he wore an expensive grey suit. Over his arm, he carried a new pair of overalls. As soon as he was in the room he smiled charmingly at both of us and shook us by the hand. Sid, ironically courteous, offered Sumner his seat and himself sat on a tin can in the corner of the room. Sumner immediately offered cigarettes. We only took one each.

'I hope,' Sumner began, 'that I am not putting you out at all.' He enlarged his smile and looked at us both steadily in turn. 'My idea, basically, is to look at industry from the other side. One has the management's point of view, of course. But I want to know,' the white plump hand circling the face, as if he was hypnotising himself, and failing with the italicised word, 'how the *worker* feels about industry.'

'Shagged,' said Sid. 'Most of the time,' he added.

Sumner laughed. His laugh, like his voice, was steady and soft, discreet, establishing mutual sympathy and understanding. He behaved, and looked, like an MP for a constituency not to be found around here in which outward elegance was not the mark of a traitor.

'That is the kind of thing I want,' he said.

John Morgan wrote a novel, *The Small World*, which was rubbished in *The Observer*, a paper for which he himself wrote. The novelist and academic John Wain described the book, and indirectly John's friendship with Kingsley Amis, as 'failing to note the difference between authorship and ventriloquism'. The criticism mortified John. He never wrote another novel, and although Wain was similarly disparaging of Sean O'Casey later and drew an angry riposte from Hugh McDiarmid, stating that he was 'not fit to wipe O'Casey's boots', the damage was done. It always seemed ironic to me that John Morgan, who was urbane and sophisticated in a metropolitan way would be so hurt whereas Ron Berry who was totally ignored and later frequently undervalued should have shrugged his shoulders and metaphorically adjusted his rifle and pack and gone on up to the line time and time again. He never doubted himself and his confidence in himself was absolute. He once wrote to me:

> I'm the only man who can put this down with candour and good faith. I mean, after all the romanticised crap that's been done and swallowed as authentic by millions.

Lack of confidence, which might come and go, can be a crippling thing, and the next writer I want to consider is in some ways a conundrum – Gwyn Thomas (1913–1981). Let me remind you I am considering the short story only and I am one of the few whose regard for Gwyn was tempered by the different stances that he adopted, later in life, as a kind of universal joker, then a commentator and TV pundit. My admiration was for his earlier work, although I am not unmindful of the difficulties which he faced in getting published at all, and later the problems of earning a living when he gave up teaching.

I commend to you two stories both included in my two Penguin anthologies. The longest – it's more a novella really. *Oscar* unfolds before you as you read like an old black-and-white Polish film, one of those grey nightmares from the past in which injustice and villainy drive decency into the shadows, a John Bunyan-like story told with a narrative skill that is based on the American detective story. It has short staccato sentences, and a pronounced attitude in the beginning, a kind of trench-coat attitude, 'out of the side of the mouth', the bitter aggrieved voice of a nineteen-year-old whose job is to act as factotum to a monster, a man who owns a mountain. This makes him into a kind of untouchable mogul because he controls a slag heap from which poor people are allowed to scratch for coal, this Oscar who also owns houses for rent and is separated from the rest of the community in which he lives only by his wealth and power. He is not a remote ruler from a different class with a different manner of speech, but very local in his wants and desires, which makes him so understandable.

The story opens with Lewis, his employee who is nineteen, and has taken the job only because he has a widowed mother and no one else will employ him. Lewis has to collect a drunken Oscar from a pub called the Harp and then to take him home on horseback. Oscar is in a side room with a girl called Macnaffy.

Oscar was sitting by the table, his head right down on the table boards. His huge, fat body poured over the sides of the chair on which he sat. His very weight gave him some kind of balance or he would have been on the floor, or under the floor where he deserved to be, a long way under the floor, a thick stone floor. I took hold of his head by the hair and the ear. I lifted it a foot. The table boards beneath were dull and steamy from the heat of him. His jacket and waistcoat hung open and there were dark fingermarks all the way up his white shirt, pulled up, crumpled. If these fingermarks were the marks of the savage-looking Macnaffy, I thought she must have been playing on Oscar like a piano. I wondered what kind of music would come out of a hog. Brief, dirty, snorting little tunes. I dropped his head back on the table and even the sharp bang he got from that did not make him any wider awake.

The girl sitting by the fire grinned at me, as if she were trying to be friendly. I was strong and lean and must have been a great and pleasant change for her eyes after a session with Oscar in so close a room. I looked back at her, without smiling. She was no change for my eyes.

'What a bloody weight,' she said, jerking her head at Oscar. Her voice was soft and dark, which was a great feature of most women in the valley, even women who looked as if they were going to rip you open like this Macnaffy. Voices like cats' backs, the velvet of skin and purr.

'He's big,' I said, sticking my knee into the blue-serged overflow of Oscar's flesh to give a leverage.

'How the hell do you feed him up to that size? What do you feed him on?'

'Acorns. And twice a year I bathe him in swill.'

'Looks like it. How do you get him home?'

'First I drag him. Then I get him on a horse.'

'That doesn't sound like much of a job to me. Why don't you get fixed up as a waiter or a welder or something?'

'Dragging Oscar was a hard enough job to get.'

I put my hands beneath Oscar's armpits and tried to lift him. He budged only a little, only such a little as caused him nearly to tip off his chair. The eyes of the Macnaffy girl were fiercer as they glared at the still, sodden Oscar. Her face was like chalk writing something on the air. She did not have the body to cope with a man like Oscar. She flicked a burning chunk of tobacco from her cigarette which had started to burn unevenly.

'What gives him the right to think he can go around expecting girls to lie at his feet like mats to be jumped on?'

'...He owns a mountain. He can jump anywhere. There is also a big coal tip on top of Oscar's mountain and he owns that, too. And there are twenty or thirty people who work on that tip picking up bits of coal and putting them into sacks for Oscar. He sells those sacks of coal. So he's got a lot of money as well as a lot of mountain. As far as Oscar goes, there's nobody bigger than Oscar.'

'You know a lot for a kid. How old are you?'

'Past nineteen.'

'You know all about life?'

'I know all about Oscar.'

'He's most of it. What a bloody weight.'

'What a bloody life.'

The storyteller's voice is not the one we normally associate with Gwyn Thomas because he has assumed an unusual stance for him, and this is by no means unusual in the sense that many writers adopt different stances. A woman might write as a man, or a man, a woman. Sometimes a different persona is assumed. For example, there are a variety of different reasons for assuming an attitude or a stance. Lord Elwyn Jones used to tell a story of appearing for a group of miners who had attacked Sir Oswald Mosely's vehicle on an anti-fascist demonstration. One by one they came into the dock and were asked to state their occupations, and one by one they replied, 'Unemployed' whereupon the judge leant forward and said, 'There seem to be an unusual number of workshy among your clients, Mr Jones?' I'm perhaps being too obvious when I say that a writer could take up that attitude and use it for purposes of his or her own. In Gwyn's case, I think he was struggling with his feelings, above all his anger and compassion which required him to adopt this unusual, understated style.

In the story, Oscar is taken home and put to bed by his housekeeper but Lewis, the narrator, decides to return home, but before he does so, he calls in on his neighbours, a married couple, the husband, Danny, unemployed for the past nine years, and his wife, Hannah, who despairs of their lot. Danny, who is in poor health, challenges Lewis about working for Oscar.

'You ought to know different. You got some sort of brain. But you work for Oscar.'

'Oh, it's a job Danny.'

'But that Oscar's a hog. You've said that yourself. God knows how many times. Your old man would have kicked you over the roof for taking money off such a crap. Somebody'd be doing the world a kindness to put him out of the way. But you help us keep him in the way.'

'As long as he gives me pay, he can be any sort of hog he likes.'

'That's not the point,' said Danny in a high, excited voice, and I could see that something was worrying him and that he would like a long argument with me or even a quarrel to relieve his own feelings.

Hannah jumped to her feet and her lips were small and bitter as she looked down at Danny.

'That is the point,' she said. 'Let's be glad somebody can have a job and keep it. So long, Lewis.' She pushed her chair out of the way. 'I'm going to bed.'

She left the room. Danny's mouth, which had been hanging open, closed tight and his grey skin flushed as if a brush were being drawn over it, hard.

'She meant that for me, Lewis. Last week I got a job. I waited a long time for it. There should have been an eclipse to celebrate, but there wasn't and that was just as well. It was a job carrying sacks of coal. I found after a couple of hours that I couldn't even carry a sack of coal and they had to pick me off a pavement. Jesus, Lewis, I felt bad. Not just because the only job I've had in nine years finished almost before it started. I felt bad inside, too. I went and saw the doctor. He said my heart is bad. By the look of him as he said that it must be very bad. But he couldn't have looked any worse than I felt. So what are the chances of me working again? Not much now, with people knowing how I

> finished up on the ground after carrying one sack for Simons the coalman. I didn't tell Hannah what's supposed to be wrong with me. She'll guess that. Oh, hell, Lew, just think what kind of life she's had. That's what makes me sick. I lost my work seven months after we got married. I was healthy enough then, strong enough. I could have dug a whole mountain away if it would have helped Hannah and if there had been a mountain that did not belong to some bastard like Oscar. The doctor said strain was my trouble. He's talking nonsense. It was plain, simple bloody worry that ate the strength out of my heart. But now, I'm not worrying. What if I die. I won't lose anything by getting rid of myself, and Hannah might gain something. That's a hell of a thing for a man to be saying who's still pretty young, but I'm saying it and I mean it.'
>
> 'A hell of a thing,' I said.
>
> 'And I'm not going to be so daft as I've been.'
>
> 'What you mean, Danny?'
>
> 'I've been afraid. Afraid of Oscar, afraid of policemen, afraid of offending anybody in case I made things bad for myself. Now nobody can make things worse for me. Funny how good knowing that makes you feel.'

There follows another agonising tirade which is the most revealing piece of writing about the 1920s and its consequences upon the unemployed that any Welsh writer has undertaken.

The narrator does not interrupt.

> I kept my eyes on the fireplace. A lot of what Danny had said had slipped past my ears but I had the feeling that all his words were bunches of nettles being drawn up and down the bare sides of my body.
>
> 'Where are you going to get your coal then, Danny?'
>
> 'From Oscar's tip.'
>
> 'Oscar'll get you put in jail.'
>
> 'What's the difference? I'll be up there tomorrow morning.'

There now follows a terrible inevitability. The next day the tipping machinery on the mountain breaks down with the result that the pickers are sent home so that when Danny appears, he is isolated and alone. When Oscar appears on horseback, he carries a shotgun. An altercation takes place and it looks as if Danny is going to get the better of Oscar but he does not. Recovering, Oscar fires a shot into the air which causes Danny to fall badly. As Oscar rides away it is clear that Danny is dead, of shock.

Subsequently, Lewis, the narrator, neglects to tell the coroner at the inquest that Oscar had a shotgun and worse happens, as Oscar gets off scot-free and finally makes advances to Hannah.

It is a bleak tale in a bleak place, but Gwyn is making statements about unimaginable hardships and deprivation that he feels he must write down. The narrator says directly:

> I thought Oscar was lucky indeed to be able to clear out of his head things he had said and done not more than two days before. If you have the courage that comes from never having been slapped down, cheated or made hungry, you can perform this cleaning out process and think nothing of it. Only those whose poverty seems to have existed from the earth's beginning have to put up with being dragged down, down below the surface of the dead chains of past years, past days. The poor hug to their hearts all the yesterdays they know have not been lived and the burden is a heavy one.

This is a very different Gwyn Thomas to the famous TV persona of later years. In this, and stories like *The Teacher*, it seems to me he is driven to make statements to enter that area of necessariness defined by Elizabeth Bowen. It's just as well to remember, too, that Gwyn's grandfather started work in the Cymmer pit at the age of seven and was luckier than some for he had survived two explosions underground, and came out from the pit after one such disaster, only after scrambling over the bodies of his father and two brothers. I mention this because we never really think of the effect of such monumental deprivation upon the family, the women in particular. Gwyn's mother died when he was six in a state of exhaustion, and while, I suppose, every generation arrives fresh in a sense, the effect of such seismic events is perhaps immeasurable. I was to witness this myself in an indirect way later and it falls into that area of experience that I have already mentioned in connection with Rhys Davies's mother. The Workhouse, the War, the Western Front, these are but words until we examine them in terms of consequences bearing down upon individuals.

My grandmother lost two brothers, and a son as a result of the First World War, and a son in the second. As a child I lived with the consequences of that. I listened endlessly to stories of 'things as they might have been', of the days the telegrams came. In a cupboard upstairs was a mud-stained officer's tunic, a Sam Browne, a holstered Luger pistol, gallantry medals, as well as the brass shell cases that everybody seemed to have. I had a direct link with those objects and the events have always interested me, but in almost everything I have read, there is something missing. It is as if something happened in 1918 that has never been satisfactorily explained. It was first of all, a common experience.

Richard Hughes (1900–1976) observed:

> We were ... unlikely to live much beyond the age of nineteen, and (we) accepted this as the natural order of things, just as mankind in general accepts the unlikelihood of living much beyond eighty or so... So generation after generation of boys grew big, won their colours, and a few terms later ... were mere names, read aloud in chapel once. As list succeeded list the time of other little boys for the slaughter-house was drawing nearer, but they scarcely gave it a thought as they in turn grew into big boys, won their football colours.

I have been drawing attention to the forces, events, peculiarities of birth and circumstance that go to take up a writer's stance, in particular the attitudes of certain Welsh short-story writers. There were, in fact, few Welsh short stories dealing with the First World War, apart from Frank Richards' stories of regimental life which Hemingway greatly admired. The poets seemed to say it all. But just think, for weeks in 1916, casualties averaged some 10,000 killed or seriously wounded every day: while the British press carried nothing but good news from the front.

So what I am really asking in terms of a writer's stance, or anybody's stance for that matter, what are the consequences of being lied to? And what are the consequences of silence in the face of such calumny?

Of course, it is not always only the cataclysmic events of history that directly affect us but people. I spent the entire years of the Second World War with my grandmother, as everyone else was away. If she went out in the blackout, I went as guard to several houses. Her widowed friends were all of the same generation. There were medals and mementoes in nearly every house. I listened endlessly to stories and opinions, and who is to say what their influence was upon me? Dai Smith has said that the women in many of my stories are the truth-tellers and I know that there was a generation of women who were not afraid to speak their minds while many men drew back. We learn, we are influenced, by charged moments that later stand out in our lives, with a sense of joy, of pain, of multiple pleasures, of warm affection. I am finally not so sure that you can ever complete the picture of influence.

I began with a neat definition of the writer fish, *Anableps anableps*. But seeing is not everything, nor a level stare, 'seeing life steadily and seeing it whole'. The whole story is also composed of great tides of feeling which inform us equally, as do a myriad of happenings, chance encounters, accidents of fate, deprivations.

It occurs to me that almost all the stories I have selected to discuss have a sense of the shortness of life, of mortality. It is to do with age, and place. My age and my place, and the writers at my elbow. If I were a young member of the audience now, I would feel impatience and want to reach out to the storytellers of a much later generation, to Raymond Carver, say, or the new women writers of the present. But they too have had to learn to move their elbows freely. For every generation, what the writer has to do is to induce a few nods!

Consider the marvellous and lyrical short-story writer from Denbigh who, like Alun Lewis, did not live to see his full potential realised: this is Geraint Goodwin (1903–1941) on going back to the sanatorium with TB when his condition worsened.

> It was as though one had broken the pane in a hurricane lamp and the flame suddenly leapt to burn itself out – one felt a desire all at once to rush out of the hospital, to rush out to the mountains. I felt that I had been trapped and I wanted to rush out just as I was. I might die here but I could never die in the mountains.
>
> (*The Heyday in the Blood*, 1936)

I nodded at that. Not eight miles from where I am standing, I saw a gypsy boy go out of the bathroom window of the TB hospital after just one day. He could not stand the pyjamas, the sputum pots, the smell of disinfectant, the injections, the polished floors, the whole regime. He was heading out, and upwards to the fields. I recognised what Goodwin was talking about. He knew. The reader's nod then, is a precious thing, the writer's final unseen reward, the ultimate accolade, but where it comes from, only the writer really knows. So here's a final thought. Those who speculate as I have been doing, should tread carefully, mindful always of the text which is the only solid thing we have, and all the writer wanted us to have. If they are not careful and suitably diffident, critics bear the same relationship to the writer as the bookie does to the race horse, handsome in his check suit, but ever forgetful of the fact that the real joy is that the horse has bothered to run at all.

SCREWING THINGS UP

It was not exactly an art gallery. More a space, an upstairs chamber with a pitched roof crisscrossed by roof beams and narrow stained-glass windows for light. Not the best light for his show, the painter thought, but, after all these years illuminating his people and places, better than the nothing on his home patch which had been the case no matter how much praise or interest was shown elsewhere. A few private buyers locally but no interest or purchase from educational or municipal sources. Nothing of his lifetime's work was hung or displayed publicly in the valley where he had been born and where, ceaselessly in a haze of wonder at what he saw, he had worked most of his life. Looking and painting. Making it new, making it true.

The offer of a curated show of his work in the town at the entrance to the valley settlements had come from a newly arrived community coordinator for the arts and regeneration. The ersatz building she had taken over as a centre had once been the town hall, a stone-built confection of turrets and brass-studded doors and oak staircases, and gently raked benches on which the elected representatives of the people sat in cogitation and deliberation at a time of coalfield expansion and untold prosperity. The furnishings had been stripped out and the gilt-edged portraits in oil of successive mayors had been hung elsewhere, in the new local government hub further up the valley: a pagoda structure of blue glass set between green wooden frames located alongside the artificial lake which had been created on top of the waste ground of a former colliery. Here the expanded and centralised workforce, officers and clerks and councillors of the enlarged local authority, met and deliberated on the future. On the site of their previous incarnation as administrators and legislators they funded 'leisure and culture': notably, yoga classes, salsa lessons, keep fit, origami and knitting crafts, choral singing, watercolour drawing and, yes, the occasional exhibition of the work of local amateur artists. The painter had been uneasy about accepting the invitation he received but the assurance that the space was to be all his own and the selection and hanging of the work was to be in his own hands was enough persuasion. The Exhibition of Contemporary Valley Art as it was coyly called in the publicity leaflets, and over which he had had no control, was to be in place for four weeks.

The painter looked around the upstairs chamber, a long and narrow room but with good height built into the Victorian mock-Hanseatic structure, and felt he had judged the mix and size of his work, some canvasses brought in by loan from museums and private collectors, well enough for the space. On opening night, no speeches made only a cursory welcome from the centre's coordinator and the chair of the council on duty attendance with some colleagues, there were around thirty people circulating, squinting and sipping warm orange juice or tepid straw-coloured white wine in nubby plastic glasses.

There were canvases, six feet by four, impastoed with globs of oil paint or ridged with lines of acrylic; there were watercolour sketches on ragged paper and mixed-media works, square or oblong, in which chalk marks dialled down the vibrant colour of streetscapes and the velvet seduction of ink-blue skies. He had included work across the spectrum of his styles and over the years. Sombre self-portraits in profile from the late 1940s were in olive-green tints and biscuit-brown hues for clothes, and his eyes were melancholic and wild, staring out to an unseen distance. The next decade had two violently autobiographical takes on him and his new family: one of man and wife crossing the recently introduced zebra crossing on the valley floor, she pushing a pram, the painter jaunty in coat and titfer and clutching an exuberant bunch of flowers as all modern life unfurled before them; the other a wide lens cinemascopic trio waiting at a bus stop, this time his one basilisk eye stares out in dread at the loss of all sweet certainties to hand. His abstracts were darker and darker, black rectangles swallowing the white light of illumination or egg-yolk yellows defiant against the environment of blocks of cobalt blue. Any semblance of naturalism or figurative realism was shucked off as he strove to find the dynamic of the place which obsessed and held him, its very meaning requiring a transformative interpretation, not the shutter click of its outwardness with which he had begun.

At the far end of the room where the roof made a generous triangle so the space below opened out, he had placed what he considered to be his master statement of intent and execution. The canvas was eight feet by four, its immensity almost covering all of the tapered length of the newly white-washed plasterboard wall. He had had the painting mirror plated to the wall with heavy brass fastenings which were deeply screwed in on either side of the canvas. Two men, clutching their insipid urine-coloured wine in their unbreakable plastic glasses, had paused in front of it. Councillors both, guardians of the public purse and municipal probity, quietly conversing. They lingered in front of the work, static in intense concentration of every inch of it. The painter noticed them, felt absurdly pleased, detached himself from the congratulations of a small group of invited guests, and moved towards the two admirers. The painter stood silently behind them and looked over their hunched shoulders at his masterpiece.

The background was a variety of blues, here bright, there shadowed, and variously across it from top to bottom was a sinuous, undulating watery bright blue river flanked by the straighter lengths of road with the headlamps of toy cars all along it. Terraced housing, or rather the roofs and pine ends, was inverted and thrown sideways or diagonally to the centre point of the picture which was a cone-ended rocket shape within which ghostly outlines of a man, the painter, walked upstairs or stood in doorways or gazed out of the blue-paned windows at the heat of the burnt-orange and purple-red ambience which consumed him. Every motion in the painting was one of climbing up or swooping down the flattened landscape as if in a medieval mapping of this unlikely habitation in which humans swarmed and begat themselves. The men were sometimes framed by doorways as if they were in their coffins. At its margins bands of stars bound it together and somewhere an easel of creation could be located within a house without the walls of blindness. It depicted in phantasmagoric fashion an upside-down world. Its strange familiarity derived from its very otherness, a vision and not a dream of how and where and why people had lived and worked in and under an epicentre of modernity of which the painting was a prophesying parody. The painter knew that with its making he had found the revelatory vision of home, universal in its singular uniqueness, which he had forever sought.

The men before him and his painting were still muttering. He moved closer in as the man now on his right-hand side spoke and waited for his companion's reflective response.

'Fucking ridiculous, Abe. I agree. What clown did this?'

'Too true, boy. Never seen nothing like that. What's the title in the brochure again? Valley Landscape With Figures. Makes no sense to me. I reckon one of our kids could make a better go of it than the way that man has done. Bloody colours are all wrong as well. Where's the green, the black, and the Rhondda greys, eh?'

The painter was startled. Taken aback. He felt, quite uncommonly for him, the need to explain. About perspective. About colour chromatics. About juxtaposition. About the proclivity to dream which the place and its history induced. About having to see beyond surface things if the meaning of things and their discovery in shapes and the music of colour were to become clear. After the fog of clichés. After the opaqueness of emblems as the stage props of a culture deserving to be prised open, from within, as a new mode of stagecraft, ultimate truth-in-the-waiting. He hesitated. Then he ran out of time.

The councillor to his left was jabbing his finger at the side of the painting, first on one side of the canvas, then pointing to the other side, at the mirror plates pinning the work to the wall.

'And just look at that, mun. Look at those bloody screws they've put into the wall. Fresh painted that was, I know for a fact when they take that bloody thing down off of that wall there'll be huge holes in the plaster. That'll need to be filled in. The whole wall will need to be painted again. More expense. Unnecessary expense for the council, for the ratepayers, if you ask me. Cos who else is going to pay for the repair work. Answer me that, Abe. Answer me that.'

The painter said nothing but he had decided to buy a large tube of Polyfilla to donate to the centre. Only fair perhaps, he thought, if he had been responsible for screwing it all up.

AT HOME

RHYS DAVIES AND HIS 'TURBULENT VALLEY'

Looking back at my growing up in Tonypandy with all the paraphernalia of a finished history and an absent historiography all around us – so no unemployment, no wars, no sickening poverty, no readily identifiable enemies and oppressors – it is the case that whether in school or on the street, at home or from the lending library, there was no available touchstone of our identity to finger and ponder over. I mean, apart from familial and communal memories, no paintings, no films, no dramas, no short stories, no novels about us, who we were and had been, except maybe for some music and the individual fame of some actors and singers. Casting around in the recesses of my sense now of a mind being gradually made aware of the oddity of that vacuum as teenage years came, I think my first intuition that there was something, after all, to discover would have come at the end of my school years when a copy of Gwyn Jones' *Oxford Book of Welsh Short Stories* (1956 originally, so for me, from its 1960 reprint maybe 1961 or 1962) came to hand. Given my other reading matter by then – an early plunge into Chekhov, a taste of Hemingway, bloodbath with Dostoevsky, a first reading of *War and Peace* for I was obnoxiously precocious – I was not overly impressed by the mix of Gothic tall-hatted tales and winsome whimsy he had assembled other than the stories of Dylan Thomas which I had found elsewhere for myself and relished their suburban thirties surrealism. I was more interested, too, in the connection my Spanish teacher, Gwyn Thomas, had to the Rhondda than in his 1940s sardonic stance and the transatlantic transference of a comedy idiom more Groucho than Karl. Not that I intuited that then or until much later on. And then there was, for me, the intriguing fact that Gwyn Jones had also chosen two stories by another Rhondda writer, this time one

I had not heard of although he was, aged fifty-three in 1956 according to his given dates, a senior member of that select tribe. Rhys Davies, I learned, was also from Blaenclydach, slap bang on our street's doorstep, just a walk away across the lower slopes of the coal tip and up the cwm at whose dead end my grandfather had worked for half a century in the Cambrian Colliery. I registered that connection more incisively than I had liked either of the stories on offer. Decades would pass before I would begin to appreciate how crafted and echoing of life his best work, especially the short stories, were. Through his brother Lewis, like Rhys upended from Clydach Vale into lifelong exile in England, a sizeable monetary legacy allowed my friend the entrepreneurial litterateur Meic Stephens, to establish the Rhys Davies Trust, which I would serve as chair for many years, to support and promote Welsh writing in English and, if possible, in concentric circles radiating out from the epicentre of mid-Rhondda.

*

On Census night 1901 the (probably underestimated) population of the Rhondda Valleys was 113,735 and rising. One of the newest additions would be Rees Vivian Davies, born on 9 November in mid-Rhondda, the very epicentre of this spectacularly booming coal society whose population, among the fastest growing in the British Isles, had, since 1871, soared from 16,914 in the parish of Ystradyfodwg to its city-like proportions as the new century began. Nor would it stop there. By the time Viv was twenty, and already Rhys in his own mind at least, the Rhondda Urban District Council was the second largest conurbation in Wales, set to peak at over 167,000 in the few years of boom that remained to it. This was the essential Rhondda experience ingested by the adolescent and young adult before he shook its confines off in every sense but one: and that was the way its private, individuated meanderings beneath or within its more public framework of events haunted and informed his mind and imagination.

Most of that swelling population were, unlike Rhys, in-mi-grants and increasingly coming from further and further afield as this carboniferous Eldorado beckoned them down to the First World War. This was even true of Rhys's own forebears, for although his parents, the Tonypandy grocer Thomas Davies and his stern schoolmistress wife, Sarah, from Ynysybwl, were as local to mid-Rhondda as you could be in this overnight building frenzy, their origins lay in West Wales, in that Carmarthenshire which gave his writings a glimpse of lost bosky Celtica to counterpoint the mongrelized streets of his own Wales. In his lean fiction and in his elaborated autobiography, both places and people are tinged with lost worlds and current compromises. Sometimes the falsity of the juxtaposition rings its own warning of grotesquerie and caricature and, at other times, is weighted with a sentimentality too sweet to be other than sickly. Yet even these emotive representations speak of the insufferable burden of being born a writer in this particular Rhondda: too big, too bewildering, too panoramic to comprehend fully. It is in the interstices of this confusion, among his ambivalences and evasions, that the twenty-first-century reader can really observe how closely Rhondda marked Rhys and how intensely Rhys documented Rhondda in his imagination since, as he wrote at the end of the chapter entitled 'Clydach Vale' in *Print of a Hare's Foot* (1969): 'Hailing from a less raw and dangerous place than the Rhondda, it took my mother some time to subdue her puritanic irritation with the turbulent valley. But I was born into it.'

'Born into it' he certainly was. No better vantage point would he have had than from living behind and above the grocery shop, named the Royal Stores by his father, set across the road from the Central, a raucous pub, and halfway up the road which straggled steeply up Clydach Vale as it debouched giddily from the settlement of Tonypandy below. The Rhondda Fawr. Again, the numbers overwhelm before we can put faces to them. Almost 70 per cent of the male population aged twelve and over were employed in the mining industry. The population was young and notoriously fecund, in and out of the marriage bed, as both rates of birth and of illegitimacy left averages way behind. In mid-Rhondda alone, north and south of Tonypandy, there were 12,000 miners at work by 1910, producing half of the total coal spewing out of the Rhondda to Cardiff and the world. And at the top of Rhys's tributary valley lay the Cambrian Colliery, itself the heart of D. A. Thomas's overwhelming Cambrian Combine, an amalgamation of pits that fuelled Thomas's global interests in shipping, patent fuels and newspapers. 'Raw and dangerous' it was, too, but a backwater it was decidedly not.

Just before Rhys Davies celebrated his ninth birthday, the 1910 industrial conflict at the Cambrian Combine exploded onto the streets as the Tonypandy Riots and brought imported Metropolitan Police, Lancashire Fusiliers and 18th Hussars into the valley. He writes vividly, especially in his 1969 memoir, of the autocratic D. A. Thomas, the future Viscount Rhondda, and of the technicolour clashes, lasting over a year, which gave Tonypandy an ever-reverberating fame in the annals of labour history. Yet his several accounts are essentially a diorama rather than an analysis. This sense of the relationship of these visceral moments to the longer time sequence which connected them to the successful national strike of 1912 for a minimum wage is as attenuated as his grasp of the progressive movements being incubated then and there in the Rhondda, for both pragmatic Labourism and quasi-revolutionary forms of syndicalism.

Thus his sense of the crowd's frenzied action in destroying the commercial property of the township on 8 November is a compound of moralising as a lament that Welsh spiritualism and perhaps Welsh ethnicity had forsaken the place and a contemporary annoyance at the 'slavering and barbaric eyed' colliers who, 'repelled' by the police in their attack on the Glamorgan Colliery at nearby Llwynypia, had 'vented their rage' on the innocent shopocracy. His writing in this vein (in *My Wales*, 1937) exhibits little of the empathy or the political insight his Blaenclydach contemporary, Lewis Jones (1897–1939), showed in *Cwmardy* (1937). But, then, Rhys's politics, conditioned perhaps by his Liberal father or just withering on the vine of a greater indifference, were never quite typical of his native ground. This was, in another sense, the lack of a unifying principle or philosophy which another near contemporary, Glyn Jones (1905–1995), remarked on in a review of Rhys Davies's novel *A Time to Laugh* in the magazine *Wales* in that same year,

1937. By then, apart from some short stays and increasingly infrequent visits, Rhys had been, via London and Europe, long gone. And in his absence, the workforce was cut in half; unemployment among those that remained, whilst thousands migrated, soared to over 40 per cent and was stuck there by the mid-1930s. 'Red' Rhondda now existed but its labours were expended in marching and talking.

So his account of the 'turbulent valley' in *My Wales* (1937) is particularly intriguing since it oscillates so dramatically between the raucous world which had cradled him but not held him, and the despairing society whose quiescence in the downtrodden 1930s he deplored. It is as if, at one and the same time, he is driven to acknowledge the (vanished) power to fascinate which the Rhondda of his first two decades so abundantly possessed and the (evanescent) pity which its humanity could invoke in him.

In one tone we can hear the cold-comfort hand-wringing simplicities of a back-to-the-soil *naiveté* but one in which an ironic gleam is not far away:

> It is merely one of the disagreeable and ruthless activities of modern life that hundreds of thousands of workers have to be left abandoned when, because of breakdowns in the world's commercial system, the accumulation of quick fortunes is no longer possible in the region. These workers are merely unlucky to be caught in the fag-end of an era.
>
> The only cheerful thought one can offer them is that they still have Wales. Surely they can forget their woes in applying their undying energy, now that most of the great coal owners and ironmasters have departed, to giving their land once again to its former cleanliness. It is doubtful whether salmon ever again will consent to leap the cascade of Berw Rhondda, but surely those huge offensive heaps of colliery rubbish called tips can be used in sweeping up those derelict works rusting in the Welsh rain which, as ever, falls to fructify green produce as well as to enter the decrepit shoes of the unemployed. After the ugly 150 years' interruption from the outside world, perhaps Wales can now return to its former pastoral unison – if it can afford.

> And, if the million or so abandoned people who cannot be absorbed elsewhere return to that elementary condition of wresting the simplest of livings out of the soil, they surely will not be bitter. Why should they be! Generations of their ancestors, and themselves, have obtained share of the industrial spoil, measured out carefully according to the economic laws of the times. No fury, no bitterness, no lamentations, should be felt. They have had the interesting opportunity of helping to build an historic era which placed their country in a wealthy and respected position among the nations which do great business over the seas of this faulty world. This should be a comforting memory to them in their solitude.

Taken at face value, this has the breathtaking candour of a Madison Avenue copywriter in search of a Development Agency commission, only that is to cross-pollinate decades and lose historical context. For Rhys Davies that context was the 1930s and there is enough elsewhere in his work to allow us to drop that tincture of irony into his otherwise Olympian dismissal of those toiling souls, apparently without mind or matter to hinder them. Indeed, over a third of his so-called 'travelogue', *My Wales*, is devoted to chapter 3 and 'The South Wales Workers'. They sit uneasily amid chapters on the 'Eisteddfod', 'Welsh Players', 'Welsh Characters', and thoughts on 'Words' and 'Holiday Trip', but it is as if the social currents of his turbulent valley will not free him from their tug. He postures, he tut-tuts, he exoticizes and he caricatures but, steadily, he is, in small things more than large, faithful to what he has seen and known, and so necessarily punctures the jibes and inflated generalities of outside accusers.

> To strike at such a time [in the 1914–18 war] with every piece of coal valuable and with a dangerous shortage of men to work the basic industries [because of the high volunteering rate of miners!] was criminal and not to be borne. The miners were taking advantage of the country's helpless plight. This was the time when people wrote to the newspapers and said the miners ought all to be poisoned, imprisoned, starved, put between the opposed rows of machine guns in Flanders etc; never mind,

> nemesis would come to them. They were bloated profiteers (who were not?); they bought pianos which they couldn't play (sometimes two); fur coats bedecked their wives; they washed themselves in whisky; they bought farms and kept other women; they wore evening 'tails' when they set out in the morning for a few days by the sea, and the ears of their daughters (who were baggages of sin) dripped diamonds; they went into Cardiff for evening trips and made that respectable city redden with shame. Further notoriety fell on the area.
>
> I saw little evidence of this shocking gaiety. Pianos were certainly bought, by musical-minded colliers who for long barren years had craved these instruments, suitable furniture in a land of song. I saw women I had known as gaunt and shabby grey shapes come out of their little dark dwellings amazingly gay with a few ribbons and a feather or two. They went excitedly to the Welsh seaside towns for a holiday (many of the swank English resorts used to turn down applicants for accommodation from such places as the Rhondda). New, wonderful comforts were suddenly and pathetically in their grasp. Some did not know how to use these comforts, having been without them for so long. Life had become a bit of a fairground – though, because of sons and relations in the trenches, a threatening fairground.
>
> This little period of fake prosperity, a few years out of the hundred and fifty, was really the last flourish of the old vigorous life peculiar to South Wales. The district became, as the war finished, less of a place enclosed by its own mountains, by its special problems, as an Eldorado flushed with wealth over which there had been terrible local battles and a period of Welsh civil war.

The First World War really was a cultural as well as a political watershed for Wales. He summed it up, again sharply in focus, as a change in outlook beyond mere economic shifts or ideological winds; it was an education in and out of the classroom which had affected the kind of Wales that would now exist for the long remainder of the twentieth century: 'Schools had done their work, the Miners' Federation was an organisation of portentous influence, the Great War had given the final jolt to a consciousness that had never been very aware of the world beyond the mountain.'

He was not the only one of his generation to name the post-war years – especially after 1926 – as ones of summation or even closure. His own major response – in the trilogy of novels he then wrote – *Honey and Bread* (1935), *A Time to Laugh* (1937) and *Jubilee Blues* (1938) – was to impose a fabular pattern on the chaos of detailed life that had rushed in and out of the mining valleys since the 1840s. His abiding talent, however, was for the miniature. In that form – notably in the short story or in slight vignettes – he etched over and over the profiles of individual men and women trapped, released, crushed, saved or just discarded by the weight of human indifference and the insistence on filling in the blank page of human existence with our own distinctive markings.

He was then, fortuitously and happily, 'born into it' to let us feel, intimately, the sights, sounds, smells – the synaesthesia of the private – that lay within this apparently grim human habitation. To the contemporary outside eye, such as this London reporter sent down in the wake of the 1910–11 disturbances, the picture was of a tottering mayhem not so much landscaped as vomited into shape:

> [Tonypandy lies]... in a narrow winding valley confined by squat denuded hills upon whose blank sides tower huge mounds of rock and rubbish excavated from the numerous coal tips. The river, sometimes almost dry, sometimes rushing down in tempestuous flood, but always pestilential with all manner of garbage and offal, is crossed and re-crossed by the railway over which, all day and all night, roll the never-ending coal trains on their way to the distant sea-port. The high road, where it may, runs its course alongside the odorous river, but for the greater part of its length it has to hug the steep slopes of the cheerless hills ... long rows of steep gardens rise sheer from the roadside to a line of small stone-built four-roomed cottages. A paved alleyway at the rear, the length of the terrace, gives access to the houses, and from this narrow alleyway, another series of gardens continue the ascent to a similar row of cots, and so the terraces rear them-

> selves until the topmost is reached from which the roadway, the pits, the railway and the river are seen in panoramic array. Each alley has one waterspout, common to all the homes in that row. The two tiny back rooms are darkened by the overhanging gardens of the higher terrace, and the houses are so low that a man must stoop before entering.

But Rhys Davies knew, from experience and observation, that if you did indeed stoop to enter you uncovered the secrets of living and dying for which he was so inquisitive and which, in this context of an embattled community, he would purvey so skilfully and compassionately.

At times, Rhys Davies's witnessing of all these crossed-over lives – not least from the custom and practice of pre-industrial society to industrialised routine and urbanised habituality – is almost anthropological. Not least in his highly fashioned, or is that manufactured, autobiographical writings. Again and again, however, the incidence of happenings in a life were alchemised into the significance of what was, after all, merely incidental by the magicking of fiction in which form human relationships can be reconfigured into a meaningfulness otherwise only latent in an actual time. Thus, in 1969 he 'remembered' for his memoir the schoolboy visitation of the recently dead, undertaken with his friend Jim Reilly out of curiosity and from a morbid fascination with what was all too common an event in that pre-1914 Rhondda, and which he had by 1942 transformed into the haunting vignette 'The Dark World' into which he had stooped, so young, to enter.

The custom was for adults to call at homes where windows were covered by white sheets to signal a death within in order to pay respects to the deceased. Although schoolboys, they pretended to have a passing acquaintance with the dead, often a young person, and in turn, might be given a glass of small beer or a morsel to eat after a viewing of the laid-out body on a trestle table or more often in a bed upstairs. In the story, Tonypandy and the precincts beyond, into Llwynypia and Penygraig, is forever swathed in cold grey mist, a few gas lamps feebly spluttering and persistent rain in the few weeks before Christmas.

Thomas Morgan is the son of shopkeepers, and Jim the son of an Irish miner, himself set to go underground. But the adventure into the unknown unsettles Thomas when, by chance, they enter a house where he himself is known – to Elias, the young widowed collier, and the mother of Gwen who has died giving birth to a still-born baby. She had been a servant in the Morgan household and Thomas had carried messages between the sweethearts, himself an alibi in their trysts before Gwen's removal into marriage:

> Elias looked older, older and thinner. Thomas kept his gaze away from him as much as possible. He felt shy at being drawn into the intimacy of all this grief. The old woman kept on quavering. At last Elias said, quietly now: 'You will come upstairs to see her, Thomas. And your friend.' He opened a door at the staircase and, tall and gaunt, waited for them to pass. Thomas walked past him unwillingly, his stomach gone cold. He did not want to go upstairs. But he thought that Elias would take a refusal hardly. Jim, silent and impassive, followed with politely quiet steps. He opened a door at the staircase and, tall and gaunt, waited for them to pass...
>
> In a small, small bedroom with a low ceiling two candles were burning. A bunch of snowy chrysanthemums stood on a table beside a pink covered bed. Elias had preceded them and now he lifted a starched white square of cloth from off the head and shoulders of the dead.
>
> She was lying tucked in the bed as if quietly asleep. The bedroom was so small there was nowhere else to look. Thomas looked, and started with a terrified surprise. The sheets were folded back, low under Gwen's chest, and cradled in her arm was a pale waxen doll swathed in white.

Now, for Thomas, the game is over. Outside in the rain he is riven with terror at the memory he carries from the dark world he has seen. His friend, Jim, is impassive, even scornful – 'What's up with you!' he jeered. 'You seen plenty of 'em before, haven't you?' The boys push and shove each other, fighting in the mud before they part.

In *Print of a Hare's Foot* – where it is also clear that Gwen, but not her death, is based on the Davies servant Esther – the factual visitations that winter, frequent and blackly comic, remind us of the basis of the story. The relationship between Jim and Rhys, however, is both more personally intimate and more fated as a parting.

> Jim Reilly remained my close friend until he left our school to go down the pit and I left to go on to the 'County' in Porth, which made a change of position inevitable... We viewed a dozen or more corpses that winter. On one occasion it was a candle-lit baby, from whose white, white face a silent woman drew away a piece of black-edged notepaper.

Their paths will diverge with no choice in the matter and as abruptly as the passage from life to death they have prematurely seen on their nightly forays. What Rhys Davies renders, here and elsewhere in his fictive delving into Rhondda's theatre of absurdities, is the return of memory as the reproach against the living made by the dead, denied even the fleeting aspiration of life as they are consigned not by illness or biology but by the pathology of a sick society, to their everlasting dark world:

> Jim would often lapse into vague reveries. Then prim absences into the privacies of a girl clouded the freckled, strong-chinned face under his fringe of yellow hair. One August afternoon, a few months before he left school to go down the pits, at fourteen, we went searching for bilberries in the rough grass of a mountain top. Failing to find any of the luscious purple fruit, Jim sat down and, bored, unbuttoned his knickerbockers and showed me what he had. It was very fat and seemed a burden to him. 'In Ireland,' he said morosely, 'they give us stirabout.' He had seen his father's when the old bastard stood washing pit dirt off before the kitchen fire – 'It's smaller,' he added...
>
> He went down Number 2 pit of the Cambrian. He told me his mother shortened an old pair of moleskin trousers belonging to one of his two brothers, and, philosophic about everything save

his father, he accepted this and all his lot without complaint. I did not leave our school above the slaughterhouse until after the next term. Meanwhile I saw much less of Jim; as a collier boy his way of life was different. I had been a pupil in the county school two years when, arriving back one afternoon, I was told about the brown van taking him home some hours earlier. He had been killed by a fall of roof. It would not take shape in my mind. Refusal of it remained locked in me. I could not go and knock at the door of his window-shrouded house to offer my respects. I dreaded seeing the white-draped windows. But I stayed home from school on his day and, at the last moment, sped up to the house for the second funeral I went to.

You do not, either in the end or in the beginning, go to Rhys Davies for the fact-of-the-matter, you go to him for the matter-of-the-thing: and in this his growing consciousness of his own sexuality as being different from the public aspect of Rhondda life became one insightful window onto that world. A sidling glance to reveal what was hidden and so was revelatory of others. You can tell immediately, especially if you too were a native of a mid-Rhondda still caught in its coalfield heyday, how intuitively he understands, too, how those rear alleyways – our gulleys – were a network of passageways in which, in the open, so to speak, communication, gossip and sexual congress could and did proceed apace. He had the social geography of this place at his fingertips of sensibility. His Rhondda was, after all and in a literal sense, a world of strangers. They needed to find out about each other, as did all immigrant societies. There were established enclaves in particular chapels, or in particular underground districts of the pits themselves, where natives of one far village or another or those who clung to Welsh in a Rhondda where well over half the population still spoke it habitually down to the 1920s, could congregate and comfort each other. Inter-marriage was a mode of reinforcing such identities and quite common. In both public houses and in shops, men and women, usually separately, could exchange the coin of fresh recognition and old renewal. But it was in those back lanes that quiet conversation, gambling, fighting and the exploration of physical love – when the mountain tops grew too cold and the seaside was too remote – actually happened. He is, in all this, an incomparable guide. Yet it is never as some kind of superannuated Baedeker that he takes us by the hand. This is the Rough Guide to the Rhondda – its packed spaces of noise, its sudden spilling of light onto darkness when cinemas or variety theatres disgorge their audiences, or the sour mash smell of smoke-fugged saloon bars and the sticky sweetness beneath eiderdown covers as pink face powder is washed off by the ravenous kisses of the young. 'The pits were working full time now,' he wrote in *Print of a Hare's Foot* about the immediate pre-1914 years, and

> Saturday nights burst with the vigour of a big explosive cabbage... Shops, open until midnight in good times, gained lost ground. The pubs rang and shouted with language. Enmities were settled on the road outside ... and I liked the forgiveness of all things and people that followed.

His is a more relaxed, almost always engaged, account of the people's swirling life than the one his mentor D. H. Lawrence contrived for the Nottinghamshire coalfield. Rhys Davies's fictional colliers, though they can be depicted as subhuman, are never quite as frightening in their distance, earned and unshareable, as are Lawrence's when we glimpse them, sexually charged carnivores squatting on their haunches and leering, with Gudrun and Ursula in *Women in Love*. Whatever Lawrence wanted, and raged because he could not find it, for himself in his relationship with those colliers, with his father and their damned acceptance of whatever life brought, it was not the lack Rhys Davies felt. The only other South Welsh writer who even comes close to the missing dimension of those too easily hastened lives was Alun Richards who, like Rhys, is able to make us see through the eyes of the women who, far from being the marginalised sector which social and economic truisms would have us swallow, were the psychological factor which continuously, if from a private margin, kept the issue of humanity itself at the forefront of Rhondda's history.

It all comes together in a marvellous late work which is more an enamelled piece of anecdotage until the terrible clang of its ending than one of his delicately crafted short stories. The story – 'The Pits are on the Top' – is set in the Rhondda of the Second World War. This is not the rip-roaring place of another wartime's prosperity. Too much of the pall of the interwar years and the miserable knowledge those decades brought hangs over it for that scenario to have any credibility. Nor will any startling discovery or revelation or brutality be uncovered, as was common in his greater stories. The tone is almost that of a quiet documentary, and all the more effective for it. What makes it sing is the setting – a bus journey from the valley's bottom to the top of the adjacent cwm, from Tonypandy to Blaenclydach, in a 'bright noon light' that is prismatic through the winter snowflakes – and the interaction between the passengers who add nothing to what they hear – of the death of a young woman's brother-in-law from bronchitis (or is it silicosis?) – to pass the gathered information between themselves like the natural dreadful thing it is whilst they observe the young collier and his girl who sit, uneasily, among them.

It is an inverse journey, away from the escape route of the larger settlement and back to its originating pits. It is grimly about endings and the way a man-made world causes that to occur too soon. The bereaved sister-in-law bemoans the cost of the wreath she has had to buy.

> It was composed of red tulips, white chrysanthemums and two long-tongued orchids which were the colour of speckled toads. She eyed the wreath with uncertainty and went on with her complaint:
>
> Fifteen shillings, and in the summer a bigger wreath than this you can get for seven-an-six. The price of flowers! And soon as I've taken this up I've got to come down again and be fitted for my black. Potching about!

Whether it was folk memory or actual recollection that caused Rhys Davies to find that seemingly innocuous phrase – 'The price of flowers!' – is neither here nor there. The echo of it is pregnant with the memories of an earlier Rhondda when, in the summer of 1910, colliers and their wives greeted the appearance of the conciliatory miners' agent and future Rhondda MP, Dai Watts

Morgan, with the bitter cry of 'What price are flowers, Mr Morgan?' just months before they wrecked, in the November riot, the shop on Tonypandy Square which boasted two hand-painted signs 'Studleys, Fruit Merchant' and 'Wreaths to Order'. In those years, apart from the fact that about a half of all recorded Rhondda deaths came about from accidents underground, colliers were dying of 'pulmonary consumption' at eleven times the rate of any other occupation. By the 1940s, at least, the medical arguments about 'pulmonary consumption' had been extended beyond 'pthisis' and 'bronchitis' to acknowledge the work-induced diseases of pneumoconiosis and silicosis. The women on Rhys Davies's bus discuss, with passion and knowledge and despair, whether the dead man should be dissected:

> 'It's a wonder,' said the fat woman, 'that they didn't open him up.'
>
> 'But the plates,' said the district nurse, who had her black maternity bag on her knee.
>
> 'He had the X-ray plates took not long ago and they didn't show anything.'
>
> The fat woman did not like to dispute with the district nurse, but, pushing the load more firmly into the basket, she said judiciously: 'Oh aye, the plates! Funny though for him to go so sudden; a young chap too – I wonder,' she turned again to the woman with the wreath, 'your sister didn't *ask* for him to be opened up, like Joe Evans and Dai Richards in my street was, when they went. It's worth it for the compensation. The pit's got to pay for silicosis, haven't they!' Indignation had begun to seep into her voice, before it subsided into doubt: 'Of course, there *is* a lot of bronchitis about.'
>
> Another woman who was nursing a baby voluminously wrapped in a thick stained shawl, said: 'There's two men got it in our street. You can hear them coughing across the road. Jinny James's 'usband one of them and she do say it's the silicosis.'
>
> 'What d'you expect,' said another, 'with their lungs getting full of the coal dust and rotting with it.'
>
> 'They can always have plates taken,' said the district nurse officially and looking down her nose. She leaned across to the woman with the baby. 'How's Henry shaping?' she asked,

> peering at the pink blob of face visible in the shawl's folds – she had brought Henry into the world.

All this time the slender, still young Dilys Morgan sits beside her powerfully built collier boyfriend, stocky Bryn Jones, and listens to their words and his persistent cough. She senses they are waiting for her to become 'one of them' and her resentment is tinged with an almost inexpressible fear. The engaged couple, Bryn without a muffler and hatless against the cold, leave the bus:

> His shoulders were broad, his limbs and hands thick and hard. The snowflakes turned into a grey liquor in the warm grease on his brisk black hair. The faint bluish pallor of his face was a little more evident. This week he was working on the night shift.
>
> They went down a side turning. They lived in the same street. But before they reached it he put his hand in hers and stopped her against an old building where there was shelter from the whirling flakes and wind. It was a bakehouse, and the oven was inside the wall, they could feel the heat coming out. He would not be seeing her again until Sunday.

In less than five pages, Rhys Davies brushes in a cycle of Rhondda life, one universal in its sketch of births and sex and death, generation on generation, and delicately precise in the quiddity of this valley pavane. Dilys, to be married in three months' time, cheers up and leaves the Bryn whose child she will surely bear and whose wreath she will certainly carry on another bus – 'she felt ... that she was lucky really. He was in a reserved occupation and he was a good miner with a place of his own down under ... he would be by her side for her to look after him.'

This is a near-perfect cameo, so good for its passing moment that it could be wished Rhys Davies had never left his 'turbulent valley' at all so that, for its long time, he might have stayed to capture its complete rhythm. Too much to ask, maybe, and perhaps the wrong request for, with the real end of that long time, we may finally now appreciate how vital those moments were and how exceptionally gifted was the wondrous writing talent that caught them, as they fell, one by one, into his imagination.

JOHN HOPLA AND THE TONYPANDY REVOLT

When, in the late winter of 2013, they finally cut through the panelling that had been put up on the wall of the club's redecorated room, they found his head-and-shoulders again. He had been damaged. Perhaps it had occurred when he was in transit from the Llwynypia Workmen's Institute and Library from whose stone-quarried frontage he had cast his eye up the Valley since 1916. The double-fronted building set back and above the road had, like most of its cultural kind, seemingly outlived its purpose after the final industrial rites had been given to the coal industry in the 1980s. It was pulled down and, maybe, the damage done to the plaque followed on from that hasty demolition. A fragment of the white marble had been chipped from the high Edwardian collar cinched tightly around his neck. In his new location, the NUM Club in Clydach Vale just half a mile away, he had, at first, been put on view again. Indoors this time. Then, as the NUM Club morphed into a full Social Club in the 1990s he had disappeared for over a decade, hidden behind that panelling and so, perhaps, it was that which had necessitated a slice off the aquiline nose of his embossed half profile to accommodate its now lying flat, as well as hidden. History was thus cached, his history, hidden and hurried away from the embarrassed gaze of a later and lesser time. At least the plaque had not been taken down, though inane graffiti had dishonoured it with its vandal smear when they left John Hopla behind the wall.

When all dust, old and new, was settled, after the centenary recall of the events in mid-Rhondda in 1910, the so-called Tonypandy Riots, local memory for details was stirred. John Hopla's significant role at that cusp time for modern Wales had not been entirely forgotten. The plaque's recent odyssey was traced. The memorial to him erected by his contemporaries and friends was rediscovered. Behind the wall. Damaged. But recovered and restorable. Those who cared now did what he and his own comrades would have done. They formed a working committee. The committee became an active society, the Hopla Memorial Society, to raise the necessary funds to make the plaque ready for a new site.

In the centenary year of Hopla's death in 1914 the shining new plaque was unveiled, safe and high and up on the inside wall of the former Engine House of Lewis Merthyr Colliery, the Rhondda Heritage Park since the early 1990s. His had been the impulse to effect social change, what we might now call his cultural creativity. Heritage, for him, would only have been a stepping stone to historical understanding and civic growth. Accordingly, the newly formed John Hopla Society, through their educational and civic activities, has served to act like yeast in the wider consciousness of what was once the epicentre of 'American Wales', John Hopla's world. The world he helped to turn upside down.

* * *

Two men died as a direct result of the Cambrian Combine strike in 1910–11 in mid-Rhondda. The first was a collier, Samuel Rays, who died according to the coroner from a blow to the head by a 'blunt instrument' on the night of Tuesday 8 November 1910, in the affray between baton-wielding police and striking miners. This was the clash which led directly to the riots and to the destruction of the shops in Tonypandy itself. Blame was never assigned to the police for the death of Samuel Rays. They certainly claimed no credit for it. They could scarcely avoid the trail of involvement in the second directly attributable death, that of John Hopla in April 1914.

Jack Hopla died on a Friday at his home in No. 5 Ardwyn Terrace, a dog-leg row of houses at the top of Gilfach hill and just below Ely Street and the open mountain beyond. From there he could have stepped out onto the hill which plummeted down into Tonypandy, and seen to the left, in the enclosing cleft of Clydach Vale, the Cambrian Collieries whose three pits gave their name to the combine of coal concerns assembled in mid-Rhondda since 1907, whilst below him just up the main valley at Llwynypia were the Glamorgan Collieries, their three pits at the core of the great capitalist combine and at the epicentre of the infamous twelve-month dispute, 1910–11, which Hopla helped to lead.

It would be a dispute over the price for cutting coal in 'abnormal places' which would make the Ely pit of the Naval Colliery in Penygraig the spark to the upheaval in mid-Rhondda and the catalyst which brought all the collieries in the Cambrian Combine group into a united counterforce. However, the size of the Glamorgan Colliery workforce in Llwynypia alongside that of the Cambrian Colliery in Clydach Vale is what added heft and leadership. In fact, Hopla had been to the forefront of a direct clash from the Glamorgan Colliery with the managerial high-handedness of Leonard Llewellyn over similar wage rate disputes in 1908. That standoff ended, after strike action, in a partial victory for the men and Hopla's rapid advancement as, aged twenty-seven, an elected local leader the next year. Whichever road eventually led to 'Tonypandy', it seems the starting point, as Daryl Leeworthy has shown us, was Llwynypia:

> The twenty months or so between the settlement of the 1908 strike and the events that led to the Tonypandy Riots were marked by continued tension... If in the spring of 1910 it seemed as though the Glamorgan Colliery could spark a wider dispute, in the event it was the Ely Colliery and its unworkable places that triggered wider industrial action. The dispute at the Ely Colliery broke out in August. At a meeting of the Llwynypia lodge in early September, Hopla warned that 'if Mr Llewellyn ... was out for a fight, then the men would give him such a fight that that gentleman had never seen before. A few days later, Hopla insisted that his lodge was ready to join their comrades from the Ely Colliery if needed. 'If the management were going to stop 800 men because of 80', he remarked at a mass meeting, 'then the men themselves would bring about a stoppage of 8,000 ... the Llwynypia men would be with them in this battle.' The Llwynypia lodge joined the Cambrian Combine dispute on 1 November 1910.

From that moment, Hopla, together with lodge colleagues from the wider Cambrian Combine, notably Will John, Mark

> Harcombe, Tom Smith, and Noah Rees, guided the strike through the Joint Strike Committee.

If Hopla's rise to prominence was meteoric so it was on a trajectory set from 1908 when a widening of a localised strike for a living wage became, for a short while, a world turned upside down in an upsurge against the globalised liberal capitalism which had exerted a social and cultural hegemony, beyond the economic and political, over the lives of their mushroom communities. This, as Hopla's brief but stellar career shows, was root-and-branch stuff made personalised.

When he died, he was chairman of the Glamorgan Collieries Lodge, as he had been since 1910, the trusted and appointed checkweigher to the men at the colliery since 1909; president of the Llwynypia Workmen's Institute, chairman of the Llwynypia Medical Scheme which he had established to help sick and injured miners and their families, chairman of the Llwynypia Workmen's Committee, and since 1911 an executive member of the South Wales Miners' Federation from the Rhondda District. His strongly avowed wish to unite his Christian faith with socialist purpose was made flesh in his own persona.

His funeral in Trealaw cemetery on the Wednesday following his death, at just thirty-two years old with a widow and two children left, was that of a prince fallen among his own. He was, it seems, universally mourned. His funeral cortege was over a mile in length. Its ranks, were, as expected, swollen by the hundreds of miners of the combine collieries whose cause he had urged with such ardour as secretary of the Cambrian Combine Committee brought together to conduct the strike and under the chairmanship of his friend, Will John, who would himself go on to serve as Rhondda's Labour MP from 1920 to 1955. Among the mourners, there would be, too, the powerful miners' agent, D. Watts Morgan, who along with William Abraham MP (Mabon) had urged compromise and caution during the whole of the inflamed dispute. And there were a clutch of younger, local labour leaders who, since 1910, had increasingly infiltrated the ranks of the liberal, shopocracy-dominated Urban District Council.

Hopla, in death, even united the nonconformist chapels of the district. He had been an active member of the English Congregational Chapel, and the formidable James Nicholas, the Reverend Minister at Moriah, and an Independent Labour Party supporter, officiated at both the house and the graveside. He was flanked there by his equivalents from Ebenezer, Bethel and Trinity. Perhaps, in all the circumstances that had preceded Hopla's death, most remarkable of all was the solemn presence of officials of the Glamorgan and Naval collieries led by the most reviled coal owner's representative during the year-long strike, Leonard W. Llewellyn, the general manager of the Cambrian Combine. This went beyond respect. This was a moment which these participants at the funeral understood with an intimacy we can scarcely comprehend 100 years or so on. They knew the larger answer to the personal question encapsulated in the tragically early death of one of the Rhondda's most significant figures.

They knew the path to Golgotha he had chosen to take. And now, in lockstep, they were compelled to march with him as the Llwynypia Drum and Fife Band, of which he had once been a member, took him to his grave with a driven rendition of the 'Dead March' from Handel's *Saul*. Jack Hopla had marched with the band before, in military precision to the beat of the drum and the keening of their flutes, when 10,000 had descended from the Rhondda in December 1910 to protest the trial at Pontypridd Police Court of their Gilfach comrades for alleged intimidation and violence. Jack Hopla was at their head then. Perhaps this would be why his enemies would seek to cut off his influence and example as soon as they could. Perhaps this is why Dai Watts Morgan would say at the graveside, in a tone as regretful of Hopla's stubborn pride as it was chiding of his wilfulness, 'Mr Hopla was a man not only of words, but of deeds as well, and as a consequence he had to suffer.'

He had to suffer. The consequences of such suffering would be death. Jack Hopla died from chronic endocarditis, a severe inflammatory disorder of the inner heart. His health had deteriorated as a result of the hard labour in prison to which he had been sentenced, and declined rapidly thereafter, from his early release in April 1912, until his death. Hopla, along with Will John, had been singled out for punishment in the wake of the collapse of the strike in September 1911, and so in November that year, both were put on trial for incitement to riot outside the Ely pit in Penygraig in the previous July. The authorities had stayed their hand in January 1911 when Hopla had been fined and bound over on a similar charge, but his card had been marked, as the Chief Constable of Glamorgan, Captain Lionel Lindsay, stressed to his superiors at New Scotland Yard prior to Hopla's first inconclusive trial:

> Irreconcilable minorities are under the leadership of John Hopla and William John, the two most dangerous leaders at the present moment. I am pleased to report a good case of intimidation against John Hopla and William John. They will be tried as soon as possible. With these two men out of the way, the movement must collapse.

The opposite proved to be the case. Only after the inability of the men and their families to maintain the strike through another winter did the authorities dare turn to the removal of those two 'dangerous' men. That the specific evidence cited was tainted to identify targeted individuals is crystal clear. Constable John Jones reported of the stone throwing at the engine house of the Ely pit in July 1911 that 'Inspector Williams told me that one of the men who threw stones at us was Jack Hopla's brother. They were all strangers to me.'

The 'strangers' were finally assembled before the Assizes Court in Cardiff in November 1911 where, despite testimony to their good character and actual evidence that the leaders had tried to intervene to stop the stone throwing, John Hopla was charged with incitement to riot and the assault of two police inspectors.

Henry Hopla, his brother, was sent down for nine months' hard labour. Both Will John and John Hopla received the maximum sentence possible of twelve months' hard labour apiece. Just over two years later, Hopla would be dead. Through his short lifetime, I believe, we can now see how the forces at work in his time and place interacted to reveal him as a lightning conductor of the transformative social storm that broke over mid-Rhondda in 1910. He is that significant.

* * *

John Hopla was born in 1882 in Pembrokeshire into a large family who migrated almost immediately after his birth to the booming centre of industrial Britain, the Rhondda Valleys. He grew up, matured indeed, in confluence with all of the dynamic world around him. Rhondda's population, well over 180,000 at the time of his death, had increased more than threefold during his short lifetime. As he grew up, to the south of Tonypandy the Naval Colliery Company sank four new pits between 1880 and 1910; to the immediate north, the Glamorgan Colliery Company had opened up three pits in the 1870s alone; and at the top end of Clydach Vale the Cambrian collieries were three in number by the turn of the century.

Social and cultural life followed the coal bonanza. Local businessmen and landowners established a free library in Tonypandy in 1899, and built Judge's Hall in Trealaw, with a billiard room and reading facilities and meeting hall in place by 1909. Brick by brick, Hopla would have seen a world-in-miniature being assembled in and around Tonypandy. Chapels for worship and a police station for order; theatres and music halls and public houses; and a commercial infrastructure along Dunraven and De Winton Street to serve the workforce, 12,000 colliers alone by 1912, who crowded, and overcrowded the bands of undulating terraced houses stretched out across the almost perpendicular slopes above the arteries of river, road and, crucially, the rail which brought the trucks in and took the coal out.

Despite its basic amenities, from education to public health after the UDC was established in 1894, this was a world seemingly at one with itself in its shared economic purpose and in the structure of its social ordering. The lodestar of consensual behaviour, William Abraham (Mabon) Rhondda's Chief Miners' Agent and Member of Parliament since 1885, personified the triple conflation of Liberalism in politics, Nonconformity in religion, and the interest of Labour, upheld within an economic framework which the men and their representatives could adjust but not control. That was the received wisdom and the network of common interests which had been created to serve and sustain it.

Consider, then, the photographic image we have of Mabon, his arms outstretched, almost in ecstatic flight as his oratory of praise and acceptance of this world soars above his listeners as they look up to him on the platform outside the Llwynypia Workmen's Library and Institute in 1906. He is presiding over the unveiling ceremony held on Mabon's Day, the holiday granted annually to the men, on Monday 2 July to honour the statue erected to Archibald Hood, coal owner and originator of the Glamorgan Colliery in the 1860s. Hood had died in 1902. He was a noted philanthropist in the early days of Rhondda coal exploitation. Mabon had said that 'We know him, a friend of the working man', and exhorted the audience of colliery officials, local notables and miners' leaders, to look to the hills for inspiration. The statue of Hood, looming above them from the steps of the forecourt of the institute, more prosaically pointed down the hill with an outstretched arm to where his pioneering venture, with almost 4,000 employed, was now thriving.

Thriving enough for D. A. Thomas, Cambrian's relentless owner, to buy it and incorporate it within the year into his gargantuan combine of pits, soon to be responsible for over 50 per cent of all of Rhondda's coal output and to become one of the most completely self-contained organisations, with patent fuels and shipping concerns added on, in the entire world.

As John Hopla, aged twenty-four, stood in that crowd and looked up to Hood's statue, already a mark of the past, and listened to Mabon's silvery words, in English and Welsh, the fustian oratory of the triumphant Lib-Lab settlement, he could have had no real clue as yet of what pressures would soon pull asunder the assured world assembled for us to see in that one telling image.

If we are to understand how that world was, within a decade from 1906, turned around we will need, with Hopla and his colleagues, to feel again the weight which the pressure of the

Cambrian Combine now brought to bear on all their lives. By 1908, the Cambrian Trust controlled its own collieries, those of the Glamorgan Coal Co. Ltd., and the Naval Colliery Company itself. By 1916 the trust's coal output in the Rhondda Valley was almost five million tons. Ruthless managerialism squeezed the margins between productivity and profitability. What had seemed hopeless cases of geological faults and outmoded work practices to some became, in the hands of D. A Thomas and his energetic mine managers, entirely soluble issues. Pit by pit. When he was told in the autumn of 1910 that in his creation of the Cambrian Combine he had 'bought a few sucked oranges', D. A. Thomas responded that 'he did not mind if there were a few more sucked oranges about. With Mr Llewellyn (his general manager) to look after them, they were prepared to go on dealing in sucked oranges and Cambrian marmalade.'

Once collieries were working, once the pits were sunk and the seams opened up, the management of any mine was severely limited by the circumstances of geography and geology. What was potentially controllable, however, was that cost of production which lay within the labour costs of the workforce, and in pre-1914 South Wales the labour cost was around 70 per cent of total production costs. Hence the common policy of all coal owners was to resist legislation whether to increase safety or reduce hours, whether to legitimate union negotiations or accede to any modest wage claims.

By 1910 in mid-Rhondda the uneasy accommodation fitfully arrived at around these matters came to a head in the Ely pit of the Naval Colliery, where a seam, worked experimentally for a year, was shown to contain such a large amount of stone that the men would not be able to make a 'living wage' if allowances for 'dead' or unproductive work were not granted. On the contrary, it was not the Cambrian Combine's policy to agree to past custom and practice, nor to make any new allowances. The stalemate which followed led to the dismissal of all 800 men in the Ely pit from 1 September 1910 and, from 1 November all the Cambrian Combine workmen in all of the other collieries withdrew their labour.

Will John and John Hopla now formed the Cambrian Combine

Workmen's Committee to counteract the behemoth of the coal combine. They had grasped, of course, that what was at stake in the Ely pit was the fate awaiting them all if it was not combated there. They resisted ceding control over these local matters to either the federation officials in Cardiff or wider afield. Nor, despite the fact that there were ideas and issues about workers' control or syndicalism in circulation among many local leaders – notably Noah Ablett, Will Mainwaring, W. F. Hay and others – is there any concrete evidence that the local leaders were personally driven by any deepening radical ideology. They were the coming men, for sure, but men coming from that commonality of social and cultural underpinning which made them a bridge from the world of Lib-Labism to the future hegemony of a Labour-led Rhondda. Their politics were rooted in a religious faith and belief in just rewards. The fissures opening up would prove to be those of a social abyss as much as an economic divide within an industrial relations dispute.

So when they strove to represent the interest of their work comrades before 1910, they did so not only aware of the specific demands around the collier's living standards, but also, holistically, of their lives within the community in general. In addition, from the frequency of extreme injury, those underground accidents which curtailed the ability of any family's bread earner, they would sense the corners being cut underground, with 595 deaths recorded from explosions and other fatal incidents underground in Rhondda collieries between 1902 and 1909. They would know that for every 1,000 live births in Rhondda that decade, almost 200 infants had died before they were twelve months old. They would know that, pit by pit and seam by seam, divide and rule was management's answer, and that any thought of a minimum wage to be paid for work performed by all colliers anywhere, irrespective of bargains and arcane deals, was a point of minimum justice scorned by the Olympian owners.

What then spilled over from the initial strike action into the riots of 7 and 8 November 1910, and subsequently in further attacks on shop owners, wholesalers and strike-breakers, was an inchoate cry for such justice to which Will John and John

Hopla, swept along on this tsunami of fury, could only respond as they did. By being at one with the men. By channelling their protest. By refusing the compromises of the past since they were no longer compromises in effect but rather submission to the dictates of others. Those others who had, in reality, made the world entire in which they had all come to work and to live. Tonypandy, 1910, in a flash, lit up the limits of the framework of their existence. To live as men and women fully was to engage with the remaking of that given world. It would not happen overnight, of course, but after 1910–11 it was equally clear that there would be no irreversible retreat.

After their prison sentences had been reduced by six months, John and Hopla returned to the Rhondda in April 1912 to be greeted by a mass meeting of celebration at the mid-Rhondda Athletic Ground. Both were now among the youngest elected members of the SWMF executive, and Will John had also been made a miners' agent whilst still in prison. Hopla would resume his duties as chairman of the Glamorgan Colliery workmen, and all that entailed in work for the wider community. As they rose that day to the applause of those for whom they had sacrificed so much, both men could already argue that they had begun to win. Their very release had been occasioned, after much petitioning, by the fact of victory in the National Minimum Wage strike which the Miners' Federation of Great Britain had conducted, and thereby won, for the first time, a minimum wage for all British coal miners.

They could reflect, too, that for the first time the representation of Labour-held seats on the local council was matching that of the Liberals, and the trend was inexorably going the way of Labour representation overall. Revolution had not, and would not, occur but evolution into a deeper form of a juster society had been set in motion by their revolt in Tonypandy. John Hopla had been at the heart of it.

Not everything that had happened to them could have been easy to accept, or been acted upon in certainty. Yet there was an inevitability to the life Hopla had led. We can only glimpse it in shadows, through acts and images more than words or memories. He died too young for the solemnity of historical reflection. His life was a dance with the fiction of what could be subsequently imagined into reality. The novelist Rhys Davies, born in 1901 in Clydach Vale, sketched Hopla in the character of Melville Walters, activist and organiser, in his 1937 novel *A Time to Laugh*, in which the strikes and riots of 1898 and 1910 are conflated but whose essence is the continuity of consciousness which Melville will seek to instil into the wild thrashing about for change brought on by others.

> The house became a secret centre of the insurgent elements in the district. The men who went there were mostly the rawest stuff. Often Melville felt himself helpless before the crude fire of mutiny that shot from them. Perhaps he had already burnt himself out in hopeless visions. He had taken part in the first riots of the present strike and had been in misery, sick with a sense of futility. But consciousness of a sacred duty still gnawed at him, he felt driven on to some bitter fulfilment of his being... The history of the miners was a long tale, dark with squalor, noisy with yells, savage with violence, smelly with sweat ... from the beginning of the (last) century to this year, when he, Melville, supposed he'd soon be doing a stretch of hard labour for his organising ability.

Sure enough, Melville will go to jail in fiction as Hopla did in life. Rhys Davies, however, even in fiction gives us the man as he must have intuited him in real life and, surely, when from 1916 he viewed the lifelike medallion of Hopla placed on the wall of the Llwynypia Institute.

> Melville sat at the table, drumming his fingers against it. His face was haggard and alive with a keen fierce light. He was good-looking in a remote non-physical way, as if his features were transcended by some glowing spirit looking out from them, fierce with some inner half-tragic strength. A mat of black hair was shoved forward untidily over his high forehead, his long lips were of a thin pure curve.
>
> The quality of his voice was harsh, but his words, as he spoke them, seemed to be torn out of his mind in a weary agony, so

> that he was listened to with wonder and attention. 'You know,' he said, 'you can steal if you want to. I'm against it personally, but that might be a limitation peculiar to myself.'

John Hopla did not need to steal either, for his victory would, even in death, be given to him.

Consider, then, finally the year 1916, two short years after his death. In February, another large crowd had assembled outside the Llwynypia Workmen's Institute. This time the memorial dedication was for Hopla himself, for a workmen's leader, not for any coal miner or dignitary. The marble tablet of his likeness had been fashioned with extreme care by a local craftsman and it gazed directly from its place on the wall onto a group not dissimilar to the one pulled together ten years previously for the then new statue of coal owner Archibald Hood. From the wall, it looked over Hood's shoulder and into the future. In the gathering were the members and officers of the institute, of course, and Labour leaders of Hopla's own generation, but also the general managers of the various Cambrian combine collieries who now had nothing but praise for Hopla's dedication to duty, for his hard-working ability and his good sense.

Closer colleagues than these, his comrades indeed, said he was 'a genius', 'a man in the true and fullest sense of the word ... who had sufficient courage to carry out his duties wherever they led him ... a man of high ideals ... a born leader of men who never lacked courage to act in that capacity.'

And he had won, for his was the first-ever sculptural memorial erected anywhere to any leader of Labour in the South Wales coalfield, and cohering around this image was the memory of an actual presence and of his creative activity among them. His 'work till death', as his memorial tablet said, had indeed made his 'life immortal' by giving it breath in the lives of others.

* * *

In just over thirty years from Hopla's premature death – from the beginning of the First World War to the end of the Second World War – much of what he, and his contemporaries had dared to contemplate from the unlikely location of a raw, but not yet Red, Rhondda, had emerged from the chrysalis of their imagination and from the cocoon of their struggle. His co-conspirators, Will John and W. H. Mainwaring had been, respectively, the MPs for Rhondda Fawr and Rhondda Fach since 1920 and 1933. They sat, in 1945, in a parliament led by the first-ever majority Labour government and they helped pass the legislation for national ownership of the coalmines, for national insurance for the injured and disabled, for widespread educational opportunity and, of course, for a National Health Service. As the dedication on Hopla's plaque stressed in its bundling up of his public services – beyond that of the miners' representative and spokesman – into the cultural appurtenances of the institute, its books and debates and leisure, and his leading of a 'Medical Scheme', what was done on a large scale across the whole country after 1945 was there in embryonic form before 1914. What achievement. No wonder he was revered and, dying so young and tragically, remembered as unsullied by any subsequent defeats or retreats. What fascination, too, there is in his short life. Above all, in the way he seemed to be central to the pace of change over 1910 and 1911.

When, setting out on my own academic research, I had interviewed W. H Mainwaring in the Oxford home of his daughter in 1968, I knew so little that I was eager only to be told things by the man who had been a member of the Cambrian Combine Committee in 1910 and a co-author of *The Miners' Next Step* in 1912. The pamphlet, in particular, had carried its legendary aura and status – as proponent of industrial unionism, workers' control, rank-and-file activism and No Leadership proposals – with it into the 1960s and subsequent re-prints. In 1912 *The Times* had devoted an editorial to it, one astonished by its intellectual power and its implicit insolence in even emanating from such a place as mid-Rhondda. Will Mainwaring gave me an original copy when our conversation had ended. But what had I learned? My notes tell me that he saw Noah Ablett as a talkative schemer and alcoholic and reserved his praise for his own mentor, the stalwart Noah Rees, whilst Arthur Horner, the communist future president of the South Wales Miners' Federation, was airily dismissed as a 'Boy Scout'. Others, including Hopla, were barely mentioned. Perhaps I had not asked the right questions. Or perhaps the subsequent events that unfolded after Hopla – the bitterness between the Communist Party after its birth in 1920 and the Labour Party chastened after the defeat of the General Strike in 1926 or maybe the deflation of any so-called Direct Action politics in the long march of Labour to power in 1945 – had all conspired to push Hopla out of sight and out of mind.

I wish I had known, in 1968, what I finally learned from the research in 2013 which helped me write an account of him for the Hopla Society. For if I do not believe in Ghosts, I am no longer so sure about Spirits. And, after all, the world of 1945 when I was born in Llwynypia was nearer, in all things material and many spiritual, to that of 1914 when Hopla died, than we are, all of us now, to the immediate post-Second World War years. What I discovered was uncanny, but what leads me on to these concluding memory traces of places and events is only the rational outcome of what happens when you taste the madeleine cake, or in the Rhondda dunk the Marie biscuit in your tea.

The uncanny bit is that when, in 1947, my parents returned to the Rhondda from Yorkshire they did not go back to my grandfather's house in Ely Street, Tonypandy, but into lodgings, or rooms as would have been said, in the sawn-off terraced row below topmost Ely Street. We lived in the front room of No. 6, Ardwyn Terrace. I shivered a little, in the middle of my writing about him in 2013, to find that John Hopla, too, had lived in Ardwyn Terrace with his family, and died downstairs and next door in No. 5. Other rooms. Other walls. Other times. But then there was, too, the continuing, wider world and spaces of Tonypandy, both in the 1910s and the 1950s, spread out below us.

It was possessing intimacy with that topography – of streets and roads and back lanes and public space, knowing where and how waste land and mountainside and quarries encroached on what was built for dwellings and shops between the Glamorgan collieries in Llwynypia and on down past Pandy Square where the Lady with the Lamp drinking fountain, erected in 1908, still stood in the 1950s, and being aware of shortcuts by the river bank and along the railway lines, above as well as below the main highway, alert in other words to the relationship, in time and topos, of humans to all that jumbled environment – which, in sum, had given me as a research historian the native-born's key to the unfolding of the Tonypandy Riots on 7 and 8 November 1910. That, in other words, neither geography nor chronology allowed a hitherto and long-accepted narrative to stand: of a mass demonstration of miners driven back from the Glamorgan Colliery's Power House to the Square and, so enraged, being turned into a riotous mob intent on vengeful destruction. My alternative explanation, a social pathology, would reveal a crowd attuned to express the hidden undercurrents of their society via the spontaneous articulation of the riot. Neither ideology nor politics was needed to analyse the social outcome of that economically induced fever in mid-Rhondda. And certainly not any dismissal of their revolt as a mindless irruption of violence.

The historical argument I advanced back in 1980, and published in *Past and Present*, still, by and large, does stand and allows for what I thereby called a 'Definition of Community'. As the strike catapulted on for the following twelve months only to end in the defeat of 1911, impelled and corralled as it was by the forces of police and military who proved so necessary to its final resolution, I could only see, then, the various other eruptions of full-scale violence after November 1910 as being more narrowly defined as the clash of outraged strikers with the reinforced authorities. Although other commercial enterprises were later singled out, notably a wholesale butcher's by arson, in revenge against his profitable collaboration, the revelatory pattern I had traced in 1980 in an almost fictive formation – via the bare facts of the incensed looting of Tonypandy's shops and the catalytic confrontation between a shopocracy and its community – was not to be found, I thought, in the more basic brutality of the industrial strife unfolding after November 1910 between the occupying force of police and troops and the indigenous population. I saw those conflicts as significant, certainly, but also as lesser.

I was wrong. It was Hopla who now convinced me that they were, in fact, just as significant if only they could be read as different in shape and intent. It was the consciously directed intention behind the later sporadic riots of late 1910 and into 1911 which I now believe allows us to round out the story, to let the narrative run on from the emotional spasm of 8 November to the calculated harnessing of that social chaos. This, of course, although not in the admiring sense I would mean, is what John Hopla, with Will John, was accused of in court when they were sent down for twelve months imprisonment with hard labour at the Glamorgan County Assizes on 23 November 1911. Mr Justice A. T. Lawrence, as he passed sentence, was essentially correct, at least so far as his indictment of Hopla and John was concerned. He had said:

> You have been convicted of rioting on the plainest evidence and under circumstances which indicate that you did it deliberately and with full knowledge of the consequences of what you were doing. There had been a state of unrest and turmoil in the country for months, and you had been prominent men with all the facts fully before you. The only excuse that I have been able to see for your conduct anywhere is in the temptations which the Act [The Trade Disputes Act, 1906] under which you pretended to be acting holds out to ignorant people. That statute seems framed ... to provoke rioting and promote civil war. With these facts all before you you deliberately committed these crimes.... It is a most painful task to have to send men of your intelligence to punishment; but it must be done.

The legal root of all this casuistry was the disputed right of strike leaders to dissuade others from working and what exactly, in law as well as in reality, was a 'blackleg'. Hopla and John were singled out, as leaders, for what had occurred in this respect on 25 July 1911 at the Nantgwyn pit in Penygraig. The police cordon at the colliery had been drawn up in the knowledge that a mass meeting at the mid-Rhondda athletic ground had resolved to end 'blackleg' working in the colliery. Around 3,000 men marched the half mile to the colliery. A deputation, led by Hopla and John, was allowed by the police inspector to enter the colliery premises to 'interview the men at work', as permitted under the Act. However, the proviso was that the management of the colliery had to agree to this and, here, the under manager refused them such permission. It was as a result of this refusal that prolonged stone-throwing and repeated hand-to-hand clashes between strikers and police, with the military called into action as boulders were sent crashing down from the slopes above the colliery, led to severe injuries until after three hours the engagement ended. The stipendiary magistrate for the Pontypridd district, Daniel Lleufer Thomas, spelled out the angry bewilderment of the socially concerned and culturally consensual in Edwardian South Wales when he convicted others for a similar, though smaller, affray in Trealaw the next day, 26 July. On 4 October as he passed sentence he spotlighted the importance of language, its terms and semantics, to the establishment of Order against Anarchy:

> I want to say, clearly and emphatically, as a believer in trades unionism, that the state of things which has prevailed in mid-Rhondda, the violence which has been resorted to under the pretence of peaceful persuasion, the treatment as blacklegs of men who were not blacklegs in the ordinary sense of the term, or who would not be so regarded by the Executive of any respectable trades union, the too ready acceptance by responsible leaders that the end justified the means, even though the means included rioting, assaults on the police, intimidation, and violence practised on so-called 'officials' or permanent workers engaged in keeping the mines open, the degradation of the women-folk by allowing them to take a leading part in these and like acts of violence – all these constitute a serious indictment against trades union organisations in the district and in the South Wales coalfield.

His substantive point, as he continued in this magisterial vein, was that the term 'blackleg' should be confined to those working for less than the wage-rate set or, perhaps, should be applied to imported labour brought in to 'enable the industry ... to be carried on as if there was no strike'. Otherwise, he claimed, keeping the pits open for work by those men normally employed to do so should not bring the 'opprobrious, undeserved title of blacklegs' down upon them. Yet this was what had happened from the start, and it worsened as the dispute intensified. It was what was at the core of the intransigence of the owners and at the centre of their demands for police protection and military intervention. It was, too, as a breakpoint, the only sanction towards winning the strike which the men possessed in their weaponry. To use it, said Lleufer Thomas, they had resorted to the 'organised lawlessness as made this district notorious at certain periods during the Cambrian Combine strike'.

To be organised was to be worse than to be lawless. The law could address the latter directly in the courts. The former had to be confronted on its own territory. On the territory of mid-Rhondda, where John Hopla organised and instructed a counter army. The early demonstrations against any working in the pits of the Cambrian Combine were intended by their insistence on solidarity among the strikers to enforce the stoppage completely. This was to be the power of sheer numbers assembled in a stand-off with management. The police-led violence against the crowds outside the Glamorgan Colliery on the crucial nights of 7 and 8 November, however, had sparked the dramatic shop-smashing in Tonypandy and, thereafter, brought in fresh numbers of police and then the military who could, and would, serve to protect the semblance of work-as-normal. What ensued, if the strike committee was not simply to fold its hand and accept dictated terms, was the organisation of a counterforce. Relative passivity became directed aggression. We do not need to look far to see why, how, and by whom it was directed. The industrial tone of the Cambrian Combine strike, as opposed to the societal tonality of the riots in Tonypandy itself on 8 November, was set by what David Evans, the *Western Mail*'s industrial correspondent, called 'the great riot of November 21st'.

Once again the issue of blackleg labour was the provocative cause. As Leonard Llewellyn, manager of the Glamorgan Colliery, attempted to bring blackleg labour into the area by train from Cardiff, so every train throughout that day was stopped and searched by picketing strikers between Dinas and Tonypandy. The decision, therefore, was taken to reorder all the rail traffic and send up a train that bore Metropolitan Police as well as strike-breaking labour. When this train, too, was stopped by pickets to the south of Tonypandy at Dinas station at 8.27pm the police surprised them by charging into them to prevent any enquiry. However, when it proceeded to Tonypandy for scheduled arrival at 8.30pm it was met by a crowd in its hundreds who now threatened to tear up the railway line and attack rail property, whether the ticket office or the station manager's house. The bridge which led from lower Tonypandy to Trealaw, and from which the railway station was accessed, was packed at both ends. The fate of the train was not immaterial. Lines of communication were at stake.

Over the next few hours and into the early morning the assembled crowd, soon in its thousands, would clash with around 100 police at first, then, with further called-up detachments of Metropolitan Police, another hundred or so, and shortly with a half company of Lancashire Fusiliers, a company of the West Riding regiment and a squadron of Hussars, all also dispatched from their base in Pontypridd. Further military, two companies of infantry, were being sent in reserve to that town. Against such amassed force, batons and drawn bayonets at the ready, the strikers would necessarily quail, both that night and in the end. But not with any ease would they be subdued, for their countervailing army was led and drilled by its own possession of a different species of military know-how: terrain.

That night, dispersed back across the railway bridge towards Tonypandy, the strikers had debouched not into the town but up the hill towards Penygraig above the Naval Colliery at whose Ely pit the dispute had begun. This is the informed and incandescent David Evans:

> When the mob on the bridge had been driven from the precincts of the station it withdrew to a position on the hillside and attacked the police with stones. Both on the Tonypandy and the Trealaw sides of the valley the land rises rapidly, and clustering at the foot of the hills are many irregularly formed rows of houses

> divided by narrow streets. Well acquainted as they are with the topography of the district the rioters ... found no difficulty in securing safe and commanding positions, and their plans were aided by the cover of a moonless night and slight fog. These advantages they used to the utmost, and aided by women, who carried supplies of stones and other missiles in their aprons, they stoned the constables in the open streets below with terrible fury ... the rioting ... was of an exceedingly ferocious and sustained character.

In effect, no matter how obdurate the strike proved to break and no matter how fiercely the strikers continued to prosecute it, well into the summer of 1911, the encounter in Penygraig on 21 November 1910 was its highwater mark of both defiance and rebuff. That the organisation of that defiance – the darting in and out of houses, into and somehow away from cul-de-sacs, formations appearing and reappearing in sudden bursts – was controlled is clear. It could not have happened, then or later, without it being so ordered. It was, and in a military sense given the opposition, a case of check and countercheck until one side became exhausted. That side would, of course, be the one John Hopla headed up, the one whose inchoate energies, fuelled by a clear concept of the lineaments of a truly moral economy, he helped to harness. He was indeed a 'dangerous man' but not, as the authorities of law and order and the servants of the coal owners would have had it, because he was a leader who had forsaken his responsibilities. It was because he was a leader who followed those of whom he was a part.

The *Rhondda Leader* reported the homecoming of the imprisoned men in April 1912 at another mass meeting, of men, women and children, at the Athletic Ground in Tonypandy:

> A demonstration was held by the mid-Rhondda miners on Tuesday to extend a welcome to Mr William John and Mr John Hopla, and to celebrate their release. Some thousands attended a mass meeting ... over which Mr Noah Rees Clydach Vale, presided. The Chairman said they were there to welcome their comrades, who would find they would now have more work to

do than ever before ... [and a resolution was proposed] ... to congratulate Messrs. John and Hopla, and giving them a hearty welcome as free citizens.

Mr Owen Buckley, in seconding that, said that all Messrs. John and Hopla had done was to obey the mandates of the workmen.

* * *

Fifty years after John Hopla's death the physical configuration of his immediate world had scarcely changed and, in the 1950s, young feet, mine included, clattered up and down the same streets, bisected by the same unpaved back lanes where stones to gather up still lay in abundance. He would have still recognised all the spaces of that epic conflict of 1910–11: from the ticket office on the railway bridge to the tilted terraced housing of Amos Hill from whose upstairs windows the contents of chamber pots were thrown onto the police, from the oval of the Track or Athletic Ground to the oil-silk black of the River Rhondda. Our worlds touched even as, in deeper and better ways than the physical, his efforts had helped them change and part. For the better for those of us to come after him, and so it should be again, generation by generation. From behind the wall of forgetfulness, John Hopla's memorial has now been restored. From behind an adjoining wall to his home in Ardwyn Terrace, I was enabled by such as him to go out into a changed world, and grow up and now to pay my personal dues to his memory.

TONYPANDY: CHURCHILL'S NEMESIS

We were in the 1950s undoubtedly the pre-eminent forerunners of Margaret Thatcher's despised 'enemy within' during the 1984–5 miners' strike. In the aftermath of the Second World War when Britain's wartime prime minister was cementing his global legendary status, we treated him as the Devil Incarnate who had conspired from the high governmental office of Home Secretary to send troops into the Rhondda to ensure the defeat of the striking miners in our valley in 1910–11. With singularly bad grace, adults and children alike, we catcalled in unison whenever his name and image appeared on the screens of our picture houses and we treated, as gospel, the kitchen folklore which saw him as an arch enemy to whom, in our newly minted welfare state, no credit should be given. But what if the folklore was false, or at best exaggerated, and the Liberal Winston of 1910 was not the die-hard Conservative Churchill of the inter-war years? What if we were fingering the wrong man, as almost all his subsequent biographers and countless letter writers to *The Times* over many decades fiercely asserted in his defence? Perhaps the actual intervention, benign in intention even if partisan in execution, was in any event a sideshow, inconsequential in the larger conspectus represented by that time and place. That was certainly my own conclusion in 1978 when I turned, afresh, to investigate and found that neither the 'riot' nor its underlying meaning was quite so dependent for explication on the agencies of industrial dispute or the enforcers of the law, whether imported police or troops. Indeed I was so dismissive of the very last as a continuing issue – yes, of course, Churchill had been complicit in the eventual deployment of troops – that I consigned the matter in my scholarly article to the dustbin of an appended footnote.

In sum, and now passing for accepted academic wisdom, the Wales of David Lloyd George – future Welsh Liberal prime minister of the British Empire and Churchill's great friend and ally in Herbert Asquith's pre-First World War reforming government – first heard its death knell on the streets of Tonypandy when a spurious national and progressive myth of Welsh societal unity was exposed by the social fracture attendant upon the strike. An embryonic revolt for a social democratic future in which neither Lloyd George nor Churchill would play a part. That indeed is, and remains, the deeper significance of Tonypandy in 1910; but the persistence of what I have somewhat dismissively called – pro and anti – the kitchen folklore has never gone away. Perhaps its performative narrative still exerts the fascination of percussive forces in opposition or, perhaps, the nuanced sequence of events – showing their perpetrators as serially bewildered as the complex seriousness of being at the cusp of profound social evolution might well entail – requires another way of telling, one in which we can, definitively I hope, stop any further indignant press comment and correspondence (for, yes, he did) by acknowledging both the instinctiveness of folklore and the objectivity of historical enquiry. Winston Churchill was less guilty than Tonypandy imagined and Tonypandy was to be more crucial to him than the Great Man could ever have thought possible. It seems that the troops did matter after all, but in more than one way.

* * *

In January 1949, four years into the Labour government's term of office after an overwhelming electoral victory over Winston Churchill's Conservative Party in 1945, Richard Gruffydd Robinson, the self-proclaimed 'anti-Socialist' Lord Mayor of Cardiff proposed to his council that a new road development in the city centre be named 'Churchill Way'. The motion was carried on a split vote, with one dissenting councillor remarking that 'Tonypandy men had long memories'. Long enough, it seemed. To reverberate from post-war Rhondda in echo of the year-long coal strike of 1910–11 and the infamous riots of November 1910 when the commercial high street of that mid-Rhondda town was wrecked and both Metropolitan Police and the military were sent in by the then Liberal Home Secretary,

Winston Churchill. What followed from that action was to haunt Churchill four decades later. He tried to exorcise the accusing spirit of what he and his supporters took to be both false memory and unfair interpretation. In a gracious reply to the Lord Mayor in February 1949, acknowledging the honour being paid to him, the great war leader but defeated politician wrote:

> I see that one of the Labour men referred to Tonypandy as a great crime I had committed in the past. I am having the facts looked up and will write to you again upon the subject. According to my recollections the action I took at Tonypandy was to stop the troops being sent to control the strikers for fear of shooting. Instead I sent Metropolitan Police who charged with their rolled mackintoshes and no one was hurt... I will let you know the result of my researches.

Exactly one year later, in February 1950 in the general election campaign which eventually returned the incumbent Labour government with a much-reduced parliamentary majority but on the highest percentage of the popular vote ever recorded and more than a million votes beyond the Conservative total, Churchill gave the electorate the further benefit of his researches into the events of 1910–11 in the coalfield just twenty miles to the north of Cardiff. This time, addressing a rally at the Ninian Park football ground of Cardiff City, he stoked the fires of controversy in public. His account was adamant and clear-cut. Troops had been held back by him, at first, and later had no direct contact with the men on strike. A few bloody noses were all the Metropolitan Police had caused. He thus gave his rapt audience what he called 'the true story of Tonypandy, in order, to replace in Welsh villages the cruel lie with which they have been fed all these long years'. This was not some spontaneous reference made in the course of a long speech, nor were there any hecklers to whom he was merely responding. In 1950, the linkage between the would-be prime minister and a distant dispute was still a live issue, even one toxic enough to have all Conservative candidates briefed about the Cambrian Combine strike and for the Conservative Party to issue a circular stating that Churchill 'allowed the troops to be drafted into the area as a reserve to the police, but they were not used'.

The righteous indignation of his opponents swiftly followed. The Rhondda West Constituency Labour Party issued to the local voters their own 'Manifesto' as a 'Tonypandy Reply' to 'let Churchill know that you remember 1910 and the part he played in requesting the use of military forces'. Ness Edwards, the Labour MP for Caerphilly, and himself a former historian of the South Wales Miners Federation, told the press that 'The miners are so infuriated ... that Mr Churchill has inflicted a fatal blow to Tory aspirations in the South Wales coalfield (and that) the facts (show) Mr Churchill did use the military against the miners at Tonypandy, and the miners will never forget it'.

It would seem that between assertion and counterclaim, between myth and actuality, only one side could possibly be in the right. Enough documentation and evidence, official and reported, enough testimony from participants and witnesses existed and could be assessed to be placed accordingly on the scales. What, however, was weighed in the balance when the thumbprints of the two sides were also accounted for was something more intangible: motivations and perceptions, intentions and outcomes, ignorance and knowledge. Both parties, as it turns out, had some justification to remember Tonypandy in their own particular way. But, in the final analysis, only one of the contenders was increasingly desperate for self-justification. By 1950 the die was cast, the popular verdict was in, and on the cinema screens of South Wales whenever Churchill appeared on the Movietone newsreels his image was booed and his very name met with the hiss of collective hostility. To understand exactly why this had occurred, the significance of what was at stake in Tonypandy in 1910 has first to be understood in its own contemporary terms.

Between 1 September and 1 November 1910 the localised dispute over the cutting price of coal in a particular seam in one pit of the Cambrian Combine of collieries in mid-Rhondda had escalated from the lockout of eighty men into the solidarity strike of 8,000 workmen. This was Labour versus Capital. The Combine Trust facing down a Combine Committee of colliery lodges, an industrial clash with social reverberations which would have both political and cultural outcomes that were unheralded in the event and dynamic in the outcome. Both sides, owners and workmen, assessed their strength and calculated their strategy in what would prove to be an unyielding conflict from its dramatic beginning to its bitter conclusion a year on from the fateful moves made by both sides in the first week of November.

For the men's part, a mass meeting, organised by their joint leaders in a new committee of command and purpose, decided to make full use of the Trades Disputes Act of 1906 to picket all the collieries into a complete stoppage. This was to include enginemen, stokers, boilermen and officials so as to bring the possibility of any working to a halt. Crucially, it was agreed attempts to use or bring in non-compliant or blackleg labour would be fiercely resisted by mass picketing of all the collieries. In full understanding of the implications of this show of power, and in the light of concerted union action in the adjacent Cynon Valley, the coal owners made two tactical moves: the first was to inform Military Command, via the chief constable of Glamorgan as was accustomed practice, and as early as 2 November, that there was likely to be a request for military support of the police being drafted into the area; secondly, that the manner in which they would conduct the strike would be to invest all available police strength, local and imported, within the perimeters of one only of their collieries, abandoning the rest thereby, and so make the Glamorgan Colliery a citadel into which directly by rail, blackleg labour could be brought as a deliberate act of provocation. The latter was the name of the game from the beginning as, after mass picketing did stop all other collieries by 7 November, any requests by official pickets to talk with those at work was peremptorily dismissed out of hand by the general manager, Leonard Llewellyn, whilst Captain Lionel Lindsay, the aggressive and malleable chief constable, ordered his officers to charge indiscriminately into the large crowds gathering outside the Glamorgan Colliery on Monday the 7th and again on Tuesday 8 November. This last, ferocious fracas led to a fatality, a miner felled by a blow to the head from a 'blunt object' caused severe and several bodily injuries and, as a by-product, triggered the 'sacking of Tonypandy'.

It was only after these related but disparate events that Churchill irrevocably entered the fray. He was still intent on being a peacemaker but was now duped into taking up a stance which he had initially spurned as he was engulfed by a conflict he neither fully understood nor controlled. It was the local coal-mining interest which, above all else, wanted the army to come to Tonypandy. Unlike any extra police – Bristol, Swansea, Gloucester, the Mets, a force of nearly 1,500 men under Lindsay by 15 November – all of whom would be a cost to Glamorgan County ratepayers, the military would be a free gift for the securing of colliery property, a deterrent to the demonstrations by thousands who might thus be dispersed and, as a back-up to police prevention of all peaceful persuasion to cease working, a virtual guarantor of the striker's ultimate defeat. The latter fact would be the cause of Churchill's enduring reputation in 'the long memories' of 'Tonypandy men'.

It was certainly not the memory Churchill would have wished to induce as he was forced to react to unfolding events. To begin with he had no wish, as a general election loomed for December 1910, to endanger any Liberal sympathies crucial to ensuring the continuity of Asquith's government. He was well aware, too, that the prime minister, when Home Secretary in 1893, had been labelled 'Featherstone Asquith' after troops shot and killed two miners in that minor West Yorkshire colliery town. Further, his broad sympathies at that time were with the coal miners whose appeal for an Eight Hour Day he had supported, as had his father before him. He proudly boasted of that in 1908 when he had attended and spoke at the annual miners' rally held in mid-Rhondda. So, when he had been informed on the morning of Tuesday 8 November that the chief constable's request for troops had already been sanctioned by the War Office, and that two companies of infantry were entrained, he summoned Haldane, the War Secretary, to the Home Office and, in agreement, they halted the enroute troop train at Swindon, with only 200 cavalry allowed to proceed but under orders to remain in Cardiff. In addition, he instructed 200 Metropolitan Police and ten mounted constables to travel forthwith from London to Pontypridd to assist, if necessary, the irate Lindsay and to placate the incensed Llewellyn. His own message setting out his decisions was read out to a mass meeting of the strikers held on the afternoon of 8 November in the mid-Rhondda Athletic Ground. It had been warm in tone, if slightly ambivalent, as he both referred to himself as one of 'their friends here' in Westminster and said that soldiers were being held back 'for the present' with only police being sent into the coalfield. To the chief constable, in a telegram sent one hour later, he was firm about infantry not being used 'till all other means have failed', but left a door open by saying the cavalry would remain in 'the district pending cessation of trouble'. General Macready was to be in sole command of 'military (who) will not ... be available unless it is clear that police reinforcements are unable to cope with the situation'. The chief constable of Glamorgan would not be one to let any opportunity to capitalise on that loophole slip, and so Churchill's first plan had quickly unravelled as local police aggression brought about a premature denouement.

From late afternoon to dusk on 8h November, a crowd of some 8,000 had gathered around the entrance to the extensive Glamorgan Colliery. Inside the gates, Lindsay commanded around 100 constables, some mounted, and backed Llewellyn in his consistent refusal to allow selected pickets onto the premises to talk with those at work. When the crowd began to stone incessantly the Power House where the electric engine was maintained to prevent the colliery flooding, Lindsay chose to drive two separate cohorts of men into the crowd to drive them the quarter-mile distances south to Tonypandy and north to Llwynypia. This led to the pitched-battle clashes between baton-wielding police and pick-axe handling miners. Casualties were many and frequent, with women and on-looking by-standers randomly involved, and only ceasing around 8pm when the police retreated into the colliery gates.

The narrative and timing of these events is the crux to comprehending Churchill's next, and false, step. In essence, the version told by the police and the coal owners was believed: that 'a mob' setting out to invade and capture the Glamorgan Colliery had been foiled in their undertaking by a small but gallant force of police which, next time, might be overwhelmed. Telephonic communications to this effect from Lindsay in Tonypandy, and a telegram sent at 7.45pm from the stipendiary magistrate which confirmed he would be ready, with fellow magistrates, to read the official Riot Act upon the advent of troops, caused Churchill, in Westminster, to reverse his decision, around 8pm, by telegramming General Macready to move 'all the cavalry into the district without delay ... if the chief constable desires it'. He certainly did, and so in addition to the 200 Metropolitans who had arrived in Tonypandy too late to assist in anything, by 10pm that night, a squadron of the 18th Hussars were patrolling the streets by noon the next day. Then, in short order, by Wednesday 9 November, separate companies of the Royal North Lancashire Regiment, the Lancashire Fusiliers, the West Riding Regiment, the Devonshire Regiment and the Royal Munster Fusiliers were also on hand, either locally, or on standby elsewhere in South Wales. Task accomplished, especially for Leonard Llewellyn who had commented acidly that 'Mr Winston Churchill's actions (in halting the troops) has really made things worse', since on Sunday 6 November he had personally 'applied for military and saw the Magistrates on the Monday morning, and I told them of the seriousness of the case, and my complaint is that none of this bloodshed would have happened if the military had been here'.

What is clear is that the riot referred to by the local law authorities, and the bloodshed consequently involved, is that outside the Glamorgan Colliery and not the collective, directed rage against the local shopocracy which followed on, sequentially but not causally, in the township. Churchill's change of response was a reaction to the claim of a direct threat to the colliery premises and to the fate of the 300 horses artfully gathered underground there by Llewellyn and allegedly in mortal danger from any potential flooding. The press had a field day on that canard, too. Churchill had, therefore, on the night of 8 November intervened directly in the strike and, although he did not align himself with the ongoing, deliberately confrontational tactics of the coal owners, he was now so tarred himself in the eyes of the community. The relationship between the clashes around the conduct of the strike and the rampaging riot up and down Tonypandy's High Street on the night of 8 November is the final clarification here needed.

The social pathology indicated by the smashing and looting of the shops is revelatory of a community fracture inimical to the self-image cherished by Liberal and nonconformist Edwardian Wales. In sum, the communal leadership of a shopocracy was directly challenged in a carnival of disorder. Those shopkeepers who were multiple houseowners for purposes of rent, or operated a secret blacklisting system for bad debtors, or enjoyed a controlling level of political representation enjoying civic and social intimacy with both coal owners and officials, or who were thought to have expressed disdain for the men on strike, were purposefully targeted. Tellingly, others were not. This world-turned-upside-down was, in this fashion, on show for one night only, although it had wider social and cultural repercussions during the strike and thereafter. The fury unleashed was violent but also selective. Bewildered analysts at the time, from all parts of the spectrum, could only, and quite inadequately, blame 'strangers' or 'drunks' or 'youths', and spirit away thousands of actual participants so that they dwindled to imagined hundreds. Churchill wrote reassuringly to the king, who was deeply concerned about the fate of the horses underground, to deplore the 'insensate' action of a mob against innocent shopkeepers for whom they could have no rational 'animosity'. Explanations for this redefining of community relations would have to wait on forensic historical research. Expressed innocence, at the time, was a whitewashing, rather elastic, concept.

Nonetheless, its simplifying of a crowd into a mob and a directed, conscious knowledge of local circumstances into a psychological frenzy was a convenient explication of social fracture if the wider strike narrative, as set out by such as the Combine's eloquent contemporary defender, the newspaperman David Evans, was to be accepted. As indeed, it was for over seventy years. The key point of Evans' *Labour Strike in the South Wales Coalfield 1910–11*, written hard on the heels of the strike's ending in September 1911, was that the riot in the town occurred only and solely because the purpose of the (other) riot at the colliery had been thwarted. It was, therefore, to be all Churchill's fault by not dispatching the military beforehand as requested by owners, police and magistracy.

Churchill, could, however, take more than a measure of comfort from the messages sent to him by the level-headed General Macready who quickly took a very dim view of the high-handedness of Llewellyn and Lindsay as to the deployment of his soldiers. Nor did Macready believe their version of what had actually unfolded. That was, in fact, a pup they had sold the distant Home Secretary on the evening of 8 November. In his memoirs, *Annals of an Active Life* (1924) Macready forthrightly contradicted them, and the account of their amanuensis, David Evans:

> Investigation on the spot convinced me that the original reports regarding the attacks on the miners on November 8th had been exaggerated. What were described as 'desperate attempts' to sack the power-house at Llwynypia proved to have been an attempt to force the gateway (and) had the mob been as numerous or so determined as the reports implied, there was nothing to have prevented them from overcoming the whole premises. That they did not was due less to the action of the police than to the want of leading or indication to proceed to extremities on the part of the strikers.

Churchill was given every indication of the exact temper of the dispute, so far as the strike leaders were concerned, when, on 9 November, a delegation attended a convened meeting at the Board of Trade. Reconciling the two sides, a move spearheaded by Rhondda MP William Abraham ('Mabon') the Lib-Lab elder statesman and president of the South Wales Miners' Federation, proved to be a step too far but what was underlined by the men's delegation was that no objections were made by them to police protection of colliery property, only to police prevention, at the owners' behest, of the ability to picket as guaranteed by the far-reaching Trade Disputes Act of 1906. That was to remain the nub of it all.

Churchill showed that he understood this, and even to an extent sympathised with the complaint. The law, after all, could be invoked in more than one way. He asked the chief constable to be circumspect by not making 'small things' a cause of resentful reaction and he chafed at the disrespect shown to Macready's cooler approach when labour was imported by train or fresh working, all without consultation, was undertaken. He had written, in an even-handed manner on 16 November to Macready, to set out his objective of having the troops there solely to hold the ring:

> You should remember that the owners are within their legal rights in claiming to import labour but that you are entitled to judge time, manner and circumstances of such importation in order that no breach of peace may be unnecessarily provoked and to ensure that the authorities responsible for keeping order have adequate forces upon the spot. With this leverage you might be able to restrain or at any rate delay injudicious action on part of the owners ... you should note my pledge that peaceful picketing will be protected.

Arguably the circle could not be squared. In the months which followed, among a plethora of incidents and prosecutions and false imprisonments, mostly orchestrated by Lindsay in his capacity as the law enforcement arm of the owners, two further confrontations stand out in which the outcome of the troops' presence in mid-Rhondda was all too readily apparent to the strikers. There were running battles between the police and crowds determined to stop the arrival by train of blackleg labour on 21 November and again, in the strike's last major incident, on 25 July 1911. In both instances, as the police fell back in disarray, Macready took command. In November, in the absence of the chief constable, he ordered up fifty Metropolitans, batons not mackintoshes to hand, and then resolved the issue by sending half a company of the Lancashire Fusiliers to the hotspot of Penygraig, a company of the West Riding into Tonypandy, with a further squadron of Hussars to assist, whilst he also stopped 'the eleven men obtained by Mr Llewellyn from ... Cardiff...at Pontypridd'. In July 1911 as a result of managerial refusal to allow any persuasion of or meeting with blacklegs at the Ely pit of the Naval Colliery, where the strike had been occasioned in the first place, a crowd of up to 5,000 stoned the pit and its protective police cordon and rolled boulders down the mountainside from above the colliery. The military, again, were called in, and a company of Somerset Light Infantry outflanked the surprised strikers. Armed with ball cartridge rifles and bayonets they enveloped the crowd from above, driving them with their fixed bayonets down into the streets for the waiting police to charge their scattered ranks.

Immense suffering, hardship and privation finally took their toll. The Cambrian Combine strike petered out in despair and was formally ended after a full year in September 1911, with the men returning, sporadically, to their individual collieries on worse terms than before. Troops slowly diminished in number but were there to the end. Churchill had offended the owners by his early vacillation and his scarcely complimentary feelings about them but he had, too, effectively ended any possibility of success for the strategy and tactics adopted by the Cambrian Combine strike committee. It may well be that his inclination to bellicosity in future industrial relations disputes – in July 1911 he threatened to put 25,000 troops into London to actually do the work of striking dockers, and as a Conservative minister was an ardent advocate of troop deployment during the General Strike of 1926 – was more than enough to cement his reputation as a foe of organised labour. Yet it was, decidedly and decisively, from Tonypandy in 1910 that the judgement against him was lodged and from where, in 1912, the syndicalist Noah Ablett would remind 'you men of Tonypandy' of what happened when the state allegedly held the ring.

Tonypandy was a cusp moment, and after the defeat, the ground shifted in ways unexpected in their rapidity and profundity before the strike. In 1912 a form of the minimum wage was won by a UK national coal strike. In 1912 William Abraham (Mabon) resigned as SWMF president. The Executive Council of the SWMF welcomed the 'advanced men' into its ranks. The days of Lib-Labism were at an end. Labour representation, on the council in the Rhondda and as parliamentary seats, increased exponentially and was fixed for generations across South Wales from the 1920s. Will John, a pre-eminent leader imprisoned in the strike, replaced Mabon as Rhondda West's MP (until 1955) and in 1933, W. H. Mainwaring, an author of *The Miners' Next Step*, became Labour MP for Rhondda East (until 1959). And this is Arthur Horner, elected from prison to be the miners' leader in Maerdy, Rhondda, in 1919:

> I walked over the mountains ... through the night to Tonypandy in November 1910 when we heard that Winston Churchill had called out the troops against the miners ... to reinforce the thousands of police already in the area ... the vicious alliance of the Government and the coal owners, against miners who asked no more than a wage little over starvation level. I never forgot that lesson.

In 1936 Horner became the first communist to be president of the SWMF and in 1946 was elected from South Wales as the general secretary of the National Union of Mineworkers. The coal industry was nationalised in 1947. And in 1948 the National Health Service, prefigured by numerous Medical Aid schemes in the coalfield, was ushered in by another former miner from South Wales, Aneurin Bevan from Tredegar. 'Squalid nuisance' was Churchill's jibe at Bevan but more significantly the metropolitan press christened him, with more essential truth than geographic accuracy, the 'Tito from Tonypandy'.

It was what had so transpired in so many such ways since 1910 that caused Tonypandy to haunt the career of Winston Churchill in 1950. It was why Tonypandy allied to his name, caused Clement Attlee, in a private Labour Party meeting in 1940, to wonder whether a Labour presence in a Churchill-led government was even possible. Tonypandy proved to be his albatross, as much a social and cultural one as it was in any formal political sense, because of all that it represented as a legitimate protest against unyielding overlordship and for what it laid bare of the reality of power relationships. If there is a one-word answer to the question why the great and victorious war leader suffered his post-war electoral defeats, first in 1945 and again in 1950, then that word is 'Tonypandy', and not so much by then for what had happened, in confusion in 1910, as for what it signified with devastating clarity for and across a transformed Great Britain.

COMRADES

Not exactly footsteps, more a kind of shuffling. Hesitant but insistent. Squeaking along the corridor, turning back as if directionless, lost, forward again, searching. In his student bedroom, the Historian turned over in his hard, narrow bed. Half awake, drifting in and out of sleep and the dreaminess of the triumph of the conference's last day when he had chaired the conversation for which most of the scholarly participants had gathered. The last of the International Brigaders had gone, silently in the night, from Wales to fight, four decades ago, in the Spanish Civil War, and another comrade who had gone, as organiser and commissar, to oversee and assist the integration of that selfless cadre of communist volunteers. And between them, himself as witness and scribe and, of course, admirer, but privileged to call the former miner by his first name, so Les then, and the political secretary, Idwal, by his. From the latter a forensic recall of the details of recruitment of volunteers and the machinations of an international political mobilisation of the working class that was, he asserted to a scatter of applause from the audience, without parallel; and from Les, gaunt and shrunken now beneath the youthful slide of him posed and heroic in forage cap and calico jacket projected onto the screen behind him, wry comments on getting used to the food, the heat, the flies, and the buckets of rough red they had swallowed, and the unreliability of the ancient rifle he could be seen clutching across his body. More laughter than applause for that, and a scowl from Idwal of whom there was no slide only, forty years on, a compact presence of certainty.

The Historian hit a switch and looked at his watch on the bedside cupboard. Four o'clock in the morning. The student bar had closed at midnight. He had guided the two heroes to the student hall and the corridor of bedsits in one of which he was now awake. Outside, the footstep pattern of stop and go continued. He swung out of the bed and put his feet on the rag rug. He stood and wondered if he should look outside. The scuffed footsteps had moved on, further away. He hesitated, his hand on the metal doorknob when he heard another door open and other feet, no hesitation in their movement, enter the dimly lit corridor. He sat down on the bed and listened to a more heavily shod tread pass his door, coming up behind what were surely slippered, rubbered-soled steps, almost apologetic for being out so late, and uncertain of their next step.

In the distance the slippers had halted. The second set of footsteps, not afraid to clatter, the feet encased in heavy brogues, marched on. Beneath their steady tattoo, the Historian could just about discern, or rather sense, the slide and swivel of slippers. Their wearer, though this was not seen, was squinting back down the corridor of walls which, as they receded, appeared to converge. Along the length of plastered breeze-block walls were set at regular intervals plywood doors. The veteran narrowed his eyes in an attempt to focus. To see who was coming towards him and not stopping. Voices now.

'Idwal?' the veteran asks. 'Sat yew, is it?'

'Where you going Les? It's not light yet.'

'Aye. Couldn't sleep, Id. Same as yew is it? All that remembering and all. Went for a stroll outside, but got lost. Couldn't find my bloody billet, forgotten the number, see, and they all look the same eh.'

'Lost? You say,' said Idwal, a friend and comrade not seen in a quarter of a century, working for the Party mostly in London, or so Les had heard.

'Aye, lost, getting on a bit, see. Silly bugger.' And he smiled. Only the smile was not returned.

'Same as at Albacete, then, after they broke our lines. You got lost, then, as well, didn't you Les. Couldn't find you anywhere, could we. Missing. Presumed dead. Only you weren't were you, Les. Otherwise you couldn't have got home, could you. Not a dead hero at all, then, eh Les. Didn't tell the boys and girls any of that, did you Les.'

'That was a long time ago, Id, terrible times. I saw worse than you.'

'Not the point is it comrade. Not the point at all. The Party had to have a word, didn't they. To shut you up. To keep you for use as a valiant member of the International Brigade. You're just lucky they sent someone from King Street to have that word. Lucky it wasn't me back in Spain, if we'd found you. Or you might then have served the purpose another way, right.'

The veteran squinted back the short distance down the corridor to where the shorter man, the Political Commissar, stood his ground. The veteran felt his breath seep out of his dry mouth. The veteran's heart stuttered in his chest. The veteran stretched out a hand to touch the wall. He wanted to go home now. Not long now, he knew, not long.

Further down the corridor, behind the stiff back of the Political Commissar, the Historian opened his door. The comrade Political Commissar turned slowly in a full circle to face him.

SECOND HOMES

ALIENS

'It was always about love, however that love was mis-placed or mis-conceived. Illusory or real, but love for all that, however mistaken or just missed.'

He stands alone in the doorway of the café which he manages and part owns for a share of the profits and hopes one day to run and own outright. He stands framed either side by plate-glass windows on which are stencilled in block capitals of gold the names of cigarettes and chocolates, Wills Star and Capstan and Cadbury's and Fry's, and in wavy, undulating white lines the trademark enticement of ice creams, made and refrigerated onsite by electric motor and no longer by hand power and blocks of ice. He stands directly under his name set across the door's rectangular glass transom: Giuseppe Macchiano (Prop.). He stands with his arms folded behind his back, his stocky build flanked by the display of cartons piled artfully high behind the windows. He stands to nod to the afternoon shift of pit workers, whey-faced and hurrying, as they cross over with the morning shift, coal dust graining their faces and their clothes rank with the stink of the pit. He stands, portly and assured in his bespoke three-piece suit with his white shirt cinched at the collar by a black wool-knit tie, and he smiles as he is occasionally acknowledged by a 'shwmae, Joe' or the flutter of a hand wave. He stands welcomingly to the side as some men enter his café to leave or retrieve cigarettes, a half-empty packet or even loose single ones, to be placed for them behind the counter on a shelf before they go or have been underground where cigarettes are contraband. He stands alone, the only one of all the shopkeepers, of fruit and veg or ironmongers or bakers or butchers or haberdashers or newsagents or general stores, whose premises apologetically arc up along the bleak and winding main street of this valley's township, to front with a custodial care akin to love his establishment as it glows at his back in the uneasy late summer of 1938.

In his head, unseen and unheard by all others among whom he works to live and to whom he smiles as he dips his head in greeting, he can reflect on images from memory as they collide with these passing moments. In his head, almost every day at some time or another, he is forever twelve years old and being pulled and prodded by his black-clothed mother through an uncertain gaggle of other boys so that he might take off his cap to scrunch it in his hands to incline his head to one side in front of Signor Rabaiotti who has made his annual return to his home village, his very presence somehow swollen, as if pregnant, with an almost intangible aura of untold prosperity, and all in order to recruit able and willing boys, no girls, to accompany him down the valley on the one-a-day open-side bus to Genoa and then by rail, four or five of them squashed together to sit on the wooden slatted seats of the train's third-class carriage, whilst Signor Rabaiotti travelled in the plush comfort of first class, to rattle across the northern delta plains of Italy and on into France, changing trains at country junctions until Calais and across the Channel to Dover to work, on three-year contracts for the man who will be their padrone and so rescue them from the stone-strewn, nigh untillable, overly parcelled-out plots of dry, friable soil which supports and slowly kills their left-behind families. In his head, without reflection, he truly knows that the urgent shoving him forward and the anguished pleas his mother makes for him, not others, to be chosen by Signor Rabaiotti, are all acts of love, and nothing but love, though it is not, in 1902, any kind of love he wants to be happening. In his head, the distant feeling has receded, no rancour left any more than any meaning to the places and events which have, by now, coalesced into a jumble, unreal and unlikely, of a transit of the unknown, languages and customs, until direction and instruction from the padrone assigned him to a daily expectation of work into which he settled as he must. In his head, he sways between the fixed solidity of a present whose future he has secured and an ethereal past whose tendrils of remembrance never quite loosen their grip.

He thinks that these men, these small and wiry blackened colliers who hail him like a friend though his relationship with them is merely social through trade and from the shared warmth his café, with its central pot-boiled coal-fired stove, can give them in winter even when they have no work themselves and precious little to spend, that they can have less idea of where he came from and of what he once did than he has of the toil in the pits which have magnetised them all, natives and aliens, to this once, and no longer, prosperous place. He thinks as he looks at them and at the coal particles pockmarking their skin and considers the coal dust caking the inside of their mouths and lining their throats so that they must continually hawk up phlegm and spit it out wherever they might be that he, too, had once had layers of earth dirt and limestone grit staining his lips and clogging his nose so that every breath he took on the heat-soaked slopes of the ground which he broke with a hoe walking behind the ox driven by an older brother had a taste and texture no water could wash away. He thinks that there was no respite, either, in the daily grind of work he had been set to do, from the off, in the alien place to which the other poverty had consigned him to chip away at both conditions, there and here, by the new boon of money earned. He thinks, and wonders, at the boy he was, raised at six in the morning from a shared bed in an attic to prepare a day's ice cream for sale, penny cornets or twopenny wafers, a luxurious confection never to be eaten or tasted by its makers who stirred, by hand, the mix of cream and sugar in the enormous metal drums encased in a wooden tub and packed all around with rock salt and the ice kept cold in blocks covered by straw bales in the dark basement and the cream rotated and stirred round and around by hand until it thickened and froze and could be transferred to the containers of the hand carts which boys would then take out onto the streets to push up and down the steeply climbing roads of the terraced streets inhabited by these people so alien to him, so many of them, and more arriving all the time in those pre-war years so that noise and movement seemed continuous, until all the ice cream was scraped out and sold. He thinks of the muscles he developed within a few years on his calves and how his skinny arms grew biceps and his shoulders became broader, all ready to flex in defence when collier boys cornered him to throw stones, once chanting 'O! O! Antonio' and turning his cart over with its long handles stuck upside down in the road whilst the ice cream spooled out in an unsaleable slick. He thinks of how his sobbing became curses at them for calling him Italiano and Eye-Tie since, as he yelled back in the suddenly summoned up ferocity of his patois that he was no Italian and that he did not speak Italian and that he was, in heart and mind, from the Bardgiani of Bardi in the valley of the River Ceno.

He considers, more with a perverse pride than any ruefulness that the ability to read and write he had acquired was in English more than in Italian and all at the behest of his padrone for whom these attributes would allow some of his boys to acquire the more necessary talent of numeracy. He considers, often enough as he grows older, that he is by 1938 three times more rooted by residence in Gales than his early years allowed for in Bardi but that his own new world in that time had changed in its fortunes more than he had changed as a creature sent out to send back what he could to a family of siblings caught in the rut of their hamlet with its dust-packed floors in their one-up one-down stone dwellings whilst, for himself, whatever was ordinary in pleasure and living was subsumed by getting by and, slowly, accumulating. He considers, from his longer perspective, how lucky he had been, as his padrone often told him, to have entered under the wire before the Aliens Act was passed as law in 1905, passed to restrict immigrant labour and assuage nativist resentment, unwarranted and fearful, but nonetheless an increasing shadow over their alien lives until in 1915 Italy, his Italia by then, joined the war on the Allied side and flags and bunting could intertwine on the streets where his broken English, with a smattering of Welsh thrown in, became, somehow but how, more attuned to these defining places of his chosen life. He considers the grooves of the path he has taken, serving in other valleys and then managing in this one and with ownership to come, on his way to becoming himself, albeit in a smaller way than the networked grandee families, a padrone with, soon, a legacy of his own.

Behind him, from where he stands in front of the café, he can sense the intimate world he controls within going about his business. Behind the long mahogany counter, its grain polished and darkly burnished, shelves from floor to ceiling are filled with tall glass jars of translucently coloured boiled sweets, sticks of orange barley sugar twists, creamy mint humbugs, fading chocolate drops and the pearly nacreous sheen of prized mint imperials, and there is, too, fitted in among this array the café's set piece, with its mottled faux-marble pillars, a soda fountain with brass taps to dispense sweet cordial liquors whilst, set to one side of the counter is the steam-driven gleam of the copper cistern of a coffee machine, decorated with the relief of a fasces bundle of rods and an axe, leased from an Italian outlet in London and as much for show as profit since stewed tea was a cheaper option to drink from thick white china cups set down on the glass-topped wooden tables, each with four spindly chairs with fretwood seats for lingering customers.

Behind the lace-curtained half door in the far left-hand corner is, he knows, a living room, table and chairs, a button-backed sofa, and on the wall some bright prints of blue sea and ochre pine stands and white villas. A small kitchen is tucked away beyond the room. The pungent cooking smells of wine and herbs and garlic mingle as a welcome memory for him and the boy, and cause the two girls to wrinkle their unaccustomed noses. Behind the brass and iron bulk of the cash register on the counter near the café's outside door, there will be in attendance, he knows, the eighteen-year-old he went to fetch when he was ten, as he had promised to do, the near-orphaned from birth Giacomo, wet nursed and raised within his younger brother's family until it was possible for him to be taken and transformed into John as his new padrone had been into a Joe. Behind the cluster of furniture in the living room are, inbuilt in one corner, stone steps to two upstairs bedrooms, the smaller for Giacomo and the larger, with a recently bought double bed, for himself and his wife.

He sighs, almost audibly, his breath puffed out into the soft afternoon air of the street, with the grateful satisfaction that an almost complete and carefully shepherded family can cause a man, once alone, to feel. He sighs, inwardly, at his luck or judgement perhaps in employing the two Thomas sisters as urged on him by their widowed mother, attractive young women she had all but implied to attract and enliven customers, her younger daughter the eighteen-year-old Dorothy, and Mair, just twenty-four herself but also widowed when her husband of only three years of marriage had died under a rockfall in the pit. He sighs with the pleasure of content when he closes his eyes to think of Mair, his pregnant wife, resting on the sofa in the living room which he has furnished, the birth of a new life imminent for both of them. He simply sighs just because it has all come to this in a dream as much as in any manner of reality.

He wonders how he had found the courage, or was it wit or gall, to ask her, fair and small and under his unrelenting if sidelong gaze from the beginning, but always with respect, to marry him, past any youthful prime, balding and jowly, or why she had agreed with only a disquiet about his religion, easily dismissed by him, assuaged by the civil ceremony he arranged. He wonders how much her mother had encouraged it, for the security of the unexpected catch of a steady provider, of food and wages and comfort, the travails of widowhood put aside, and he wonders, too, how the unexpected readiness of their love-making might promise him a deeper love to come from a baby for both to cherish. He wonders, from all the change this prefaces with its promise, and for the first time in all his sequestered time, what harm might encroach on them from a world he cannot influence and which he has, largely, let pass him by, unbidden and unwanted. He wonders whether, as she enters more fully into his compartmentalised and distinct world, he has made it clear enough to her, and perhaps to others in the common and native life that is hers not his, that he attends the monthly meetings of the Fascio, consular and business encouraged, not because he has embraced whatever fascism is or who Mussolini might be, though some compatriots do so and all swear an oath of allegiance to an admired Il Duce, but only because it is a means of connection and aspiration. He wonders, nonetheless as she reads to him alarming newspaper rumours, if it is time to become a British citizen, in name as well as deed, and, too, for Giacomo whose English is so much better already than his own. He wonders, fleetingly, about what such a formal step might entail for all of them as they go into a future life of uncertain outcome.

He remains, his stance on all substantial things unaltered by any passing fever of speculation, convinced that the past has been faced and overcome. He remains unrepentant that, the one and only momentary time he returned to Bardi when the Great War had ended and Mussolini and any New Italy were not yet in full sight, he had left behind the bride he had found there, only for Theresa to die in childbirth, himself not yet established enough to have taken her with him back to what was still a relative land of plenty. He remains staunch in his belief that Giacomo was best cared for back home, with money sent and a promise for him to fulfil when a decade has passed and a new one had begun. He remains, then, determined to be rooted in the place where his caution and his labour have seen him survive against odds he could not have countenanced if he had ever envisioned them, yet against which he had manoeuvred to create a new life.

And so he stands teetering on the heels of his feet, rocking almost imperceptibly from side to side outside his café, and inside himself he girdles together all that has been dearly gained and all that is dear to him, deep within himself for the love of it, and for them, and he stands four-square and steadied as if he is the guardian of light, the beacon light of his café, shining out beneath the gloom of the leaden sky and the clump of dark hills which hems them all in, and the space he inhabits is timeless, the café a theatre of performative defiance, and his life its own aria.

* * *

Mair had read aloud to him from the working man's newspaper, the crusading *Daily Mirror*, for 27 April 1940.

> Now every Italian colony in Great Britain and America is a seething cauldron of smoking Italian politics.

Black Fascism. Hot as Hell.

Even the peaceful, law-abiding proprietors of a back-street coffee shop bounces into a fine patriotic frenzy at the sound of Mussolini's name.

We are nicely honeycombed with little cells of potential betrayal.

He had held Maria, his infant daughter, close to him as his wife read what passed for news. It felt more personal than that. He could see it unfolding in the way there were, all the time, fewer and fewer customers. He planned as best he could. He arranged with the other family, to whom he remained tied and indebted, that Mair would run the café if necessary and keep the accounts for as long as the war and his maybe absence might entail. He signed all that was necessary for this to be clear and legal. His main concern was for Giacomo, youthful and disbelieving and protesting. He railed against such injustice. He denounced Mussolini and cursed Giuseppe for his open attachment to the Italian network that had sustained them. '*O, mi figlio*', Giuseppe muttered in despair, and so what had been unsaid was, at last, open between them. He told, too, the wife he had taken as his own, and she told him she was not twp and that they must all act together.

Before the blood-spattered disaster at Dunkirk in May and the seeping fear of defeat which came despite all the bravado of public rhetoric, Giacomo left them. In the night, no moon to penetrate the blackout, clutching a suitcase, no torch to light his way through the back door of their yard, down the unmade lane to the river and on to the iron bridge and across it, turning right and up a cinderbank to where it flattened out and led to the back entrances for Miskin Terrace. He opened the unlocked garden gate of number 62 and went past the brick lavatory down the steep path to the steps of the outside yard of Mair's mother's house where the widow still lived with her younger daughter, Dorothy, who waited to open the door to him. He was to have the upstairs back bedroom with access to a roof space if needed. He was not to look through any windows or go downstairs or leave the house for any reason except to use the outside lavatory by night. The women would do all else for him.

Mussolini, to whom Giuseppe had regularly sworn his meaningless oath of allegiance, declared war on the Allies on the tenth of June and, thereafter, the round-up of all male resident Italian nationals was swift and unrelenting as even some of those who had become British citizens were arrested. Local police came for the men. No exceptions were made for local knowledge, trustworthiness or friendship. The officer who knocked on the door for Giuseppe Macchiano apologised to Joe who was packed and ready and shrugged his understanding. Questions about the darkly handsome assistant, young Johnny, were deflected by Mair who told the policeman he had just panicked and disappeared. Maybe to London, she said. Giuseppe was transported for internment in the Isle of Man, there to await, with hundreds of others who had been rounded up as enemy aliens, deportation to a Commonwealth country for the duration of the war.

* * *

The sisters take it in turns to cwtch the child in the café's living room or to serve at the counter. The customers who still come cluck sympathetically about the plate-glass window boarded up after a brick was thrown and had shattered it one night soon after Giuseppe's arrest. Dottie moved in to help out and only visited her mother by day. No one asked directly about the whereabouts of Giacomo. The whisper was solely that he had gone, as if disappearance was another species of innocence. Not everyone was convinced of that, though the police had searched the living quarters of the shop. Dottie confided in Mair that Ted Williams, a collier-turned-soldier who had been sweet on her and tried to win her affection more than once, had stopped her in the street one evening as she left her mother's home and, in drink she said, had speculated about the convenient vanishing trick of what he called her Eye-Tie Lover Boy. Out of sight was not out of mind so far as he was concerned, he said, and that she'd better not get into trouble for it herself. When Dottie glared at him and pursed her lips tight, stubborn and defiant, Ted had softened his approach. He said he wished his leave would not end so soon, but that somebody had to go and fight for the country, didn't they, and one day he'd be back again. For good. She had wished him 'all the best', stepped past him on the pavement and hoped that 'all would be well' with him. He stood stock-still outside her mother's front door as dusk fell and watched her walk away.

The tip-off came in the form of a handwritten letter which had been posted locally. The same policeman who had arrested his father had knocked on the door and asked the sisters' mother if he could come in, as information had come to the attention of the authorities that an enemy alien had been seen on the premises. There was no resistance. Giacomo was taken into custody. The constable called in at the café to chide the sisters for the concealment they had arranged. The sisters were unrepentant. Everyone knew Johnny was no threat, they said, and the policeman knew it for a fact, didn't he, and all who knew the boy. And in any case, they wanted to know, who could possibly have betrayed him. The word and its concept hung in the air. The officer had no answers to give them, he said, only that the letter writer was a patriot who genuinely considered his duty had been to write the note. Dottie told the police officer, who had been known to them all their lives, that no one could be so cruel or so stupid to believe any of that if they knew any of the facts or circumstances. So who, they chivvied, and why? The officer demurred. No address was given and the letter writer was anonymous. But the information was correct. The suspect had been duly apprehended and, he said, that is that. Mair would not let it go, however, and she pointed a finger at the policeman and said it must be someone wicked, someone who has a grudge against Giuseppe, against Johnny, against us. No, the policeman said, trying to mollify them. No, no evidence of that kind at all, only the scrawled initials at the bottom of the page, 'E. W.', and that's not enough to go on. But for Dottie that was enough.

* * *

The pre-war cruise ship *Arandora Star* had once been opulently equipped for 400 well-to-do passengers to enjoy the sun and sights of the Mediterranean coastline. Wartime service saw her painted grey and armed for ferrying troops. In late June 1940 she was commandeered for the transportation of German POWs and the Italian internees, some 1,600 altogether, with the Italian contingent as four men in two-berth cabins on the lower decks. The crammed ship sailed from Liverpool for her destination in Canada on the first of July 1940. The Macchiano men, father and son, had found each other in the camp and were together as the *Arandora Star* left port.

Giuseppe, momentarily bereft at the capture of his son, began to envisage a post-war future, whether back in Wales or in Canada, depending on the conditions and prospects in that quite unimaginable place. To contact the sisters would be the first, most important thing. The talk between them, and the others with whom they mingled during the forty-five minutes' exercise on deck allowed each day, was of other homes: of Bardi and the rash of contiguous villages they had left behind in the Ceno valley. They remembered, with some wonder, the journeys each had undertaken and the outcomes for which they had settled. Giuseppe confided his own long-held plan to buy out his senior partners in the café and how eventually it would be for Giacomo and Maria and whatever other family might yet follow. His father probed gently into his son's feelings for his wife's sister, feisty Dottie, the smiles and gestures between them noticeable and telling for anyone who cared to notice, as Mair certainly had and told him. His son brushed the implications aside and said time enough for such things. And besides, there were others, always others weren't there, as his father had discovered for himself. Father and son, in a peculiar enforced fashion, were content to be fully together as themselves and at long last.

Still only half-awake in makeshift bunks at seven in the morning of the second day at sea, the ship's engines thrumming enough to make the vessel vibrate, then a jolt at first as much as a noise which followed, percussant and afterwards rippling, so that the ship seemed to creak and moan. Alarm signals like disturbed banshees. A clatter of feet. Doors slammed open and shut. Everywhere everyone shouting. A confusion of bodies in the narrow corridors. Was it an internal explosion or a torpedo into the ship? No one knew on the lower decks. A panicked scramble to get out and up the stairs. Bodies falling. Arms and fists pushing and hitting whatever was in the way. Water entered the corridors with more and more force. Men slipped and fell, were trampled on. A sudden shift in the ship's position as she listed to an impossible angle. An inrush of sea into the body and veins of the *Arandora Star* which was sinking bow first into the depths of the sea which swept Giuseppe Macchiano down and away from his son as a roar of white water pounded at speed down the stairs, the gangways, the corridors, churning and hurling the men in its path into open cabins and against the walls in a swamp of drowning before the ship lurched one more time and then sank head first as she upturned at a ninety-degree angle and disappeared into the deep as Giuseppe could only cry out in despair and love, '*O, mio figlio*'.

* * *

Along the length of the curving main road, the windows of the shops were either boarded up with plywood or whitewashed all over and blanked out. Their former purpose, and that of the café in their midst, was finished as one millennium ended and another began. When the café was finally closed, the only fixture to be retained was a glass-framed case screwed into the wall behind the counter. It held a yellowing newspaper cutting. Maria, the sixty-one-year-old childless proprietor of the café after the death of her mother, knew the words of the page scissored out of the *South Wales Echo* by heart.

Disaster at Sea

One hundred and twenty-five miles north-west of Ireland the transport ship the *Arandora Star*, taking POWs and deportees to Canada, was struck by a single torpedo from a Nazi U-boat in the early hours of 2 July. She sank to the bottom of the sea within twenty minutes. Some men jumped into the sea from upper decks and managed to swim clear of the stricken vessel. Lifeboats could not be released in sufficient time to save the lives of 75 Nazi POWs and 486 Italians who perished. It is estimated that 49 of the Italians being deported had originated in the Ceno valley in northern Italy and were, for the most part, engaged in the restaurant and coffee-shop trade in South Wales where many of them were well known locally.

* * *

After the war was over and loose ends could be tied up, Mair Macchiano had bought the café outright with a bank loan, and she and her sister Dottie ran it as before. For decades nothing substantial inside or outside was changed. It was a timeless time-bound place, practically a shrine. Mair died, widowed twice, in the early 1960s, forgiving no one and blaming nobody. Her sister, Dottie, never married and never forgave one in particular, the one whose initials had been scrawled at the close of the letter of betrayal: 'E. W.' It was murder by any other name, she would say, and repeat to anyone who cared to listen, even in her eightieth year, to her own denunciation of Edward 'Ted' Williams who had sent the young Giacomo to his death.

When the twenty-first century came, aunt and niece ended Giuseppe Macchiano's dream and left his valley to live quietly until death at the seaside. Ted Williams had long since emigrated to a new life in Australia.

* * *

When the area's new police headquarters was moved to a more central location, shelf upon shelf of manila-bound files of yellowing paper, correspondence and memoranda mostly, were transferred to the reorganised Public Records Office for sorting and reassigning. There were folders of local reports and letters. One note, written in blue ink on lined notepaper and with no date, nor address nor full signature, read:

Dear Police,

To whoever this may concern.

This is to tell you that the Italian called Johnny who serves in the Bracchi on Cardiff Road is hiding out at 64 Miskin Terrace where the girl, Dottie, who also works in the café lives with her mother, the widow Joan Thomas. I seen him in the back garden more than once to use the lav and it is him for sure. My boy Ivor never came back from Dunkirk and those who killed him should not be free to live here.

Trusting you to do your duty.

Yours faithfully,

E. W.

An archivist's research identified the note as a wartime letter of denunciation to the authorities in June 1940. On an attached filing card she had typed out her further findings after consulting the census returns for Miskin Terrace in 1931 and, there being no wartime census made in 1941, that of 1951:

Those in residence in 64 Miskin Terrace in 1931 were:
Joan Thomas (Housewife; widow), aged 35
Mair Thomas (Daughter), aged 17
Dorothy Thomas (Daughter), aged 11

Other relevant information. In 1931 the residents of 62 Miskin Terrace, the even-numbered but adjacent next-door property, were:

Ronald Wilson (Collier), aged 46
Edna Wilson (Housewife), aged 38
Ivor Wilson (Son), aged 13

In 1951 only Edna Wilson is recorded as still living in Miskin Terrace.

* * *

It was always about the distortions effected by love; love blind as to what fate might engender; love indifferent in either hope or despair for what might be brought about; love beyond hate or revenge but not grief; always love, wilful and unyielding, and which would make all it touched suffer for its sake.

THE BAILEY REPORT

'Here he comes,' said Geraint Owen, the sound engineer, to his cameraman.

'At last,' said Mickey Britt. 'Stand by for irruptions, and assorted earthquakes, Ger.'

The two men were dressed for the weather, any weather, in Corporation-issue black anoraks and wide waterproof trousers. They were dressed for waiting. They both looked down the funnel of the terraced street, houses on each side for almost half a mile and cars parked nose to tail, to where the street sloping down to the valley bottom abutted onto the main road. At the junction, where only double-yellow lines were free of vehicles, the car they recognised as his had stopped, and parked on the double-yellow lines. It was a silvery blue Bentley, a coupé, with amber-tinted windows and low-slung doors which closed with an assuring clunk when he stepped onto the pavement and shut the one on the driver's side. Right hand over left shoulder, without looking, he locked the car electronically.

A. J. Bailey was a man in late middle age. He had the broad but loosely held shoulders of a middleweight boxer and the heavy legs of an Olympic oarsman, so he appeared to be longer above his tapered waist than below it. The late-November morning was dank, edged with a coldness seeping down from the hills into the streets, but he wore neither overcoat nor raincoat, and no Corporation anorak, against the chill, only a bespoke single-breasted suit of grey worsted over a cobalt-blue shirt with a button-down collar left open at the neck. As he strode up the street toward the waiting team he ran a comb through his thinning sandy-coloured hair, and he whistled, rather tunelessly, to himself.

At the far end of the long street, Donald Thomas, executive producer, sprawled across the back seat of a leased Corporation Volvo saloon. It was a diesel model, painted in forest green and with brown leather seats to match a walnut dash. The car came in the middle range of hired vehicles deemed suitable for someone at executive-producer level; Donald Thomas curdled with resentment at the car's silent signifying of his rank. He hated what it registered, that he was nearer sixty than fifty, and that this was it for him. He had his eyes closed as he sat and waited in the car. He drummed his fingers against the headrest.

From the front seat of the Volvo, May Onions, his PA for over a quarter century, had been keeping watch. She half-turned to the back, 'He's here, Donald,' before staring back down the street past the patient, immobile Geraint Owen and Mickey Britt. In the Volvo, Donald Thomas opened his eyes, but only to glare at the back of the seat in front of him. 'Oh, he is, is he? At fucking long last … at fucking long last … as fucking usual.' Then, with a wrench of the handle, he opened the rear left-hand door of the Volvo and pulled himself up, and into the street. After the warmth of the car he shivered in the outside air and buttoned over a heavy cable-knit sweater, his fur-lined suede coat around his stomach. Not much of a belly, he felt, given his height, almost six foot, but maybe, he'd decided, enough of a belly to drive him to a gym someday soon. He ran a hand through the muss of black curls, with only a hint of becoming grey around the temples, and rubbed his prominent nose between finger and thumb. The twat, he thought. He stood stock-still as his presenter approached with a studied nonchalance, an insolent ease, which Donald

Thomas hated even more than he disliked the Volvo the Corporation had bestowed upon him.

The late arrival waved at the crew of cameraman and sound recordist as he drew near, and blew a kiss, one made somehow into a lascivious gesture by sliding it off the palm of his turned over hand with a puff of his breath, to May Onions. She sucked on her lower lip and turned her back on him as she reached for a clipboard of notes in the car. May wore a woollen black bobble-hat over her auburn hair and a shiny black coat of stitched panels over blue jeans and suede ankle boots, so that she was, apart from a freckled face and sage-green eyes, quite covered up. The presenter smiled. He swivelled to greet his producer.

'Morning, Colonel,' he said. 'Are we set? Best get cracking, eh?' and, infuriatingly, he treated the annoyed recipient of his off-hand delivery to a lop-sided grin which was not contemptuous at all, no need for that, just intentionally dyspeptic in its effect. On Donald Thomas, that is. No apologies, and absolutely no explanation, for this, after all, was Bailey, and Donald Thomas knew in an instant, as he had been forced to know it many times before, that his anger, without any real means of redress, would be futile, and that even reasonable complaint, albeit merely verbal, would be self-defeating in the face of the tantrum it would undoubtedly cause. So, he just grunted, in a mutter of an aside, 'For fuck's sake, Bailey,' and gestured vaguely to the patient, indifferent crew who had balanced their Styrofoam coffee containers on the bonnet of their white Ford Estate car, and were waiting for the action to begin.

Bailey strolled across the street to talk with Mickey Britt. In the recent past the cameraman would have had an assistant to lug the gear, to set up the camera and even to pull the focus for the shot, but no longer. Nor was there a lighting man with his array of blondes and brunettes and redheads, the aptly named devices, to derive or deny tint and colour from the glare or dimness of the natural light. Nowadays there was only the camera, its reduced operator, and a soundman to mike-up or point the muffled microphone to the talking head. Bailey often reflected on the incremental disappearance of the latter, of people like himself, from documentaries and factual programmes. Yet, thank God! he would add, not from the gritty nit-picking of the investigative reports in which he had long specialised. His gift, so to speak, and he'd conclude looking at the accumulating pension pot any freelance was required to feed, the gift that kept giving … for a while yet anyway. He suddenly felt, and looked, genial.

'Where do you want me, Michael, me old mucker?' asked Bailey of his cameraman, and both nodded at each other in the shared recognition that any star presenter knew with whom his best interests rested. And it was certainly not with any producer.

Mickey Britt gestured towards the backdrop behind them where the sloping street began to climb further upwards to the mountain which was more of a protuberance than a peak. It was one of those squat, rounded hills of bracken and boulders which clamped a sullen presence over all the vistas to be glimpsed from the valley's floor of road, rail and river. To the left of the hill where it abruptly fell away and flattened out as if a shovel had cut into it was what they had come to investigate, or rather to show since the actual investigation researched by May Onions and scripted by Donald Thomas, would be revealed by the footage Mickey Britt had already taken for Bailey final voice-over in studio. What they were about 'in situ' was precisely that to add the authenticating touch of actual presence and perceived involvement - the Bailey trademark.

In the near distance, through the camera's viewfinder, men in yellow slipover jackets, and all with white or orange hard hats on, could be seen moving around the site. The soft thrum of dumper trucks mingled with the harsher revving of lorries in a suspension of whiteness, a dust flurry which never settled but floated among and beyond the encircling railings and open gates. This, in plain view, was the Mynydd y Caws waste disposal site, an open refuse disposal unit, set down on the cleared ground of a closed colliery's former tip. That signifying pyramid of coal, once teetering to an insolent height over houses and a school, had been levelled and grassed over after the Aberfan disaster of 1966. But the debris of industrial waste, just like the waste which had once spewed over these valleys, was still being recycled here for use elsewhere. If Bailey did irony he could have joined up the dots. Only Bailey did not do irony. Nor did he have any discernible political allegiance, not even cynicism or compassion. In life this made him, for those who did, like Donald Thomas, almost insupportable. On the box, however, it made for a strength of conviction that had all the direct simplicity of the best acting.

'We'll use that behind you, Bill,' Mickey Britt told him. 'You can assume it, there, over your right-hand shoulder. It'll be in sight all the time … for the viewers … great picture, Bill.'

Bailey allowed the liberty with his name. Some could, and some could not. For Mickey Britt, fellow incomer two generations removed, and as monoglot English a Celt as Bailey himself, there was no problem. Anyone else, though, had better know Arthur Joseph Bailey as 'Mister Bailey' or call him 'A.J.', or, better still, just 'Bailey' if they knew what was both good for them, and appropriate for him.

Donald Thomas had stood off to one side. He ambled

forward in a proprietorial shuffle and with a self-announcing cough. He looked through the viewfinder as if his opinion of the shot was the one, in the first and last resort, which mattered. Bailey had already moved centre frame. Donald Thomas jiggled his bent-over head in approval. Mickey Britt took a final look-see, and gave Bailey the thumbs-up. Donald Thomas moved between Bailey and the camera. He held out his hand. May Onions hurried forward with a script. To check … to be certain … ins and outs … for continuity. He conferred with Bailey who simply shrugged. Geraint Owen confirmed there were: no aeroplanes, no cars, no vacuum cleaners, no music, no troublesome kids, no rowing households: only the ambient buzz of traffic and industry and a soughing wind off a bedraggled copse on the otherwise bare bones of the hill. Perfect.

'Right,' said Donald Thomas. 'A run-through?'

'No,' said Bailey, 'Come on. Let's just go for it.'

Mickey Britt chortled, and looked up at his producer, and then slyly at Bailey. 'One-take Bill' was what camera crews had gratefully christened him. He never 'corpsed' with the private, inexplicable inner glee at the absurdity of his role; he never fluffed a line or suffered sudden memory loss; he never tried to better what he'd already accomplished the first time. All this, over many years, had been a constant source of friction with his various producers who remained determined on the self-justification of having various takes from various angles: 'For choice in the cutting room. Just in case. You never know. In the final edit.'

So far as Bailey was concerned, such professional belt-and-braces trainee school stuff was a waste of time, his time, valuable time when money at business conferences and government seminars and training videos was begging to be made elsewhere. This time,

Donald Thomas didn't bother to argue the toss with the insufferable Bailey. He would get Mickey Britt to do some hand-held GVs later, for mood and for case of editing, but for now all there was to do was to mutter, 'Yeah go for it then. Ready, Mickey? Geraint? Right. Camera rolling.'

Bailey rocked slightly on the balls of his Gucci-shod feet. It pulled him, almost imperceptibly, into the camera's lens. His face was immobile and his light-blue eyes seemed transfixed for the heartbeat or two in which he said nothing. Then he half-rotated his upper body but without ever taking his eyes off the camera, to suggest the presence of the Thing behind him. His voice when it finally came out of the silence he had created for himself, was in a resonant, rumbling, buttons-holing conversational tone. This was to be the opening of the programme. It was to be a signature Bailey piece to camera.

'Look … there … behind me. Would *you* like it behind *you*? Behind *your* street? Looming above the rooftops of *your* houses? Lurking in the air above the fields where *your* children are at play? Would you? I know *I* wouldn't.

'But that's where they've put it, though, this *Thing*.

'That's where *their* Council has put it. A state-of-the-art refuse site, *they* say. The Mynydd y Caws Dump. And I say Dump, because that's what they do, that's where they dump, on open ground, close to these streets, not just household waste but un-treated building materials, plastics, chemical matter, toxic stuff some say, biological and pharmaceutical discards.

'And I'll tell you this, as I stand here in this street on this workaday morning, it's noisy, its filth is in the air, and it stinks in my nostrils. And the good people of these streets have to listen to the *Thing*, see the *Thing*, smell the *Thing*, and breathe in its noxious fumes, day by day and night after night.'

Bailey adjusted his stance and took a pace nearer the camera. He gave the camera a wry smile, an over-the-garden-wall confidence: '*They* … the Council … *They* say it's all within acceptable limits for legal emissions. *They* say it's not a health risk, or indeed any kind of hazard to public health. It's safe. It's necessary. It's well-managed.'

His smile became a grim memory in an instant. '*They* … the People who live here, who have to live here, say the *Thing*, that *Thing* behind me, has caused birth defects, chest problems, stinging eyes, sore throats, premature deaths of the young, and of the old, and a terrible psychological blight on all the lives of those who have no choice but to live here.' He paused. The tone was level once more. 'Who's right? And who's wrong?'

Bailey let the silence wrap itself around him. He looked deep into the camera. His knife-edge of a mouth widened to a resolute crease, and he said: 'Well, there's only one way to find out, isn't there?' He turned his back to the camera and walked with a slow, purposeful step up the slope of the long terraced street towards the mountain and its tumorous waste tip. After no more than fifty yards, he pivoted on his heel and lengthened his stride until he was almost back to his starting point.

'OK, Squire? You get all that?' he shouted out as he walked, but not to his producer, only to the cameraman who, again, gave him his customary thumbs-up signal. Donald Thomas gnawed at the sore spot on his bottom lip. He waited for Bailey to be within earshot for a whisper.

'Fine … fine … though you missed out on the health statistics we discussed, and the reasons for its being there in the first place, and such stuff. So we'll need to pick that up later, in studio, won't we? One way or the other. But since we were so late in starting, we'd better break now, hadn't we? For an hour. Be back, at the gates, while it's still light.'

This last was mostly for May Onions who looked down at her clipboard and then, in a voice louder than Donald Thomas' musings told everyone that there was a chippie on the main road or an Italian for frothy coffee and corned beef pasties, if they preferred, and outside the gates to the dump in an hour then, at one-thirty, OK?

Mickey Britt and his sound engineer began to pack up their equipment into the back of their car. They would drive it wherever they were going, no matter how near or far it was, and park it in full sight to foil the 'thieving bastards round here'. And everywhere else they ever went. May Onions glanced at Bailey, trying to gauge his mood, and assess his needs now that Donald Thomas had exerted producer's timetable control. But Bailey said nothing and did nothing, other than to give them a perfunctory nod. He jangled his keys in his trouser pocket as he walked away from his colleagues. He zapped open the Bentley, slid into the driver's seat and turned the car around in a tight circle before accelerating away onto the main road where a passing van had to brake and sound its ignored horn.

'The bugger,' Donald Thomas said. 'The bloody, arrogant, self-centred sod … the bastard.'

May Onions saw his point. She had acknowledged it for herself some time ago. No point in going there, though, she thought. She enquired instead, 'Coffee, Donald? Join the boys?'

'Sod that,' said Donald Thomas. 'And sod him, too. Come on, there must be a pub around here. I need a bloody drink.'

* * *

Donald Thomas fished out a twenty-pound note from his wallet and asked May Onions to 'get the drinks in' whilst he 'paid a visit'. His PA took the money and pulled a face behind his retreating back.

'I expect that includes you, boys. Mickey, what's yours? And Geraint?'

Drinks were ordered, and fetched to their adjacent but separate tables. A large whisky and soda for Donald; pints of lager for the boys; and a lime and soda with ice for May. Home-cooked ham and chips to follow for the boys, with ham rolls for her and Donald.

Donald Thomas returned and sat, in a glum contemplation, slightly to one side of their table. It was warm, a steamy iron-radiator heat, in the back bar of the cavernous red-brick Victorian pub which they'd found in the town. He took off his sheepskin coat and threw it over the back of a Windsor chair. It fell to the floor. May Onions retrieved it. She hung it up on a peg. She gave him his change. She sat down and waited for the mood music to begin. She knew it would. Donald Thomas always simmered before he boiled over. The crew were quietly sipping their drinks and tucking in. She nibbled at a chip. She waited. Donald Thomas had not touched his drink or his food. Instead he stared, as in a trance, at the cone of weak sunlight which was being beamed through a blue-and-red lozenge of a stained-glass window so that it funnelled through the air a mote of dust which flickered, particle by particle, in a whirling suspense.

Donald Thomas was not actually thinking. He was free-falling. Into his own past. A past that had once been so full of promise. Like himself. Into the present he tumbled. So unfulfilling. Like his unfulfilled self. Was it his fault? He couldn't see why. He still 'had it all', as a former controller had told him, back then at the beginning, and indeed thereafter as he occasionally inched his way without real conviction or desire, up to the famed Third Floor, but where he never secured a foothold beyond being there 'in an acting capacity'. His telegenic looks - the phrase used in the 1960s for being conventionally handsome - had weathered but had not deserted him. Some had even thought his brooding eyes and sensual lower lip had a touch of Richard Burton about them. It was the same lip he was biting now. And, he thought as he bit it, he'd had a proper degree at Oxford, not like Burton's wartime dalliance there but a second class in PPE at Jesus. The Welsh College, as it was known, despite the fact that its Welsh intake was in a minority even then. Still, lifetime connections could be, and were, made among those who would, chrysalis-like, turn into the professionals which a Welsh secondary education, whether good grammar or minor public schools, intended for their academic caterpillars: barristers and solicitors, civil servants and professors, executives and diplomats, administrators and managers. Playing rugby football was not, of course, compulsory but it had added a sheen to the polish to be brought to becoming a 'Professional Welshman'; and he'd been good enough, once or twice, to play not just for his college as a loose wing-forward but also for the university seconds, the 'Greyhounds'. College societies allowed him to brush up on the hesitant Welsh of his boyhood, the tongue his solicitor father and housewife mother had scarcely used at home between themselves, or in the family at all, in the city in which, as with so many post-war contemporaries, they had settled after their own college education. Donald was to be set on an even more upward social path. Paths to be trodden carefully and gratefully in exactly the way of others like him before him. Yet by the sixties, more enticing opportunities, particularly for those of his generation and upbringing, were accruing almost daily in a country busily creating a living, for some at least, out of itself as a cultural artefact. There were new highways that could as easily to be taken to public prominence, the fame that whispered of fortune, as any of the more traditional routes to security and comfort. If he had made a mistake at all in the early days of his broadcasting career, it was only perhaps in scorning the steady labour, and subsequent rewards, of the offered management training courses. He was, so many sirens assured him, with his looks, his intellect, his charm, his sonorous speaking voice, his quintessence of being a modern man in a Welsh idiom, a star in the making. And from the off he had loved the attention he had been able to gather for himself by being, however instantly or briefly, at the centre of the moment, those moments only radio and television could conjure. He was a Presenter. He was a Personality. He was a Face. He Voiced Over. He read the News. He chaired and he interviewed. What he never became, as if there was an ingredient missing in his make-up, was a Broadcaster.

Donald Thomas, sometimes despite himself, knew exactly what that meant. That there was a disjunction between the ornament he was and the function to which he aspired. That, unlike other professions with their guarded and self-sustaining worlds, the true Broadcaster had to both reach out to and yet reflect the audience. But most of that audience was indeed other. His colleagues, sensing this, and besides, not possessing his other attributes, readily took to those roles behind the camera, and so away from its relentless gaze, which higher executive positions or strategic production thinking could, along with higher salaries, bring them. He bridled at the tedium of committees and baulked at the even temper required for management team work, notwithstanding the compensation available in the darker enjoyment to be derived from the backstabbing of Corporation politicking and the arse-licking of superiors. He clung, for far too long, to his original, narcissistic dream.

Over the decades Donald Thomas, stalwart and veteran, was increasingly channelled as a presenter into those adjunct programmes and early-evening series whose softness and cheapness could accommodate his now less than compelling presence. Worse, when he complained that such output only buttressed or perhaps occasionally tended the changes shattering their accustomed world - the pit and steel closures, the destruction of established ways of life, the uncertainties of politics, from left to right, the uneasy rhetoric of a nation revived, former class divisions papered over - then, on the Third Floor, wise heads nodded and decided to find a way to use his talents, to note his desire and placate his ego. He was, all said and done, one of their own. They made him a producer … a senior producer … an executive producer … a producer by any other name for all that.

Donald Thomas was to be involved, as he had wished, in the big events, the big issues, the pressing matters, the state of the nation debates, in all of the glamour and gravitas which the Corporationi hoarded as the rightful cultural capital of the nation's broadcaster. He worked hard to shape and direct these productions so that they might, in their turn, affect that culture. His ambition was no less than that. Yet, ruefully, and even as he chopped off as many of the Talking Heads of others that he could manage, he was inwardly confronted by the stubborn, deep and instinctive knowledge that though he had failed himself to be that automatic and personal connection between lens and living room, he had need of that power wherever its detestable source lay.

* * *

Bailey... Bailey...Bailey... the surname beat a persistent tattoo inside Donald Thomas's head. He reached over to pick up his drink. Bailey. He gulped down some of the whisky and soda, snorting as the bubbles darted up his nose. Bailey. They always turned to Bailey. Whose principal concern, the producer so often lamented to those above him on the Third Floor, was only money, the fee, the dosh, spondoolicks, the loot, pounds, shillings and no fucking pence in the presenter's own reiterated mantra of demand. Bailey. Donald Thomas, whose own name credit-ended every decent programme Bailey had ever made let out an involuntary sigh.

How much he, Bailey, lacked. How much he, Bailey, seemed oblivious to all around him. Did he even know that, out of his hearing, for his temper was as ferocious as his fists were quick, they called him 'Billy Boy'? Like a chirping budgie with an appetite for seed and an ever-open beak. Once a secretary, star-struck maybe, had sung 'Bewitched, Bothered and Bewildered' at a Christmas do and dedicated it to her 'Pal Billy'. Bailey had applauded her 'lovely singing voice'. Someone had once christened him 'King Arthur' in ironic tribute to the discrepancy between Bailey's day-to-day behaviour and the regal flaunt of his TV persona. He seemed aloof, disinterested, untouchable. And then the green light went on and he was none of these things.

Donald Thomas said to May Onions as if she'd been sharing his thoughts all along, 'The thing is, May love, the tosser is such, such...', and he paused to let the exact and appropriate word arrive from his Oxonian hinterland, 'such a boor!'. It was as if he'd had a sudden revelation, or a returning one anyway: 'He's boorish, so ipso facto, he's a boor.'

May Onions remained silent. She was not, herself,

quite clear how Bailey was a boor, or what the category of boorishness fully implied. She wondered if it was a categorisation people like Donald Thomas invented, required even, to denote people like Bailey. To distinguish themselves from those others who were not, ever, capable of being like them. Donald Thomas was unaware of her lack of certainty. His own absolute conviction was now both infinite and specific.

He sipped at his double whisky. His reverie returned. Time was when, at the start of their careers, he'd tried to be sociable with Bailey. Never, even in those days, Arthur or Joseph days, certainly not 'Bill', and 'A.J.' sounded too boardroom, so it was always to be 'Bailey', and no closer than that for Donald Thomas. He invited Bailey, and his wife - Rita, a nurse he recalled - to his house. His own wife, Nerys, had taken a day off school to prepare the dinner. None of that sickly pink prawn cocktail and glutinous boeuf bourguignon stuff which the world and his wife were dishing up at that time, usually to be followed by a crème caramel and the blue stilton with dimpled crackers. They were to have something to which the palate needed to pay attention, something, for that time, exotically different. When the 'Sopa fría de Ajo y Almendras con Uvas' appeared in its crock of white china, Bailey's eyes had directed his nose to sniff. At the first spoonful of the thick, white, bread-soaked liquid of ground almonds, water and garlic - almost a perfect replica of the deliciously refreshing soup Donald and Nerys Thomas had tasted in the hills of Andalucia the previous summer - Bailey ran his tongue over his lips and glanced up first at the dutifully slurping Rita, and then at his hosts.

'Supposed to be cold, is it? Only asking, my old flower, but I've got a grape in mine, too. Afters first, is it?'

He had spooned up half a bowl and declared himself to be 'full as a tick' and 'ready for mains'. In those days the great oenophile had not achieved his transubstantiation out of the form of the beer-swilling Bailey, but he smacked down a glass or two of good claret with a hint of the wine-bibbing future he might yet care to embrace. A platter of rice and pine nuts dotted with minced lamb meatballs and a layer of sticky brown dates and gooey orange quinces steamed onto the table in an aroma of sweet fried onions, and with the subtle herbaceous hints of Middle Eastern spices. 'Oh, good,' said Bailey, 'main meal and pudding in one. We'll get home early, Rita.' The invitation was never reciprocated and, so far as Donald Thomas could recall, he never set eyes on the wife of the surprisingly uxorious Bailey again, though from time to time there was abrupt news of children being born whilst he and Nerys, her choice more than his, kept their parallel careers on track, and the lives of the executive producer and the headmistress of a primary school in the city proceeded in agreeable, childless fashion.

Donald Thomas chewed it all over again. 'You see, May,' he said. 'Someone like me looks at a Bailey and well, should, in some ways, admire him. And why not? He didn't go a particularly good school, one of the second-rate grammars in the city, and he didn't have the advantage of an Oxbridge education. Not even a university one … the local poly in fact … some kind of Mickey Mouse law and accountancy course. He never practised either. A stint in the army hoping for a commission, but he gave that up to marry. Pregnant, probably, knowing him. Straight into local news reporting and then broadcasting … despite having no Welsh … not even passable Welsh, like mine was then … so, yes, of course, to be admired.' Donald Thomas drained his glass. 'But then why, oh why, is he so bloody obnoxious?'

It was not, of course, a question. Not one of any kind. In any case, May Onions had no answers to questions she would never have posed to herself in that or any such way. For her, Bailey was a phenomenon, a force of nature even, difficult and undeniably unpleasant when he chose to be, but, as she also felt, utterly distinctive, to the point of being unstoppable, whereas Donald Thomas was, well, nice enough, self-deprecating, charming when he stopped whining, but self-absorbed where Bailey was self-directional. She had been sucking up her pale-green lime-and-soda drink through a colourless plastic straw. She finished when the sump at the bottom of the glass filled with air and made its slightly farty sound in the mouth at the final suck. Donald Thomas had not stopped talking to himself of course - so she tuned in again.

'And what's all that army stuff all the time with him? Where does that all come from? He was only there long enough for basic bloody training. I'll tell you why … cos he's a snob underneath it all, underneath all that weepy stuff about council houses, an abusive, alcoholic and then absent father, and a saintly mother out scrubbing floors for her Joseph. Onwards and upwards for him. He *loved* swanning around an officers' mess, I bet … losing his twang quicker than he could wink. I bet he sucked up there. Colonel! Major! Captain! Sergeant-Major! General! My arse.

'Let's face it …we put up with him but for how much longer? He insufferable … Tony Hancock on speed! Decades out of date and snide to boot.'

Donald Thomas needed rescuing. They could all feel it. May Onions didn't know where to start. Mickey Britt was pensive. He'd heard the diatribe, in one of its many forms, and more than once, from his nominal boss. Since Bailey and he were akin in their upbringing so far as working-class parents of second generation Brummie origin went, and with a disciplining yet socially limiting education to match, he could himself understand and so excuse Bailey's mix of combative aggression and touchy sensibility … more readily, anyway, than Donald Thomas ever could. Mickey Britt even admired the brute manner in which Bailey had spurned the drummed-in, leaden persistence of the know-your-place education which they had had in common. Bill Bailey, Mickey Britt knew, was no gent, and never would be. Donald Thomas, though, personified the caste, at least in its local guise, and was always courteous to his staff colleagues. As a mark of respect for the issue before them, an attempt at reassurance for Donald Thomas, in a gesture of almost professional solidarity, Mickey Britt tried to help with a definition of his own, one closer to home.

'Yeah, Don,' he said, his own original inner-city vowels as sharply defined and slicing in intonation as ever, 'proper old fuckin' ba-a sta-ard when he wants, inne?'

Donald Thomas coughed in disdain at the distasteful language. May Onions flashed Mickey Britt the chiding look of an intermediary smoothing matters over for the great and good. Geraint Owen, as he had learned to do since leaving the north for the south, kept his private thoughts close to himself. May Onions decided to intervene, but in lesser, more amused vein of recollection.

'Then again, Donald, what about the time we were filming the Welsh restaurant-in-the-Dordogne story, Michelin stars for Merthyr-born couple, and all that? Lovely meal, wasn't it? But A.J. so grumpy, and off to bed early, only the adjoining hotel I'd booked, corporation rates in play, wasn't to his liking, so he came back to the restaurant and I had to drive to that chateau on the edge of the town.

Set in parkland … lovely … and charming English-speaking proprietor … nice-looking, too.

'Anyway, our man barges up to reception and blurts to the young woman behind the desk, "Bonjour, my Cherie, chamber large, yes?" And the owner steps in and says he's had my call and reserved a special room for the "Famous Corporation" and before he can finish, speaking perfect English, mind, Bailey jumps in and says, "Splendido, my frère. But, listen, this is just for moi, see, so ensure, comprendee? that it's a Grand Chamber with private sale-de-bain. Gracias mucho, count." The marquis, I'm sure he was, looked as if a dog had vomited all over his Aubusson. That's a carpet, Mickey!'

Donald Thomas permitted himself a pouting smile.

'Yes, you told me over the cognac later. Embarrassing git … what he is, at heart, what he truly is, because I don't believe he doesn't know what he's up to, is … feral.'

Mickey Britt had liked the modest French hotel May Onions had booked. But he had also seen the Dordogne chateau when they picked Bill up in the morning. He had waved from a sun-dappled terrace, the remnants of his breakfast of freshly squeezed orange juice, coffee, rolls and croissants, scattered in disarray before him, and the marquis laughing with him, but in service at his side. Mickey Britt had sensed a flush of pride rising. One of our own. In the pub, now, he considered that 'feral' was perhaps 'fair do's', but that Bill Bailey was better understood as 'fierce and fearless'. Donald Thomas pushed his empty glass to the edge of the table. He watched Mickey Britt and Geraint Owen snaffle the untouched ham rolls. In the far corner of the echoing bar-room an old man left his high stool at the bar. He shuffled over to an old-fashioned jukebox set against the wall, inserted a coin and punched a button without looking. In a whoosh of slithering strings the chord-roasted tones of Nat King Cole swooped in and warmed the room:

Unforgettable, that's what you are.
Unforgettable though near or far
Like a song of love that clings to me
How the thought of you does things to me...

'Oh, Christ!' said Donald Thomas. 'That's the tin lid, that is. Come on, let's go.'

* * *

Two o'clock outside the gates, Bailey had not appeared. The camera was already up on its tripod in a fixed position. To the north-west of the council refuse site, the winter sun was fast sliding down the mountain ridge. Bailey refused to give his mobile number to anyone; besides, it was permanently off, subject to his view that he used it to reach people when he wanted, not when they required him. In the back of the car Donald Thomas and May Onions sat in silence side by side. She wondered if she should pat his hand ... or perhaps not.

Donald considered what he had heard other people in command call available 'nuclear options'... an official complaint ... a dressing-down ... an enquiry ... a sacking ... or perhaps not. He sighed.

May Onions looked again at her own option. His hand ... then at her right, free hand. In her other hand, the left, she held her mobile. It buzzed and she grabbed it with the hand that had been momentarily free. She pressed answer. It was Bailey.

'Hiya, love ... A.J. here ... been delayed ... on the way, OK? Fifteen mins ... see you babe.'

'Well,' said Donald Thomas. 'Well? What excuse has the shit got this time?'

May Onions contemplated the moods to come. She rehearsed in her mind the tempers that would fray. She surveyed mentally the best outcome for the show. She acted in its best interests.

'It's his mother,' she said.

'His mother? His fucking mother?' gasped Donald Thomas.

'Yes I should've said earlier, Don, but he asked me not to. Was why he was late this morning, too. He said he didn't want to cancel or make a fuss. She fell in the night. She's in sheltered accommodation, you know. On her way to the loo. They only found her this morning. They called an ambulance. Hospital. It seems she's broken her hip. They, uh, after this morning's shoot, A.J., uh, belted back down the dual carriageway to see her. She'll have to have an op. She's about 96. Not his fault this time.'

'He could have told me directly. I'd've postponed it. But that greedy bugger would've seen a loss of earnings elsewhere on his packed schedule!'

'He is close to her, you know, Donald. He was only eight when his father left.'

'You swallow that d'you, May? The absconding pater familias, the old lady taking in washing and doing cleaning to keep Saint Bill in school? Jesus, May… '

'As a matter of fact, Donald, yes, I do,' asserted May Onions. 'And he just said he'd be breaking the speed limit to come and finish the prog, so give him a break, OK?'

Donald Thomas shook his bushy head from side to side. Incredulous, rather than denying her plea, he slumped back into his seat. May tapped on the window. She gave Mickey Britt and Geraint Owen the ubiquitous thumbs-up - waiting time over soon.

Inside the chain-link fence, dumper trucks were using their shovels to cut avenues of access between the piled-up refuse. Mickey Britt took a few more GVs without his producer needing to ask. The man who'd played Nat King Cole in the pub was clumping unsteadily up the steep dirt-track road to the site. He nodded to the camera more than to operator and walked up to the Volvo where Donald Thomas, his window closed, still sat. He rapped hard on the window. May Onions put her chewed-up biro and clip-board down on the next seat and pressed the button to open the electric window on her side.

'Yes?' she said. 'Can I help you?'

The man at the open window was in his late seventies. He wore a thin black mackintosh over a grey polo-neck jumper. He was unshaven, a grey stubble pocking his scrawny neck. His breath was a waft of inhaled, rerouted and exhaled untipped cigarettes and the woody sweet after note of draught bitter.

'Aye,' he said. 'Perhaps you can. They told me, back in the pub, that you're filmin' up 'ere bout that tip, and stuff. S'right?'

Donald Thomas had opened his eyes. He leaned slightly across his PA. In a protective manner, not sure where this was leading.

'You 'aven't got council permission, 'ave you?' the old man said. 'Permits 'n 'at.'

Donald moved his hand closer to the window. 'Hang on mate,' he said. 'Hang on. That's not entirely fair, you know. And, besides, I think you'll find we're here to help.'

'Help? Help? You're jokin' are you?' said the man. 'Don't talk to me 'bout help. This will be another sideshow, a circus, a news story. A joke.'

In the distance, beyond the old man's grizzled head, Donald Thomas could see Bailey trudging up the road. The old man shifted his own stance to follow the producer's eyeline.

'Is that that Bailey, then?' he asked.

'Yes,' said Donald Thomas wearily. 'That is indeed that Bailey.'

'Well, I'd bloody well like to have a word or two

with him as well then, right?' growled the stranger. 'He needs telling something he does, if he's with you, that is.'

'Yes, fine,' said Donald Thomas. 'Fine. You give him, my friend, if I may be so bold, the benefit of your considerable experience, and clearly your correct and entitled opinion. Go ahead. Be my guest. Just give it to him … preferably with both barrels.'

Bailey was yelling, 'Sorry, boys' as he approached the camera position. He offered May Onions a hand wave as thanks. May Onions scrambled out of the car. She said, loudly enough to be heard, 'Sorry to hear about your mum's fall, A.J. … hope she'll be all right.' Bailey made a puzzled frown. 'Eh?' he said and then, recovering, 'Yes. Ta, she's OK, I think. Last time I looked anyway.' Then he almost bumped into Donald Thomas and the producer's newfound friend, both standing in the road and in his way so that Bailey said, genially enough for him, 'Move over, chaps … we've got to do this pretty quick, eh … before the light goes. All in my head, Donnie, no worries … don't you fret … here I am … will be word-perfect … as agreed … just for you, mon General.'

The old man did not move. He jabbed out a nicotine-stained finger at Bailey. The distended knuckle wobbled as he waggled it in Bailey's blank face.

'I've been wanting to meet you for years, I 'ave.'

'Really?' said Bailey. 'Why's that then, Tosh?'

'I'll tell you why,' said the old man, and he wiped a work-swollen hand across the spittle of his lips.

'I'll tell you why,' he repeated as Bailey waited.

'With all we have to put up with … patronising buggers coming up ere when it suits … and only then. Patronising buggers, like your lot, coming up ere, as if from another planet, takin' your bloody pictures, makin' us all out to be 'opeless, dim-witted, doo-lally-tap, 'elpless left-overs, relics. As if we 'ad nothin', done nothin', 'ad no history to speak of, just remnants, to be sorry for. No idea most of the time of who we were, leave alone what we are now. What we actually may still be, 'cos there's no clue in their 'eads, is there, of what might be in our 'eads, that we might be thinking, behind the closed doors of those 'ouses none of them ever thinks to enter and ask, when the curtains are drawn and we're not being given parts to play, uh?'

The old man was shaking. He seemed to have run out of breath. Bailey set his lower lip into a Bailey jut.

'And your point is, soldier?' he said.

'My point is, Mister Bailey,' said the old man, 'is that you, and I'd say only you, seem to understand the half of what I've just told you. I dunno much about you, but I've seen you giving those buggers set above us, by themselves most of the time, an 'ard time, whoever they are. I know you're not from 'ere, not one of us, directly like, but you can't 'elp yourself can you? From being with us, as well, to expose them, to chivvy the buggers, beat 'em up when they don't answer the questions they don't want to hear, and which you still ask. And, if you 'ave to, bring the fuckers down, uh?'

'Right-o,' said Bailey. 'Couldn't have put it better myself, could I Donald? Now, if it's OK with you, Sonny Jim, I've what we in the business call A Piece to Camera to do. Stay and watch if you like. But behind the camera, please.'

Bailey shook an outstretched hand. He walked past the old man. He winked at a crestfallen Donald Thomas. Mickey Britt pointed to his marked position, and asked, 'What the fuck was that all about?' Bailey took up his position in front of the camera. He said, quietly enough, 'Fuck knows, Michael, some local paysan Donnie boy picked up. Shall we do this, then? Get it over with? I've got something on in town at five o'clock, got to change first.'

Bailey's face was suddenly shadowed into seriousness by some inner mechanism he controlled when he needed it. Mickey Britt checked, and approved, the light. It was just sufficient, a glimmer which penetrated the whole and made a chiaroscuro cameo from which Bailey could shine out. Geraint Owen asked for a soundcheck. Bailey said, 'Tiddley Tum, Tiddley Tum, what's the price of a sack of coal nowadays, Down the hatch.' Mickey Britt respectfully raised an eyebrow for Donald Thomas to start proceedings officially, but the producer was gazing into another space and it was May Onions who said, 'Go for it, then A.J.'

Bailey had not lost his concentration. He moved, but again only fractionally, to animate his stance, and he began, and ended, in one take.

'Here in this valley, indeed in all our industrial valleys, there have lived people of quality: vintage communities, created out of appalling conditions by the people themselves. Self-confident people, proud people, whose very existence has shaped our history, yes, the history of all our nation, like no other force in the past 100 years. They deserve, in these latter days, better than this. To be dumped upon. Like this … thing behind me. You know, I have concluded that this is not a question of who's right and who's wrong, of statistics or efficiency savings, of managerial capability or scientific expertise. It is, quite simply, a question of common humanity, and of our duty, all of us, to that humanity, as it exists, on the ground, here. On *their* front doorsteps … in *our* backyard. There is only one feasible conclusion to draw from our investigation in this programme. That Thing over there should be stopped. It will be stopped. It must be stopped. To let all who live here, who choose to live here, who have the right to live here, listen again to birdsong not diesel engines, to breathe fresh air not noxious fumes, to smell spring on the mountains, not scent death in their valleys.'

Bailey counted one-two-three to himself. He shifted his head, so that his eyes seemed to glitter with a new force.

'This programme has been, as always, a calling card on behalf of the people who matter. You. I'm A.J. Bailey, and you've been watching the Bailey Report. Thank you and, until next time, goodnight.'

* * *

Donald Thomas thought: 'Christ … he thinks he's a bloody American.' May Onions decided it was 'cheesy', even for A.J.. Mickey Britt confirmed it was 'a wrap'. Geraint Owen wandered off to record 'some wild track'. The old man applauded and slapped Bailey on the back as the presenter strode past him. Bailey, without looking back, waved a hand at them all as he left the scene.

COUNTERACTUAL

The old man watched Bailey retreat down the street. He saw Pigeon slide off the low cream-coloured concrete windowsill of a garishly painted terraced house. Bubble-gum pink for the walls and baby blue for the woodwork. He saw Pigeon flip a half-smoked cigarette in Bailey's direction and wave him away with a vigorously waggled V-sign and a muttered, 'Piss-off outahere.'

He waited for Pigeon to turn on his heel to walk towards him. The old man looked past Pigeon to check that Bailey had reached his car. He had. He had paid Pigeon no attention. The car, with the TV Presenter at the wheel, moved off in a hurry. The old man walked slowly towards Pigeon. When they stood face to face on the pavement in the middle of the street, Pigeon looked down at the old man, ready for him to speak first. In the silence between them Pigeon was impatient. He shouted loud enough for an audience.

'Wassa 'bout butt? He's offa telly innee? a tossa there. 'Ee can fuck off forrastart, an all. Saaright, butt?'

The old man tilted his creased and pallid face up towards Pigeon, so closely that his stubble almost scratched the teenager's scrawny throat. 'Yes, he is,' the old man said. 'And there's no real requirement for you to speak like that now that he's gone and they've finished filming. And they are out of hearing so long as you desist from shouting.'

'Sorry,' said Pigeon. 'It's just that I thought you'd said we had to keep it up … under all circumstances.'

'Yes, by all and every means. But only when it is necessary for them. Not between ourselves, eh?'

Pigeon took off his NYC back-to-front baseball cap. He looked back up the street where the TV crew were packing up their gear.

'Are they really that thick?' he asked.

The old man sighed. 'No, not thick exactly. Just a trifle obtuse, where other people are concerned. They can't read our signals readily. We don't go around with coal-black faces anymore. Our politics no longer frightens them. We are no visible threat to their own conception of society, though that, of course, we hope, may change one day, again. You see, we are, in their eyes, poor. So we must be lesser. We stay here by choice, so we cannot be, oh, sacred word, aspirational. You can see why, then, it would not be helpful in the firmament of their fixed universe if we were to be discovered enjoying Beethoven, discussing Matisse's cut-outs, or reading Updike and Mailer. Or indeed, as you do yourself, be found grappling with Foucauldism as a metaphor for our auto-incarceration. We speak as we do before them only for them. It is necessary to sustain their illusion by deluding them.'

Pigeon sighed in his turn. He sucked on his lower lip and gave the old man a petulant look, one that hinted at having heard something very similar from him a number of times. He decided to try another tack.

'I know it's a waiting game. I do know that. But what exactly, whilst we wait, do we get out of it?'

'Ah,' said the old man to whom, over the years, this query had been put in the public yet secret meetings that had been held, in closed session, since the setback of the Great Strike a quarter of a century earlier.

'What is at stake, my boy,' he said, 'is not what we currently get - the grants, the funding, subsidiarity, inward investment, regeneration projects, public works of art, entrepreneurial pods, electrification of the rail network, touring concerts and opera, visits from our national drama companies, and every other species of economic and cultural munificence we can garner - no, what is at stake is, first, why and how we get it. And the answer to that is by being, stubbornly, us and by staying, very much bloody-minded, where we are. Think of it this way, too,' he said. 'Imagine if the Sioux had not gone, quietly in the end, with Red Cloud onto the reservation. Imagine if they had been able to stay out on the Great Plains with the resurgent spirit of Crazy Horse in their veins. Well, we have managed that, haven't we? Inside our own heads, I mean. Together, still, in ways they are not. Nor have ever been.'

'But then?' said Pigeon. 'After all this, then what?'

The old man clasped the young man around his shoulders. 'The values which validate us, our past into our future through this present vale, cannot be allowed to shrivel up. To become, if you like, the clichés a Bailey will spin about us as tight-knit communities and the heart-warming victim syndrome. Because a pit closes, all of them in fact, or a factory closes, or even if a generation disappears like mine will soon, it does not mean that we cannot live as if the normal, our particular human contribution to history and morality, cannot be, for us, the norm.'

Pigeon moved in step as the old man took his elbow and began guiding him back down the street.

'Look. Consider it this way,' said the old man. 'The more we are perceived as different, impossible cases perhaps, the more we will receive the benefits due to our being disabled from any utility in their utilitarian world. Best to let us fester outside their city - region. Keep us quiet, quiescent you might say. The danger is if they decide not to leave us alone, to wallow pityingly about our benighted condition. For then we might be sucked into their soulless, deracinated lives of get-and-go, into their lookalike pattern-book housing on their digitally modelled estates, bombarded by their aimless electronic chatter, their faceless tweeting of trivia, their closed circuitry of surveillance and the overall tyranny of their dehumanising technological devices for which an Orwellian coinage would surely have come to St George: Social Media aka a-social Dystopia. Antisocial. Code for cod. Sharing by pairing. Paring the possible to the bone for the boneheaded.'

He stopped stock-still. A guru on his own patch. Not to be denied, Pigeon relaxed.

'If they think,' the old man said with some force applied to the young man's arm, 'If they think we cannot aspire to be them, prevented by our heritage, our genes, our tribalism, whatever, from being able to join them, then, with a brute equivalence of motive and silent condemnatory accusation, we must strive to ensure we do not, ever, sink below them. For that would be to drown in the shit of their making without even the compensation of being ourselves the defecators of such a tragic destiny as their's surely is. So, you see, we require a holding strategy, a defence against the Midwichery of their Moonie herd. For they are the real tribalists, not us, and our togetherness, at its collective best, has always been about full individual liberation, not the falsity of having to choose from a prescribed set of options. They think, as they view our limitations, real enough I grant you, that we are the ones who are imprisoned. On the contrary, we are the ones who can be free in ways they will never, for themselves, comprehend. What, therefore, we do together, increasingly into the future and as consenting adults, of course, as citizens if you will, is something they can no longer do, and which they would prevent us from doing if they knew: to relate the one to the other, to cohere, to have common purpose for common wealth, to inherit who we were so that we may create who we wish to be, to survive as ourselves in order to live on, as ourselves, not to live, even well, just in order to exist.'

Pigeon released his arm and elbow from the old man's grip, and rubbed them. 'Mmmm,' he said and stared into the distance. The sun had sunk even below the lowest of the darkened hills. The two walked in a slow lockstep towards the bus stop on the main road. Pigeon looked at his eBay-purchased wristwatch. A fiver. Brand guaranteed. He shook his wrist from side to side to start it up again. In the gathering gloom, they sheltered behind the cracked Perspex shield of the bus stop's canopy against the wind scurrying up the valley. The old man decided that to clinch the argument, for the present, he needed another example to illustrate the necessity of defence before attack.

'D'you remember,' he reflected, 'how we were almost caught out about a year ago? They'd come up, as usual, with their fold-away camera and hairy caterpillar mikes, to take some vox pop on the latest government announcement: What do the people here think - do they think is what they really mean - of the proposed shift to reduced and universal benefits? And what they wanted, so that neither they nor their viewers would themselves have to think, of course, was the usual know nothing, chopsy, keeper of the slurred, glottaly over-endowed and strictly incomprehensible local accent. Preferably a morbidly obese, blowsy woman in her late thirties, with a fag in one hand, a can of extra-strength in the other, and an ignored baby crying in its pram. And, naturally, we were, as ever, prepared, on the lookout, ready, and able to station Tracy, after just twenty minutes in make-up in the Centre, right in their path. Irresistible. And she was.'

'And we were rumbled?' asked Pigeon.

'Almost. Almost. Not quite. Tracy had been brilliant:

'*Lookewe. Owswegonna live, eh? Ows I gunna feed 'er?* And she'd gestured with the cigarette in the direction of the child we'd borrowed and blew some smoke, not very much of course, towards the baby's face: *If ew sods or them sods takeawaysee, 'er rights, like, she'll starve to death, she will, 'onest. And I'm not 'avin aat ?, see. There'll be blood on the streets, innit? Like ah Miners' Strike all over again. Only worse, men'l see to aal, don't et worry. Only worse. And, me personal like, I got a disability, aaan't I? And my old man's buggered off n'all, see. Some piece from Swansea.* At that, dear old Tracy burst into tears and put her pudgy hand to her lipsticked mouth as she bawled. They ate it up. Made all the news bulletins, Welsh and national UK.'

The old man pursed his lips. The bus was swaying down the valley towards them. He tapped Pigeon on the arm.

'Only, the trouble was that the soundman had left his tape running for wildtrack nearby as he went off to help the cameraman load the car, and when he played it back he heard something, and we heard it clearly since Tracy and I, me in attendance naturally, had not moved: *My God. Did you see their scrunched-up, contemptible little faces. They really, truly, wanted me to be less than human, didn't they? So I gave them my best thespian works. But, you know, even then, in character, I was still human, wasn't I? Not in their prejudiced excuse for a life I wasn't. I was an oik. A scrounger. A nobody. A no-hoper. A scumbag. Well, scuttle back off to your sewer, you rats, and feed your trans-*

ferred poison to your bosses. Me, I'm off to evening class at the Centre. Short stories from Chekhov to Carver, without a Cartland in sight.

'We could see, immediately, the confusion it caused. The recording chap looked hard at Tracy. But the breeze and some sound from up the street had distorted it a bit. He was, in a sense, thank goodness, unwilling to believe what he'd actually heard. I sidled over as he replayed the wildtrack. I grinned at him. I said, 'Wassamarra, butt? Aaahs all come offa radio, mun. Schoolteachah biddy, uppa road, allus loppin' inna sum clever-dick play, or somepin, she is. Cow, mun.' I left it there. And so did they. Or else, I tell you, the game might have been up, and the first steps of revelation might have begun to suck us into their world of sensibility and submission.'

Pigeon stuck out a hand to hail the bus. The driver took Pigeon's bus fare, gave out a ticket and waved the old man and Pigeon on and into the bus with a 'Good afternoon, gentlemen'. They sat, together, at the back as the bus crawled, stop by stop, filling up along the way, down the valley to the Heritage Park at the valley's mouth. Pigeon and the old man knew most of the faces on the bus. Nearly all were among the cast assembled locally for that night's performance. The first of the season in the Heritage Park's small theatre. The committee had decided to dramatise the Tynewydd Colliery mine rescue of 1879. Exploring underground flooded workings. Trapped man. Heroic rescue work. A boy scared. Medals for bravery bestowed. It was due to start, ninety-minute tableau of dialogue and effects, rehearsed for weeks, at seven o'clock that night. The first cultural tourism coaches from the capital, generally genealogically alerted Americans, would be arriving around six. Plenty of time, the old man said, to get into costume and to melt back into

Victorian character. Then, by nine o'clock the cast would assemble again, with some invited others, in what they knew among themselves, as the Centre, to consider the lessons to be learned from further study of pre-1914 syndicalism in the Rhondda and workers' cooperatives in post-Independence Bengal. The old man would lead the discussion of the former and sit back to learn from their guest speaker's knowledge of the latter. They had all embraced the need for the long haul. Their retrieved culture would be ransacked to inform their future politics. But for now, he leaned over to Pigeon, slipping in and out of the actual present to ready himself for a re-enactment of the past.

'Oi, butty,' he said. 'Tonight, mind, when it goes dark and you're supposed to be trapped when the workings flood, remember you, David Hughes, are only thirteen, and thinking you'll drown, and die, so remember to shake with fear, real fear, because it's actually happening. Only, me, Isaac Pride, master collier, risking life and limb to tunnel towards you after you've been trapped for four days, you and your butties, me, Isaac Pride, will take you and hold you tight in my arms so that you're to stop shaking and sobbing when I say, "Now, now, boy bach. Now, now. We'll 'ave ewe back with ewer Mam in no time at all, butty. No time at all."'

'Orright, Grancha,' said Pigeon. 'Orright. Only don't kiss me and squeeze me too tight, like you did in dress rehearsal, eh? Or else some of them punters might get the wrong impression.'

JE SUIS UN AUTRE

He had died in early March but the cold weather lingered that spring of 1981 and caused coal fires to be still banked up in the grate as winter took a last grip. His body was brought back to the village by hearse for the funeral and buried afterwards in the cemetery where his forbears lay. On the day, there was late snow on the ground and old men walked gingerly to the workmen's hall where his coffin had been placed on the centre of the stage. It was draped with the original banner of the South Wales Miners' Federation and flanked by that of the local colliery lodge and a hammer and sickle flag. In over fifty years of party allegiance he had never forsaken the dream for which he had renounced the chapel beliefs of his youth. The funeral would be, as he would have wished, familial in tone and secular in spirit. That was the essence of his politics: protective and unyielding. In fiery times he had been among the most fierce but he had learned, too, as he moved up through the ranks of the union, when to give way in order to stand firm. From experience, men knew his words could be trusted. He set aside oratory for implicit dialogue. It was said of him that men knew to listen most intensely if, in speech, he clutched a buttonhole of his jacket between finger and thumb. The open secret of his mode of leadership was persuasion so that men could see why they, too, would reach those conclusions or take such actions. There was never a hint of triumphalism or of its doppelganger the fear of defeat in all he did and said because he did not fight or negotiate or compromise within such limited terms. He was concerned with lives and their betterment and the practical means to secure and hold that.

At the funeral there were hymns in Welsh but warm words of memory rather than any formality. The underlying threnody behind the anecdotes and recall was one of love for one who reached out so far by staying close.

* * *

The formal memorial meeting in his honour was arranged for later in the month. It would be held in the same workmen's hall of his home village. In the intervening weeks daffodils would push up from the sodden ground and the talk was increasingly of a nationwide strike, one to dispute the power of government.

* * *

This time, an occasion more public and political, his life was seen across the generations: from the few who could recall pre-war days and the unity through nationalisation which followed and on to those he had mentored as, sometimes, the Coal Board proved as recalcitrant over wages and hours as the despised coal owners had been. His last years in post as general secretary were marred by the closure of pit after pit but ended with the national coal strikes of 1972 and 1974, the first to bring victories since 1912, and both of which he believed stood as apogees of his most deeply held conviction: that the only individual credit worth banking was conscious solidarity of being in the frame together as a plurality. That took time to build. Some thought that kind of time had run out. The principal speech was to be delivered by the man campaigning to be the next national president of the union, the youthful firebrand of the 1970s who now spearheaded the smouldering militancy of the early 1980s.

The hall had filled up quickly on the designated Sunday afternoon. Cars and buses ferried lodge delegates from across the shrunken coalfield, and beyond. Respect was due, of course, but there was, too, a sense of new beginnings. If there was to be a nationwide strike, again, then unity was imperative. The talk so far had been febrile. Leadership of this uncertain mood needed to coalesce divergent ideas. The principal speaker was late, delayed by being in consultation elsewhere in a cabal of his most fervent local supporters. Speeches of tribute and acknowledgement had already been given before whispers from the back of the hall alerted those seated of his arrival.

The campaigner was flanked by an entourage of supporters as he weaved his way across and through a tangle of chairs and tables, nodding here and there to well-wishers and, before sitting, he exchanged greetings and handshakes with the bereaved family members. But if this was familial loss, it was also the wider familial legacy of political gain that was being assessed. The campaigner needed to take more than his own Yorkshire base with him if he did indeed become the national president, and be ready to implement the executive powers he believed would be his to use. He had already, as favourite, made it plain that union rules could be made more flexible rather than being a frustrating backstop to stymie strike action without a full ballot of all members. The campaigner presented himself as the embodiment of the direct action he, and others, sensed as being the antithesis of any scuttlebutt compromise. The wildfires of unofficial walk-outs and stay-downs which were breaking out with greater and greater frequency were, for him and them, the advance flames of what might become a revolutionary conflagration.

Now it was his turn to mount the steps to the stage where a few weeks earlier Dai Francis' coffin had been set down. The polite applause for earlier speakers became a wall of applause and shouts of anticipated pleasure. If there was destiny to be encountered, then it would be done in tandem down the narrow path Arthur Scargill had already chosen as if it was not his personal choice but the directed fate he represented in all he said and did. What he projected was something other than himself, or rather himself as a vehicle for something bigger.

So, naturally enough, all strangeness made normal, he spoke only in the third person. His accented syllables were elasticated by the pitch of his sentences and by his voice, a piercingly thin vibrato which brooked no response other than assent and acclamation.

> 'The first time our late comrade, Dai Francis, met Arthur Scargill, after a national delegate conference in 1972, he said that he had met the future leader of the British miners. He said, and in public, that the torch was soon to pass from one generation to another. From one comrade to another. From one leader to the leadership to come.
>
> 'Arthur Scargill went on, proudly, to become the president of the Yorkshire miners. Now it is time for him to become the national president. Time to meet the challenges ahead of us just as it was met at Saltley Gates in 1972.'

Here cheering broke out and cries of 'We're with you Arthur as we were then!' made him pause and raise both hands in acknowledgement.

> 'That was a key moment for the National Union of Mineworkers. The press photographs of the day show that Arthur Scargill was not to be cowed. Not by the

> police, the forces of repression. Not by false arrest and manhandling. Not by the diktat of the state, made ten times worse under this Tory government. And now, almost a decade later, these repressive agencies are mustered once again against our rights, against our communities, against our livelihoods, against the working class, against common justice. Comrades, Arthur Scargill is ready again, to lead you again, this time against the most reactionary Tory Party in living memory, against Margaret Thatcher its vile and arch leader.'

Here the shouts became raucous, the insults directed outwards more and more vivid and furious until the campaigner raised one hand, his fingers splayed outwards.

> 'Comrades, she will be defeated. If Arthur Scargill is elected your president when the time comes for it, then, when the time comes to it, your president will be, again, at the front of the struggle to the death. Arthur Scargill is telling you that nothing less will do than the overthrow and destruction of her government, that lackey of capitalism, and, comrades, as Dai Francis would have wished and foresaw the National Union of Mineworkers, your union, led by your elected president, Arthur Scargill, will build a better future for all our communities through socialist policies as the bastion of reactionary capitalism falls before our united and victorious National Union of Mineworkers.'

The peroration ended, the campaigner modestly left the stage to be swarmed over by those who were his already, and Formica-topped tables were thumped and the sprung wooden floor bounced under the tattoo of stamping feet. A memorial gathering had been hijacked as a campaign rally.

At the emergency exit door to the left-hand side of the stage, two men stood, bemused and silent. One raised an eyebrow 'Is that charisma?' he asked. 'No,' said his friend, 'that was magma. A violent spewing of toxic self-love which may bury us all. After the eruption beware the valley of ashes.' The other said that if the First Person was to lead the Second Person as if the former really was a Third Person, and the latter was Object not Subject, why, then we, the plurality, were well and truly fucked. Which proved to be, as the impersonal third-person pronoun might have put it, all too true and all was indeed to be other than what had once been or, come to think of it, than what might have yet been.

VOX POPS

MAXIMUM BOYCE

In 2023, at the age of eighty, Max Boyce saw a statue of himself, guitar in hand, erected in his home village of Glynneath. He had become a cultural icon. He has been a cultural phenomenon since his career took off with his surprise-hit, best-selling album *Live at Treorchy*, half a century earlier in 1973. It was a moment for which his particular genius was made: an instance of historical triumph poised between the successful miners' strikes of 1972 and 1974 whose significance he understood in his bones. The comedy with which he regaled that Rhondda audience in that parenthetic year was salted, as they were, by knowledge and revenge. They didn't need to be told 'Duw It's Hard. It's harder than they will ever know' because, like Max, they knew who exactly the ignorant 'They' were and how what coal mining had extracted from families and communities was as deep as it was still raw. Nor did wider audiences, quickly picking up on his spreading fame, need telling that 'the pithead baths are a supermarket now' since, as South Wales stumbled on into the 1970s, the evidence was all around them. A known and cherished world was literally slipping away as collieries continued to close and valley townships shrivelled further. Hence that historical, shudderingly hysterical, pause in 1973 as the momentary yet momentous industrial fightbacks sandwiching that year first rocked the Tory government and then caused an electoral defeat. The laughter ricocheted outwards from Treorchy until it returned as a ghastly echo in 1984–5. The enigmatic career of Max Boyce, its ups and downs, glints for us like a cracked-open lump of anthracite coal to reveal the social fissures of the past half century.

He was born in Glynneath in September 1943. His father, Leonard Maxwell Boyce, originally from Ynyshir in the Rhondda

Fach, had died a month before in a pit explosion in Onllwyn Colliery, Banwen, in the Dulais Valley. Four men had been badly burned in the Evans and Bevan colliery but, as the management told the local newspaper, 'The damage was not extensive, and work was resumed shortly afterwards.' Leonard was, in fact, fatally injured and his four workmates were hospitalised. A subsequent case, a year later, against the colliery owners for negligence for 'failing to provide proper ventilation at the place where the men were working' was proven and admitted. Mary Boyce, Len's thirty-year-old widow, was awarded '£1,750, of which £300 was for a year-old child, with £23 funeral expenses and costs'. The Boyce family would never need to be reminded of the price of coal. The sum allotted for the child was about the total wages for a whole year of a skilled collier. The boy would leave school aged fifteen and, variously, work underground and as a factory electrician, then studying for a time to be a mining engineer at the former School of Mines on the campus at Trefforest. In the 1960s Max's personal need for expressiveness would be assuaged by reading poetry, versifying in his back bedroom and singing amateurishly in local clubs in the Folk and Country mode of West Wales and West Virginia. An uncertain direction of travel, both for him and his creaking industrial society, was counterpointed by strong roots. All around the young at that time were the examples and values of men and women who truly knew where they had come from and exactly how they belonged to one another. The new generation, increasingly so, might never again be of a coal-mining or steelworking background but their parents and grandparents had been the makers of their own community genesis, and they personified a moral compass not to be ignored. The unspeakable, because avoidable, obscenity of Aberfan in 1966 was bookended by the numbing effects of pit closures – 'And it's they must take the blame' – and the working-class struggle across all the coalfields of Britain which restored miners to the forefront of the league table for industrial wages until after attrition, the NUM was outwitted and outgunned in 1985. Max Boyce's song title teased out the process of implosion with a scepticism attached to regrets for so much that was expended in vain: 'A Winter Too Late (Miners' Strike Song 1984–85)':

Did you listen then to Arthur
Do you think he was misled
Did he lead the miners bravely
Or was he much too vain
Would he call a ballot
If he had the chance again

And when the year had passed, lads
Did you wonder was it fate
That brought the bitter weather
A winter just too late.

* * *

In an Afterthought to *Hymns and Arias* (Parthian, 2021), a compendious collection of songs, poems and stories – there were two previously, in 1976 and 1980 – Max reflected how 'Some of my work has gathered dust on the shelves of time' since they 'belong to an age that has passed', but that they are included here since, too, 'they are of a certain time and place that is worth remembering and precious to me'. Indeed, running through the collection are elegiac tones resounding in deceptively simple rhythms and rendered in a diction which recalls the great poet of the earlier coalfield, Idris Davies (1905–1953). But the fissures do not all break sadly. The self-confidence of Max's post-war generation shines, too, as a celebration of life served up for a relishing of its cultural particularities in tall tales, anecdotal jokes, ancestor worship, and, of course, the concomitant triumphs, and very rare tribulations, of a glittering era for Welsh rugby football. His rocket-ride to fame coincided with that sporting glory and imprinted him with the soubriquet readily bestowed upon him by Gareth Williams and myself in 1981 in *Fields of Praise: The Official History of the Welsh Rugby Union* where we called him 'The popular Troubadour of Welsh Rugby'. In the 1970s, a decade sprinkled with grand slams, triple crowns and victories against the All Black nemesis via Llanelli and the Welsh-dominated Lions, Max Boyce was the jubilant ventriloquist of a travelling army of carousing worshipping, gobsmacked, bobble-hatted, joyful supporters. From treasured and closely guarded icons, those much-fingered 'photos of Barry John' to 'A Sunshine Home in Dublin for blind Irish referees', and on to predatory Ladies of the Night who wanted your Ticket or Debenture for favours bestowed, Max mercilessly laughed at and with a delirium of croaking tenors belting out the oh-not-so-pc 'Delilah'. In short order, he sold over two million albums worldwide. He made TV series as singer, comedian and genial presenter. He packed the London Palladium. He toured the UK to poke fun at the po-faced. He sold out the Sydney Opera House. For a time, he just seemed to have been made with precisely that time in mind.

There was more to it, however, than talent and timing. He, and his echoing admirers, were facsimiles of the Rugby XVs they invested with more than a touch of glory. Teams were transformed by them into standard-bearers: as in reports of Captain Phil Bennett's impassioned exhortation to his men in 1977 before they played England to take historical vengeance on a field of play against the white-shirted emblems of rapacious capitalism and imperialism. It was an opera bouffe act in a melodramatic Revenge Cycle. The style, the victories, the arrogance of assumption, the God-given DNA – that underground factory where a conveyor belt of Welsh outside halves were made until, tragically, they 'cracked the mould of solid gold that once made Barry John' – all such were, by clutching an oval ball, now in those unlikely Welsh hands. And the hands were, more often than not, the hands of the sons of coal miners and steelworkers – from the coaching genius of Carwyn James to the wizardry of Gerald and Gareth and Chico and Barry and Denzil and JJ and Arthur Lewis and John Bevan, and on and on, even to the gnarled resistance of working miners like Glyn Shaw and that incomparable everyman, Dai Morris who was called Shadow by his team mates, the one no one ever 'blamed', the one the children all called 'Dai'.

It could not, of course, last. Before the mid-1980s the fever pitch of an unending, assumed continuum had petered out for coalfield society, its holistic way of being, its industrial muscle, its sporting triumphs, and for Max himself. There is a poignancy in what he considered his proudest moment, when he heard the crowd in the North Stand of Cardiff Arms Park sing out his 'Hymns and Arias', that lusty lament for the actual hymns and anthems once sung with natural spontaneity. The replacement of 'Calon Lan' and a hallowed back-list was a bitter-sweet irony which signified an unspoken truth, that the paraphrase of memory had replaced the poetry of being. For Max, in mid-career, there were necessary shifts in tone and emphasis, on stage and on air, foregrounding the exaggerations of the cheeky chappie front-man, an Innocent Abroad from Back Home. But the connective nerve ends were too often frayed from now on. He sometimes looked and sounded like a relic of a past time. The surface characteristics which had amused in his act, cut loose from the hinterland of a vanishing actuality, could seem like the unwanted caricature his detractors resented. The out-sized Rosette. The Giant Leek. The Scarf, the Bobble Hat, the drawn-out accent and pantomime gestures. Not so much an archetype of a distinctive community, too much a stereotype of a diminished working class. He was being unpicked just as his rooted world was not just being shrunk bit by bit but found itself systematically dug over by the denizens of Thatcherism and all that was thereby entailed. His own limitations, though always readily understood by himself, were exposed: as a folk singer, like most if not all, he relied on the tradition. In late 1980, in the magazine *Arcade: Wales Fortnightly* which was invented to help turn the cultural tides many thought had drowned the aspirations of devolutionary democracy, Kim Howells, spokesman for the NUM in the 1984–5 strike, wrote acerbically about a perceived 'shabby sentimentalism' and a 'maudlin fatalism' in the social victimhood he detected in Max Boyce. He was not alone in that opinion at that fraught, murky time. What was being expressed was a more profound cultural unease with the generally celebratory tonality of our popular culture. The South Wales coalfield, with its stirring male choral tradition and its drilled silver and brass bands in the first, massed ranks of its musical presence, from Victorian times had never embraced the lone voice, the plangent accusations of the subversive Balladeer. Ours was the music and the lyrics of heroic Romance and soulful

Melancholy, of individual and communal fusion in common cause, not the strangulated defiance of the oppressed and the bitterness of the overlooked. In short, by the time we had reached mid-century, Billy Connolly had never lived here. Sentiment, if not sentimentality per se, was a comfort blanket we held close, one knitted with the maxims of religiose nonconformity in as Protestant a part of the Bible Belt as you could find outside that other Deep South.

What that viewpoint saw, however, was much less than meets the eye if we adopt a longer and deeper perspective. The act which Max Boyce had fashioned over the years was, like its attendant society, a masterclass in survival technique. The traits it exhibited to the prissy discomfort of some native onlookers would, in a further passage of time, only need fine-tuning to let their undeniable authenticity shine through the framework of performance once more. The nub of his ability to engage and hold an audience was entirely performative. He was, on show, the classic Trickster Supreme. He subverted the secure reality they owned by aping its absurd self-satisfaction. His moon-faced, rubbery-visaged, wide-eyed helplessness, trembling between tears and chuckles, lulled you into his Simple Simon disguise only to trick you with a sly cunning for the payoff line. Having trumped cheerful expectation, there might be a sardonic comeuppance for the self-inflated, the socially superior. He pricked pretension. He deflated the self-regarding. The Clown, claiming innocence through feigned ignorance, chided all manner of snobbery. Max, in this mode, was a great Clown, and like all such he was haloed by a protective ring of knowing sadness. To act the Fool in a world at odds with all sense was to be other than foolish. Gwyn Thomas's *Dark Philosophers* emerged from the ruins of the 1930s to engage with the deceit of sobersided truth by means of zany humour. It was a Welsh weapon. Max was in the tradition of Caerphilly's Eynon Evans who used surreal comic capers to create the radio sensation, 'Welsh Rarebit', from 1938 to 1941, which peaked across all of Great Britain with fourteen million listeners in 1949. The antics of not-as-daft-as-he-seemed Tommy Trouble and Wyn Calvin's camp signature opening of 'Elloo, Boys!' had a later personification in Max Boyce.

During that unifying wartime period in which his father had died underground, 'Welsh Rarebit' had a weekly 'Letter from Dai' as part of its American-style mix of fast-moving kaleidoscopic sound. It was written and read by Lyn Joshua, son of the evangelist Seth Joshua, as a heart-tugging account of the daily life of the various Welsh home towns of the listening soldiers serving overseas. The programme always ended, tear ducts fully opened by then, with the glycerine sweetness of 'We'll Keep a Welcome in the Hillside' for those who, one day, would 'Come home again to Wales'. The specially composed music and words were, respectively, by the show's talented producer, Mai Jones and by Lyn Joshua. Its incantatory melody and unashamed, gushing lyrics of hiraeth and home, might have been written by Max himself, then or later. This was the popular cultural zeitgeist of South Wales. One to inherit and to take forward. Max would have been old enough to see the last days of variety theatre and the so-called comic turns which enlivened it in venues like the Empire in Tonypandy and the Grand in Swansea, and in theatres across the coalfield before they became cinemas towards the end of the 1950s. There were star names on the playbills: the fishwife cackle of Gladys Morgan, the come-hither innuendo of Maudie Edwards, the gurning tomfoolery of Stan Stennett, all known from the airwaves. Their humour refracted rather than reflected an ambient world of neighbours and over-the-garden-wall rivalries. Live performance, local performance, audience and artist in tandem were the filaments of a common popular culture. Perhaps the most distinctively formed of all those variety performers was Ossie Morris (1906–68) from Port Talbot, and a worker in the steelworks until sudden fame in 1949 catapulted him from workingmen's clubs to being the resident comedian on 'Welsh Rarebit' and a top of the bill act across, though not beyond, South Wales. Ossie brought something additional, a humour which verged on the control of insolence. He could be silent, near to sarcasm in a louche persona, before unleashing his wit on his captives. He told us to wait, be patient, to be quiet if we wanted to listen, and even learn: 'Ush', he'd say, 'I must 'ave 'ush!' His every fibre, the suggestion of drink taken and deeds to be kept hidden, was cloaked in a questionable aura of respectability. He was from us and for us, the grown-up antithesis of what being a tidy boy meant. The laughter he evoked had, of course, the catharsis of release but, more, it invoked the consciousness of lives lived among promises endlessly deferred. Neither he, nor we, were in the business of kidding ourselves.

Through observation, or by osmosis, Max Boyce conveyed the same message. For his poems and songs in the 1970s he had needed that intimacy of connection which, in that decade, he had found to such memorable effect. He knew all along how it had come about. In the foreword he wrote in the summer of 2021 for the third collection of his work, he summed up his creative process:

> I put my songs and stories into the furnace of performance, altering a line here and changing a word there, until ... they are the best they can be and best suited to the gifts I may or may not have... These are the poems and songs and stories formed in the embers of that furnace.

Now some may consider it coincidental, but I certainly do not, that those performative, flickering embers burst back into spectacular flame again a year after Wales turned a tricky corner and, in 1997, voted to go on the journey heralded by devolution. The 'old' Max had been rather quiescent for a while, just as his formative society's culture had been dimmed to a shade of its former self. Yet the connective tissues from past to present were clearly vital life givers if any meaningful future was to be envisaged. The validity of a generational hands-on was essential to help revivify values. As a member of Max's own generation, I had skin in this unfolding game. In the 1990s, a part of my commissioning strategy as head of programmes (English language) at BBC Wales was to reach out, across all broadcasting genres, from news to sport to drama and documentaries, to acknowledge the cultural requirements of an audience too much deprived of a full sense of themselves on the airwaves of radio and television. Entertainment was no exception. So, in the absence of a 'Welsh Rarebit', we found a contemporary resonance in the comic devilment of Owen Money and the unforgiving, satirical pirouette of Boyd Clack's 'Satellite City'. And then there was the figure waiting in the wings, the 'new' Max Boyce. It was Chris and Megan Stuart of the independent company Presentable Productions who approached me to suggest a Max Boyce special for BBC Wales. He did not want to retread his material. He envisaged a different version for a changed time. In conversation and in discussion with all concerned, he was fully engaged and what emerged for a Christmas special in 1998 was a pared-down, stripped-back, in-your-face and furnace-refulgent star performance. The show broke all BBC Wales records for viewer numbers. The audience had been waiting for this, and Max, in a spectacular act of reconnection, did not disappoint. Audience and artist knew who they were and why they were for each other. It was Maximum Boyce.

As the twenty-first century began in Wales, with Millennium celebrations and the opening of the Welsh Assembly, Max became a singular and connecting bridge from what had gone to what might yet be in the future. His was a constant presence and reminder. If song-poems could be measured for audience impact as much as for sheer literary worth, then the academic historian Martin Johnes was surely right, in his compendious volume of 2012 *Wales since 1939*, to assert that Max Boyce's 'Duw! It's Hard' had become 'as important to Welsh culture as anything written by Dylan Thomas or Saunders Lewis'. The connective tissue was the real deal as Max had demonstrated over and over. Or else there was only the nothingness of solitary existence and the know-nothingness of throwaway individuality. Wales was not immune from the blight of social amnesia. Remembrance, then, was always more than nostalgia. The elegy sung is also the eulogy proclaimed: from child to father and mother and forbears through generations. And the colour of that saying is neither to be bought nor found except in the human traces it has left, for the colour is indelibly Rhondda Grey as in Max's great song-poem of that name:

Rhondda Grey

One afternoon from a council school
A boy came home to play.
With paints and coloured pencils
And his homework for the day
What colour is the valley, Mam?
What colour is it, Dad?
His father took him by the hand
And they walked down Albion Street
Down past the old Rock Incline
To where the Council put a seat
Where old men say at the close of day
'Dy'n ni wedi g'neud ein siar'
And the colour in their faces says
'The tools are on the bar.'
'The tools are on the bar.'
'And that's the colour that we want
That no shop has ever sold
You can't buy that in Woolies, lad
With your reds and greens and gold
It's a colour you can't buy, lad,
No matter what you pay.
But that's the colour that we want:
It's sort of Rhondda Grey.'
'It's a colour you can't buy, lad,
No matter what you pay.
But that's the colour that we want:
They call it Rhondda Grey
They call it Rhondda Grey.'

Max Boyce
Max Boyce: Hymns and Arias - The Selected Poems, Songs and Stories

THE DAME: SHIRLEY BASSEY

An implausible story at best, something scripted on speed and sieved through a crazed publicity machine. Rags, in the beginning, for sure. And even less. As a kid, legend has it that she had to borrow spare knickers from a friend to go sliding down heaps of coal slag on a tin tray. The riches to come would then have been beyond belief. Even more so, maybe, the fame that would surround her in an aura of stardom right across the world for over fifty years. And then there will be the accolade of recognition at the very pinnacle of society's establishment. But recognition of what precisely ... of raw natural talent being relentlessly crafted into the sustained achievement of a Voice?... Of the uplifting model of a lifetime of financial success in a crushing, fickle on-stage business? Of sheer dogged survival through training and diet and willpower? Of an atavistic popularity akin to and perhaps now beyond that of royalty? Or just of a woman who always behaved as if she was more than just a dame, and so finally became one with a capital 'D'.

* * *

A woman, not blandly beautiful but touching in her startled-into-loveliness look, returns, suddenly and briefly, to her home town in the last year of the twentieth century. She seems, both up close and from afar, to be in her forties though she is, in fact, in her early sixties. Everything about her, from clothes to hair to make-up, has a bespoke elegance. When she left home, aged sixteen and for the first time, in 1953, it was as a big-eyed, crop-haired and gauche teenager in the decade that was busy inventing the term, and her provincial town, already far removed from its bonanza times of half a century earlier, was a drab, workaday place. Yet now, in 1999, it too had had a make- over and was a-buzz with activity again. It had become, at long last, worthy of the title of capital city which it had borne, somewhat taken sheepishly, since 1956. The change is such that she claims not to be able to recognise it anymore. And, in truth, most of the flattening and rebuilding had been, since 1957 and with increasing pace, of the very area in which she had been born. Here, this late *fin de siècle* spate of modernising reconstruction, even regeneration, some said, transformed a city waterfront that was once a working docks into a newly urbane bay in order to house the new democratic assembly of her own country. Here, in her own, actual and mythical backyard.

It is, in fact, why she has come back on a cool July night to the space that has been cleared near the Gothic Pierhead Building, grandiose reminder of her youth, and one that will soon site the grand design of the assembly. She waits, a slim, supple, honey-coloured woman with liquorice-brown eyes that can glitter or glaze as the mood requires, to step centre stage before a shell-like canopy of electric stars, and into the open air, once more, before a huge and expectant audience; yet this one also, in its diverse mix, very much her own. She appears. Instantly recognisable; and, for these people, symbolically endearing. She is wearing their flag.

The applause crashes on and on, ricocheting off the memories of once-Stygian pubs like The Packet and The Ship and Pilot, where once she sang, and down that fragment of Wall Street at the bottom of Bute Street where the palazzos of merchants and the pillared halls of coal millionaires conspired for a greatness that never came, until it swirls back through the unreal real estate of the boutiques-that-will-be and over a smorgasbord of international restaurants. Surely, she does not forget the overcrowded apartments into which grander Victorian mansions had been turned to make rent affordable or the allure of illicit gambling and after-hours drinking that enticed men to come below the bridge to go a-whoring in Tiger Bay. For sure, she will remember the dismal grind to survive and the lively fun that accompanied it as a true salvation. So, she is wearing what is her flag, too. This most glamorous of fashion-orchestrated women is draped, and loosely so, from head to foot in green and white with the red heraldic dragon of Wales emblazoned all over her. No wonder they clap on and on until her arms, sinuous and beckoning, still them. She begins to sing, in a voice so resonant that, if the building still stood, it could be heard in the rooms of 182 Bute Street where she was born in 1937. Shirley Veronica Bassey, here on this very spot, her back to the sea, facing all Wales and singing outwards from this transformed location into Wales, is At Home. Her voice is unique. Yet it is, in and by its very individuality, redolent of twentieth-century Wales. Now, on this silent air, south of the city that had prospered and of those valleys that had foundered as both made Wales modern, it weaves itself, via television and radio, into the night, right across the nation and into the new century that is waiting, more pregnant with hope here in the bay than anywhere else. Shirley, in particular, has earned the right to be part of this. If she had stayed, just kept working as a packer of enamel pots and pans in Curran's factory, waitressed in Frederick Street, married, sang solo in The Baltimore, then it would have been Veronica's by right anyway. The joy of it, for those with filled memories as well as those with blank expectations, was that La Bassey was choosing to exercise the right. She was definitely doing it Her Way. Kitsch couture met Cymru and post-modern irony kissed national solipsism. All in all, not a bad start for Welshness in the next century.

* * *

The last time Shirley Bassey had sung in the bay was in 1957 on her first triumphant homecoming, by way of London and Las Vegas, when she topped the bill for the first time at Cardiff's New Theatre where, just three years before, she had been a scene-filling bit singer in a tawdry, touring revue *Hot from Harlem*. The intervening years had seen her solo act and her self-presentation shaped, sometimes rather savagely, by the first of a number of would-be Svengalis who thought they had seen beyond her raw vocal appeal. The journey back to Cardiff had been via one of the circuits of variety theatres which still connected the provincial towns of 1950s Britain like a necklace of lacklustre Venusbergs. Now a very stage-managed return to her own city saw this still-fresh ingénue, floating rather than swimming on a floodtide of local fame, entertain the kids of the Rainbow Club, a social and youth club which had once helped to give her room to grow the talent which, from thirteen years of age onward, she had let rip, in versions of 'Stormy Weather' and 'Bye, Bye Blackbird' and 'Somewhere Over the Rainbow', in the dingy male drinking dens of post-war Wales. Already the switch to diamantéd sheath dresses or fish-tailed frocks like the ones Jane Russell or even Monroe were modelling on the new cinemascope screens had taken this twenty-year-old torch singer into a new plush world – even if the plushness of it, so far, was confined to crushed-velvet tip-up seats in the make-believe cabaret of Variety 'turns'.

By the end of the next decade the cabaret would have become for real as she filled the Empire Room of New York's Plaza Hotel, made Hollywood's Coconut Grove shudder at her power and crossed the world over and over, from the 'Pigalle' of Paris to Las Vegas, Sydney and any London venue she chose. By then, too, the plot of her improbable life had twisted and turned – sometimes it would almost corkscrew out of control as lurid headlines captured her life in tabloid flash-bulb mode. Shirley was kidnapped at gunpoint by an estranged lover, near murder ensued; affairs, casual and profound, and Pygmalion-esque in the case of the actor Peter Finch, who was then heartbroken over her, would punctuate the years of her pomp: marriages would offer stability and yet founder, once on the rocks of suicide; and sudden death would haunt her again when her daughter, Samantha, drowned in 1985; and throughout, there was the incessant work-driven ethic that took her, in material things, further and further away from the time, when at seventeen and an unmarried mother, she was stuck, after her first doleful board-treading, back with her mother in Portmanmoor Road, Splott.

The family had moved there, Shirley, her brother and her five sisters, when she was just three. The upheaval was only a bus ride away from the bay to the vicinity of the Dowlais Steel Works (moved down from Merthyr in 1911 and a vital aspect of Cardiff's economy until its closure in the 1970s), but Shirley never, ever, quite left Tiger Bay itself. Her first baby would be named Sharon, the name her own father had given her as an affectionate tribute, he said, to the queen of Sheba. His name was Henry Bassey, a Nigerian seaman who had jumped ship in Cardiff after the Great War and found there a Tyneside woman, Eliza Jane Metcalfe, whose last and seventh child would be Shirley Veronica.

As the Second World War began in earnest in 1940, Henry Bassey, his claim on British citizenship tenuous since his region of Nigeria was only a protectorate, was summarily deported. He had, as officialese would have it, 'fallen foul of the authorities'. His life, as party-giver, bed-provider, dice-thrower and occasional ship's stoker, had come to an end before his last daughter could come to know him. As she grew up – her mother in a new long-standing partnership with another Nigerian seaman, the smart and serious Mr Mendi who became her 'Dad' – the workaday world of Splott and Moorlands School cradled her, but it was the enticing pulse of her father's Tiger Bay that pulled her in.

The early memories are of a shy, almost fearful child, crouched under a chenille tablecloth in their two-storey terraced house, listening to the beat of music at one of Henry's impromptu parties, and singing. The place in which she was singing was perhaps the strangest Wales had yet created. Accents all around her, and way into the 1950s as she kept her friends and youthful forays into life on its particular streets and byways, were, as Gwyn Thomas wrote, formed by 'the high soft speech of a hundred tongues from Africa and the East, or perhaps from the lips of a child born into the docks, an enchanting mixture of Somerset, Madagascar and Pontllanfraith'.

Even more miraculous was the manner in which the built environment had been given a domestic bedrock, a commercial purpose and a mercantile splendour that made it, uniquely in Wales, a world in cameo. In 1922, before Henry Bassey rented it, 182 Bute Street was the premises for Julius Bregartner, clothier and outfitter, whilst at 216 Bute Street, H. Berman and Co., self-styled as 'The Boston Tailors' held their own sartorial tea party, and at 165 Bute Street there was the fashion-conscious soirée of 'Latner and Redhouse (late L. Blanchard) ... noted French house'. By the end of the 1930s only echoes remained of the consulate presence that represented the nations of the world on Bute Street, but the scent of their once having been there was still intense – up and down and around that square mile, for a moment in Wales, were the consulates of the Argentine Republic, of Belgium and Bolivia and Brazil, of Chile and Colombia, of Denmark and the Dominican Republic, of Ecuador, France, Greece, Italy, Norway – pause to register it was Edward Dahl, father of the more famous Roald – of young Soviet Russia and Spain and Sweden, and all the way down the alphabet to the United States of America, Uruguay and Venezuela. As she wandered, to a welcome from all over that populated globe, she would reflect that she inherited her love of the sea from her father. Maybe. And certainly she would have imbibed it, here, from birth.

There were, of course, plenty of mean streets where the working and the non-working poor of Butetown, that city-within-a-city 'below the bridge', lived. In those streets, still, as she matured would be the boarding houses, specialists all, for the various nationalities of this special place. A Trades Directory reads like an international roll call:

Boarding-House Keepers
Ahmed, Said, 38 Maria Street; Arabian boarding house
Arapis, Manouel, 50 Bute Street; Greek boarding house
Attard, F., 156 Bute Street; Maltese boarding house
Avoth, Mahomet, 19 Angelina Street; Arab boarding house and coffee shop
Campos, Mrs, 166 Bute Street; Spanish boarding house
Guerdiaga, Fidel, 150 Bute Street; Scandinavian boarding house
Lang, Hassan Ben, 8 Bute Terrace; licensed keeper, Malay, Singapore, British subject
Low, Hing, 22 Patrick Street; Chinese boarding house
Magri, Catherine, 214 Bute Street; Maltese boarding house
Oxley, John, 41 Peel Street, Butetown; West Indian boarding house
Risman, A., 1 Sophia Street; Latvian boarding house
Rodrigues J., 18 Maria Street; Portuguese boarding house
Zamith, Manuel, 161 Bute Street; licensed Maltese boarding house

Shirley Bassey would not be the only one to find fame in the world of popular culture from these origins. The great rugby league star, Gus Risman, would tantalisingly play the amateur Union game in the 1920s before heading for professional and legendary status in the north in 1929, and the wondrous Billy Boston, son of an Irish mother and West Indian father, hit the heights before his near contemporary, Shirley, did so when, in 1953, he signed for Wigan for £3,000 and a dazzling career as an all-time great. And already, in boxing, the most cultured fighter of his generation through the 1950s would be the (almost) heavyweight and immensely popular, Joe Erskine. J. Lee Thompson's 1958 movie now seems to provide a last-documented glimpse of this mixed race and tolerant society but, at that time, was just unblushingly able to use the name Tiger Bay as its title and know, unhesitatingly, that across the globe it would be as familiar and as instantly of Wales as, say, Rhondda. The personal names would reverberate on for a while yet, as boxing boasted Eddie Avoth in the 1960s and Peter Rodrigues became the first Welshman to lift the FA Cup since 1927 when he did it, not for his home-town club of Cardiff, but as captain of Southampton in 1976. Tiger Bay, and perhaps the last real remnants of the culture and community it had created, was a lesser place then than the area had once promised. The pedimented and porticoed grandeur around the Pierhead and the beckoning elegance of the townhouses of Loudon Square had been bulldozed by obtuse planners – the Philistines were the only ethnic group not welcome in the bay or fell silent about their dream of destiny. Only in the voice of Shirley Bassey and to the acute ear in her accented vowel sounds, can we still detect that dream and, maybe, its eventual destiny.

Not that it wasn't always strictly personal with Shirley. She knew that the myth of racial tolerance in Wales was rapidly deflated once you stepped outside Butetown – and, of course, the 1919 race riots in the aftermath of the Great War almost defined the geography of race in the city – and both she and her mother stood up against the name-calling whenever it came to the young girl. Later, on her transatlantic tour of 1960, the admired and admirable Sammy Davis Jr would protect her from the casual abuse of American racial slurs. Much later, when her performances at South Africa's Sun City drew down anti-apartheid criticism, she would insist that she would never appear before racially segregated audiences. Yet her determination, at the same time, to affirm her own humanity came through in the accurate but disingenuous remark: 'My mother was white so I never thought I was anything else.' No one would label the individual Shirley Bassey unless it was Shirley herself. But Shirley Bassey the singer, at the beginning, had to succumb to the paraphernalia of exoticism that surrounded her early career, as singer and dancer, on stage. Even her first hit, in 1956, was 'The Banana Boat Song', and welcome though the break would be, she was, decidedly, no calypso singer (the closest she would ever have been to a banana boat was at Barry Docks). Nor was she quite in the mould of other British songbirds of the glutinous 1950s – not the sibilant Ruby Murray, the Clooneyish Joan Regan, the husky catch-in-the-voice Alma Cogan rooted in a froth of tulle, or the winsome Lita Rosa. Long before this, she had ruefully concluded, in duets of practice with her brother Henry, that she wanted to sound like Sarah Vaughan but came over more like Billy Eckstine.

Imitation fell away when, now being bruised by life's events, she stumbled on her distinctive singing persona and infused her voice with the secret: her captivating sexuality and its attendant vulnerability. Sometimes this would figure as a come-hither, over-the-top playfulness as in her lubricious rendering of 'Kiss Me, Honey, Honey' – where she snaps out the words 'Honey-Honey' more like an impatient dismissal than a term of endearment – and, later, meld into the draggy jokiness of 'Hey Big Spender' for whom, alone and smilingly for everyone watching, she will 'pop her cork'. Mostly, though, it is an urgent, snarling sexual predatoriness – the elongated phrasing of 'Goaal-Fingaah' matching the voraciousness of the lyrics – and, most affectingly, squeezed out, reluctantly, in her first, and dearly prized by her, mammoth hit song of 1961, 'As Long As He Needs Me'.

Her judgement about her own songs in her own career became infallible. The gut instinct came first when the spine shivered and she knew that is 'my song'; the cerebral bit was, always, 'that the storyline is something that has happened to me along the way'. Then the identification became complete and the innocuous originals, picked up like 'Grande Grande Grande' when listening to Italian radio as she sojourned in and around her favoured Monte Carlo, became transmuted via new arrangements and English lyrics, as did the resounding 'Never, Never, Never' and the heart-stopping 'This Is My Life' whose bravura defiance makes Sinatra's 'My Way' sound like a small boy's petulance.

Since the mid-1960s her experience and her range have come together with consummate ease in her professional packaging of Shirley Bassey. She has garnered endless recording awards and kept her new and retrod albums constantly in the upper reaches of chart sales. The concert tours continue to give the audiences the essence of what they require – technically adept, superbly staged and sprinkled with that peculiar baggage of evanescent pop starriness: instant nostalgia (a million Dansettes spin a myriad number of vinyl 45s and LPs every time she mouths her past on stage). Nonetheless, this is not what will ensure Shirley Bassey's memory as a singer. Sure, she, as well as anyone, can deliver classic standards, from Bacharach or the Beatles or reaching back to the jazz-pop American basis of her youth; and the Cold War spy-fest that laminated our eyeballs with the techno-cool social snobbism of Bond movies handed Shirley a video backdrop, an audience of zillions and a niche in film history via *Goldfinger*, and *Diamonds Are Forever*. But what will resonate will be the songs she delivered as if they were the personal arias of her own life.

This connection between Shirley and singing which is beyond the technical is at the heart of her appeal. When she does this, the base metal which she has sometimes polished too thin melts away and we are left with no impurities. The phrasing is unmistakable. She skeeters, word by word, almost in a recitative manner as the song's tale begins. She roars ('Hate me') and trembles ('Love me – Hate me – Love me') tearfully but defiantly ('I am what I am') to spit reaffirmation of a life back in the face of fate. It is bravura singing. The names to conjure with then, are those of Judy Garland, of Edith Piaf and Maria Callas. The latter is not over-fanciful. Her voice coach – for she works out on all parts of her body daily – Helena Shenel observed that her voice, one that is 'naturally very big', 'doesn't need a mike to fill the Albert Hall'. And the powerfully voxed opera star, Jesse Norman, rapt with admiration, asked Shirley after one riveting show, 'How do you do it? I don't do the same – I couldn't sustain the power for an hour.' What Shirley Bassey actually projects though, is not power, but love.

At the start of her career in the mid-1950s, escaping from the Carmen Miranda head-dresses of the Al Read show where another northern English despot masquerading as a comic wished to pin her down, she sought the effective disguise of low-cut simple black dresses and a doe-eyed, transfixed look to distract attention from the dreadful messages of 'Jezebel' and 'Ebb Tide'. At midpoint in her career, she exposed one silvery leg from toes to thigh in a slashed sequinned dress and allowed Morecambe and Wise to pinion her high-heeled foot on a stage set's step in a wonderfully comic downplaying of her act ('I'm a stripper at heart' she has said more than once). No one is really fooled. The voice tells of trust and betrayal, of passion and despair, of triumph and adversity. The body is inseparable from it. Its beauty is the cause of her misery and joy. It is undeniable and it is, as the voice reveals, at risk. She is still, said the lyric writer Norman Newell, a volcano on the stage. When most dormant, in her presence, she is least extinct, in the force she is about to unleash: 'On the stage I become another person. I am not Shirley Bassey the wife or mother.'

Watch recordings of the 1992 Royal Albert Hall. Her hair is like a purple cloud framing her mobile, expressive face. She wears a flesh-toned spangled top and a skirt, revealingly cut in the back, of a beaten copper colour that glints with a dull, then suddenly incandescent sheen beneath the lights as she moves and swirls. Or stands stock-still as she does for 'I Who Have Nothing'. The music swoops and soars, familiar, almost banal in its abrupt endings. The lyrics plonk as you rehearse them in your mind. It does not matter. This is all now transformed.

She stands before us. Her hands are extended slowly, modestly beseeching, put before us as a supplicant, then clutched to her breast as she tells us quietly of the bereftness of her life. Then, as the music and narrative drive upwards, her arms are thrown out, out, wider and wider, not to envelop us, but to take us in. The hands speak to us, fluttering like deranged butterflies beating hopelessly against the glass of the captivity. Finally they suggest her open-palmed stigmata.

When she sings 'As Long As He Needs Me' the body language is heavily transferred to her face. She is not afraid, as she searches for the soulfulness of the song, letting her emotion, even her tears, well up from within her, to make a pout which other singers seek to avoid. Her nose twitches, pulls down, down to the left as her mouth, now the size it seems of a third of her face, now a curved slice, lets out the tremolo sound she has mastered as much as the full-throated yowl of her be-damned-to-it-all ballads. As the meaning of her words and of her public presentation of them dawn on her afresh, her eyes open wide as if she is making love. And perhaps she is.

Certainly, at moments like this in her act, the non-threatening bump and grind of 'Big Spender' are left far behind and 'As I love you, more and more and more' reaches out reminding us of how young and determined she was in 1959, we just wait, for the ups and downs of 'This Is My Life' to end with those expressive arms pulled down, inevitably, and against her will, only to be raised in a spiritual conquering of all closures and all pettiness.

'There's something of my past in every song' is what Dame Shirley Bassey knows. She does not need to spell it out further. It is there in her voice. And her voice has used the makings of a universal popular culture of song to invest it with an ineradicable and distinctive Welsh identity. She is what we are.

1987: PASSING (IT) ON

'What dreadful people. We are really wasting our time. What is the point of all your efforts if they appreciate them so little.'

(Prime Minister Margaret Thatcher speaking to Nicholas Edwards, her Secretary of State for Wales, 1979 to 1987, after a vocal demonstration against her appearance in South Wales.)

* * *

Only, see, I hope I don't linger. Better to go sudden, isn't it. In any case, I wouldn't like to think of her having to listen to my death rattle. Nice kid she is willing to do anything for me, love her. Bit wild I know, but still time for her to change given half a chance. She won't have heard anyone die yet, will she. Not so likely these days what with people dying more out of the way, in hospitals mostly, those geriatric wards. Ach y fi. But I've always had a feeling, daft really I suppose, that I'll pass away in this bed. 'Course I've seen and heard dozens and dozens dying myself, sitting with them, waiting for them to slip away, not always easy that, and washing them after, and laying them out too, for neighbours to come and pay their respects. Paid work that was, mind. The way it was, then. And not very nice for a young woman as I was. All the same at the end, and yet all different somehow, and that old death rattle at the last. Not a proper rattle, really, more like pebbles, but hollow ones, bumping and grinding against each other, everything gurgling up from the chest, blocking the airways, flooding the passages, gasping life out. Years ago people generally died in the beds they were born in, or at least in the beds they lay in for most of their lives. Passed on they were, like this one, with the lilies hand carved into the pine headboard, and the irons to hold the base with, for years and years, an old lumpy tick mattress on top, though I have chucked that out now. It was Mam and Dad's bed before me, passed down to me and Alec after their time, and we were glad to have it. Don't suppose she'll have any looks on it, or anything else I'll leave, not clothes for sure, so they can all go to charity. A bit of my china maybe, or that nice ivory bangle I had from my Bopa Lel. I'll ask. I've had the bed from the summer my mother died in it, fifty years ago, the year the King abdicated. That was in the December, Edward the Eighth he was going to be, and the month before, as Prince of Wales, he came to South Wales to see for himself he said, and he said after that something must be done. Only then he went, didn't he. I saw him close up in Dunraven Street, in his car I mean, when he passed through Pandy, and you know what, he had make-up on. Never seen make-up on a man before, but he did, honest. A sort of orangey face powder it was, quite thick, and his hand kept rising up to flick his bowler so he seemed almost like a mechanical thing, a tiny one all scrunched up in a big black overcoat against the cold and damp. I told Alec when I got home. He said that he had better things to do than to gawp at royal wankers. Only he didn't of course, not then. Something must be done my arse, was what Alec said. And when the war came and he got back in the pit, good wages underground for a bit, it was too much for him after all that time out of work and he went a surfaceman which he never liked, with all his butties as colliers, and after the war he was on the council, sweeping the streets or on the ash lorries to empty the bins. Not much of a life was it, and if I'm honest, now that he's long gone too, I don't think, looking back, that he was ever fully himself after the first war. So many boys dead in that one, and others terribly crippled for life, some with no arms or no legs and you'd see them, for years after, on crutches or on homemade bogeys with little iron wheels, mooching about just going up and down the street or on the road, waiting at the corner or outside a pub. Pitiful it was, to see them, and in Alec's case it was there, too, but more in his head, what he'd seen, what had been done, and he was only seventeen when he went, different entire when he came home. We'd been sparking a bit, not proper courting, when the war had started, and after it we got engaged but years before we could manage to marry, and I do think that even then it was as if a light had gone out in him, one that never really not fully, came back on, ever. Lovely feller, everybody said, your Alec. And he was, I know, but still we both had to settle for less than anyone should have to do. I told her that once and what d'you mean she said and I said curiosity killed the cat, my girl, and that there are some things which are for me to know and to keep to myself. Though she is persistent that one, won't let go, so I had to tell her that we weren't all born behind a gooseberry bush back then, though I made her laugh when I told her about what we called going out courting, and she said it sounded dull, so I said, hoy madam, I've seen a bit more of life than you might think. Oh, she said, hard to believe that, and she was grinning, cheeky with it now, because if it isn't on TV or happening outside the valley, for all her generation I think, it just isn't happening at all, is it, and I told her straight that I hadn't always been stuck at home, had had lots of different jobs to do, places I'd been to, over the years, cleaning big houses in the city before I was married, serving stuck-up buggers as a live-in maid, hands all over you if they could, then after I was married, later on, travelling to the munitions factories during the war, your hands going yellow with the sulphur, making you cough and splutter, some of the girls actually killed in explosions, stomachs blown open, all hushed over at the time of course. And when people could afford to buy wallpaper there was paper-hanging, which lots of women did in houses in the Valleys, front-rooms for best or bedrooms perhaps, come in early in the morning, set up a long trestle table and cut to size wallpaper lengths and slather on thick, cold, greasy paste, and onto the wall with a brush to flatten it, and do two or three rooms in a day, all on my own, word-of-mouth reputation bringing in the work, with women being neater perhaps than men, and besides not all men being handy about the house at all, so it was good pocket money, especially when Alec was out of work or on short time. She listened to all this, a bit bored maybe, so then I said, all casual like, that oh and there was that other time when we were on our uppers, desperate for a couple of bob, and I'd catch the bus to Cardiff, all dolled up. Fitted right in, I told her. You never, she said. Only once or twice, I said. Alec never cottoned on, so no harm was it, I said. Well, you should have seen her face, I'm telling you, and I kept mine straight as a die, see, for ages and ages until I had to burst out laughing. You cow, she said, you old cow, laughing with me now. I would have liked to have had a daughter like her, even if she's too sassy sometimes for her own good. I tell her I like to think my Mary Ellen would have been like her, if she'd lived. She says, oh go on, but it's true and I think she likes me to say it because she always looks again at the snap, fading brown it is, I have in that little slate frame on the wicker table by the bed. Only three she was when she got the Dip, I tell her. She didn't know what diphtheria was, another killer of our kind that is gone, thank God, I say, like a lot of things we had to fight against. I tell her good things don't happen by accident. She says that so far as she is concerned nothing good ever happens around here anymore. Nothing happens at all, she says, but it comes out more like a question in her voice, cos it's all over and done with round here, she says, and I have no answers for her, not really, only more stories to tell her.

* * *

The General Election of June 11 has brought about a change of personnel at the top in the Welsh Office, with Mrs Thatcher's appointment of Peter Walker as the new Secretary of State for Wales set to usher in a new initiative: the Programme for the Valleys. Mr Walker, who believes the provision of major tourism and arts centres to be vital to his plans for urban renewal, said: 'In the case of the proposed Rhondda Heritage Park I consider this to be an extremely exciting project which epitomises many of my aspirations for the valleys. Based on the industrial heritage of the valley communities it will transform a derelict site with its symbols of former glories into an attractive heritage park and so help to change many of the unwarranted perceptions that still exist about valley life.'(Associated News Reports, June 12, 1987)

* * *

I just don't see where all the furniture will go to when I'm gone. Too heavy, too dark, most of it, for youngsters today. I found it hard to part with it, each piece saying something to me, the only one left now, that would mean nothing to anyone else. I tell her though, all the same, whenever she pops in to see me. I tell her how proud my mother was to put blue-and-white china on that tall pine dresser we bought from Twissler's in the first war when, for a time, there was good money to be earned, and pianos, though we never had one, put in lots of front rooms, for show mostly so never played, their tops covered by crimson velvet cloth with tassels hanging down the side. I still have that marble-topped washstand upstairs and its creamy yellow bowl and pitcher, not that we used it except from time to time, all of us washing in the bosh in the kitchen, with a bath in the tin tub in front of the fire once a week, us girls first, Davy John after. Sounds primitive she says, especially now there's indoor lavs and baths, but she can see it was fun too, all of us more together then, and neighbours walking in and out without let or hindrance. In my mind now I keep going back, all those early things, big and small, all crowding in and jumbled up higgledy-piggledy, like the very first time I got out of the train in Trealaw, six hours we'd been what with changing trains and waiting, with Mam and my older sister Nel carrying a suitcase each walking over the railway bridge up the main road into Tonypandy, and then up Dunraven Street, all the way to the Square, a crossroads really, and suddenly Dada was there, still blackfaced from the pit, and I squirmed when he went to kiss me, his moustache all bristly and wettened with beer, smudging coal dust all over my face so that I cried and pulled away, and he laughed and threw me in the air. We hadn't seen him for almost a year after he'd left to join his brother Tom, working as colliers in Clydach Vale. I had never seen so many people milling about, much more than in Blaenau Ffestiniog, all filling up the pavements and spilling onto the road, the stench of horse manure strong and the shops open though it was almost night-time proper with the electric arc lamps tawny bright in the gloom as rain began to slant in broken lines across their light, women and bigger girls out shopping on a Friday night, pay day, aprons and shawls over their dresses and some of the older women wearing men's dai caps on their buns, wicker baskets full with spuds and onions and carrots and leeks, and all chatting, with more Welsh than English being spoken, so it did not seem a strange place to us, not at all. I was just gone eight years of age then, in 1908, younger than my cousins, Mam's sister Gwennie's boy Davy John, and daughter Sarah Elin, the four of us to share a bed until we found a house to rent, later to buy. So every year since then, I tell her, I can mark off by the things which came to surround us. A deal table, wooden curved-back kitchen chairs, a horsehair sofa eventually, and then another one with button-backed chairs to match for the front room, which was only for visitors of course. And on the mantelpiece there, when Dada retired as choirmaster from Eglwys Dewi Sant, all from the north they were like us, we put the brass-faced clock in its walnut case, with its big brass key to wind it up and make it chime on the hour every hour. I still have most of it, but whenever I look at all the bits and pieces I don't really see them as you know, stuff. I see their faces, hear their voices, smell mothballs and polish, as if all was new again. Only the bigger things, more important things I suppose from what telly makes of what happened to us, riots on the Square, strikes and lockouts and war, only all that seems old and finished, and I feel sometimes that nobody seems to know, or wants to know, that we laughed a lot, and cried, yes, and, how can I tell her, dared, that's it, we dared to be giddy. I think she'll understand that. And it's the same, you know, as later, when we could go on HP, and we rushed out to buy washing machines and vacuum cleaners, and fitted carpets instead of that icy cold linoleum and that rough and dusty coconut matting. That was who we were and wanted to be, too, from having TV sets and the wireless, and going to the pictures, all a proper mark of us, and nothing to regret or be ashamed of as if we were selling out after all we had coped with. No, I think, in a way it was why we were there in the first place, isn't it, you know, moving there for work and wages, and a better life we hoped. Same the world over, then as now, and will be. Staying put when it wasn't, better I mean, that's different, and harder to explain, though lots left most didn't, and I think it was, in part anyway, because we had come to belong one to the other, and to the place in a funny way. She says she hates it here. Over and over, I tell her, we are not cemented down, so stay or go, as you please, and what matters is what you keep with you or take with you which is of us, as we made ourselves into something more, together I mean, more perhaps than at times we realised. I tell her that I know this is true, and I mean it but I can't prove it, and it's for her to find out, if she will trust me. Look, I say, let me put it another way, I'm not political or anything like that, but I say, I always vote, always have since women could vote equally with the men, only since 1929 I say, and that's because I know, from living and being here, what counts and what's what. And what's that then she says, all cocky with me. Knowing your enemy, who and what and why, I say and can see she is surprised at how serious I am being. She grins at me, but a bit awkward. We don't usually talk like this, us two, but I go on, won't leave it there, tell her she will have to find out for herself, that things always change, but one sign of it is when things are closed down and people are fixed by it, not allowed to grow, not released to be different from what went before, as we once were in this place, and did. And you can do it again, I say. Fat chance, she laughs. No way, she says. Find a way, I tell her. This won't be now forever, I tell her. It never is I want to say, and that I can see most of all that was and really mattered has already gone, or is going, being tidied away, maybe soon forgotten. There is so much to tell, and I worry that she will not be ready for what is facing us, coming for her I mean, if we just disappear, as if nothing that mattered ever was. She says I try too hard, can't keep up with everything at my age, should let go, stop banging on about 1985 as if the world had ended, only here maybe, not out there, she says. Get a life, she tells me. That makes me laugh, and we smile together. I ask her if she remembered to pop my postal vote in the box, first time for me like that and last, too, I suppose. She says, to stop me, yeah yeah, and that she'll vote when the time comes, for my sake, she says, no other reason. It's a start, I told her. Anyway, I have decided to leave her the clock, the one that chimes on the hour every hour, but only if you wind it I will have to tell her. She'll need to know that, too, in the years to come. I'll say that if she wants, in her heart I mean, I can still be there for her, if she wants, over the years to come, the years without me, her time.

* * *

I was jealous of my gran because she was dying and I wanted to. She, with a healthy appetite and a house full of possessions and a lifetime of riveting stories... And me, me with not even a thought in my head, was living. Just didn't seem right... She told me I had first pick of her wardrobe, and she told me I could have her sewing machine ... (but) she gave me more... She gave me treasured stories and examples and standards to live by, reasons to fight my way to where I want to go... She equipped me with everything I would need to begin a new forceful life of my own making. The strongest woman I have ever known handed out to me her gift-wrapped strength... Imagination tells me someday soon something amazing will happen to me. (Rachel Trezise, Rhondda Valley, December 1996.)

JUST NAMES

The University Directorate had encountered an unexpected problem. The new chair of the governors was, as the vice chancellor explained to his executive team, being decidedly 'Hands On' in her approach. In the past, the former polytechnic had secured the nominal appointment of a local businessman or lawyer or accountancy bigwig or local government panjandrum who could be relied on to be supportive in the community which the Poly ostensibly and primarily served. The Poly's elevation, however, to university status had widened its horizons from the regional to the national and as the VC had reasoned, brought the obligation, and the opportunity, to be more in tune with the evolving culture of the devolved polity.

The new appointment was considered a coup. Not only a woman but someone who, via a previous career as head of this and that within the belly of the beast that was a burgeoning and influential media, was well acquainted with the merry-go-round of committees, commissions and consultancy reports which had sprung up in place of various quangos, those unelected non-governmental organisations that an elected Welsh government had hastened to remove as an affront to democracy. She was by experience and personal connections the kind of personalised conduit into that Cymric Magic Circle which had, previously, somewhat scorned the Poly-as-was for its utilitarian stance on all things academic and societal.

The VC handled the incoming chair with the accustomed ease of a past master of the arts of administrative and governmental chicanery. Scrutiny of the university's strategy - as for international recruitment, a matter of fees above educational purpose, and inflated match-funding claims to win research funding which, in turn, directly boosted the institution's financial returns - all passed through the chair and her governing body like a gentle enema. Government ministers, courtesy of the chair's lobbying, were more frequently seen on the campus as she hosted discussions over lunch or offered day conferences tailored to present the university as a willing handmaiden for policy made elsewhere. The VC readily acceded to her suggestion for the purchase from local artists of art and sculptures to adorn the ramshackle corridors and open spaces of the peculiar mix of Victorian solidity and sixties plate glass which was the university's rather graceless estate.

These were nugatory requests, accomplished for a pittance, that could be as readily accommodated as bilingual signage and a spattering of croesos and diolchs to grace public occasions. Form over function, however, took an unwanted turn when the chair's interest in outward show came to a head over the naming of university buildings. That is to say: they had no names. They were mere building blocks and had been for as long as anyone could recall as the original School of Mines had become the Polytechnic and had metamorphosed ugly-duckling style into the University. No one, it seems, had a problem with this. The campus, its variety of brick and concrete and glass and steel teaching buildings and laboratories and offices strung out haphazardly across the lower slopes of the mountainside, was not easy to negotiate on foot but fold-away maps or direction boards were readily available to take you from 'Block A' to 'Block B' and so on until 'Block M' was reached. It was designed for efficiency. Cold and brutal perhaps but somehow at the heart of the institution's pride in its own no-nonsense approach to the purposes of higher education.

Only the new chair did not quite see it this way and, bothered when her distinguished guests were seemingly wryly amused or when one laughingly said it made her seem like a prison warden in charge of an establishment of incarceration, she began to berate the VC over this alphabetic listing. Neither indicative of pride of place or native tradition, she said, of roots or achievements. In short, not respectful of Cymru itself as envisioned by one of its Prifysgolion. Indeed, she said, having translated for the VC, as its newest member and one needing a new aesthetic of appellation. She would not let this bugbear rest. In matters great and small she began to make life increasingly difficult for the VC, querying and questioning his every decision or proposal and getting the great and the good, her valued accessories, to chivvy and chase, by e-mail and letter, by phone and by whispered word, until he reeled under the weight of the coalition of disquiet she had mustered. To fully join the club, he now learned, things, or rather building blocks, had to be indicative of how the nation itself expected to be seen. As she rather archly informed him: 'Once there may have been an Assembly but for now and ever there is a Senedd and what has been Wales will be, one day soon, Cymru.'

A special meeting of the directorate was convened to consider the renaming of parts. A collective head was scratched. Pro Vice Chancellor Robson, an engineer from east of the Pennines, snorted that, in the absence of student protests, the idea should not be entertained and that the fold-up maps were excellent value for money. The VC partially agreed, as he did with everything, but hinted at other advantages. PVC Eirlys Morris, Chair of Nursing, wondered aloud about Welsh place names and began to recite a mellifluous litany until, one or two sibilants and tongue on teeth sounds too many, PVC Mallea, from west of the Pennines, intervened in a mid-vowel pause to declare it would be an impractical marketing tool for their recruitment both cross border and overseas. He emphasised, in his most reasonable manner, the difficulties of location, pronunciation and orthography, with which the university laboured to make a wider mark. PVC Francis, Dean of the Business School, said he had consulted among the few historians left, three to be exact, within the umbrella body of Social Sciences, Humanities, Criminology and Creative Writing, and they had reminded him of the entrepreneurial past of the Valleys, its ironmasters and coal owners and shipbuilders. Why not illuminate, among the contiguous landscape of terraced housing and grassed-over coal tips, the marriage of capital and labour under such names?

The VC, a very rare thing for him to do, snapped out a cursory 'No'. Inevitable objections from the Students' Union who would, equally inevitably, propose the names of those Paladins of the People who had led rebellions, both violent and measured, against those who had exploited them and who, the VC reminded his directorate, lingered on in the time-serving ranks of those who ran every council in sight and sat, by necessary invitation, among the governing body. The VC turned to his deputy, PVC Carter, his first appointment and a former colleague in his previous polytechnic, one whose shrewdness and foresight seemed to derive, the VC had concluded, from being an Ulsterman whose accent could be, and was, modulated according to circumstances. 'Castles,' PVC Carter murmured. 'Wales is a land of castles, is it not?' he said. And he reeled them off, somehow evoking an imagery of imposing battlements, wind-bitten keeps, the romance of moats and ivy and a hollowed-out history long gone. There were a lot of 'Cs' - Caerffili, Cardiff, Conway, Caernarfon, Carreg Cennen, Castell Coch, and Harlech, of course, and you could throw in a few abbeys, Margam and Strata Florida, and cathedrals, St Davids and Llandaf and St Asaph, if you needed to make up the number. Around the oval polished table there were nods and sighs of approval. The VC opened one eye to look at Professor Carter, Dean of the Law Faculty and a practising barrister. The VC knew the plan before them would now be replaced by something irresistible. Whetting the appetite was PVC Carter's way of clinching a better deal. First, by making the original offer not at all what it had seemed at first glance. PVC Carter moved to flatter his colleagues before he set out to convince them.

'There is indeed a problematic issue, however, as I sense you are about to tell me. And, as I spoke, I could almost intuit the objections you might rightly make. A ring of castles, yes, and a Wales for consumption. But also an echo of power. Over others. Native others. Power to build was the might of overlordship based upon the dynamic of conquest. Maybe the full notion of colonisation is a tad ahistorical for the actual history as it unfolded. But, even bilingually expressed, plenty of contemporary voices would be raised to accuse us of foregrounding the coloniser writ large.'

PVC Carter stopped. He paused. He readied his more palatable suggestion for approval. 'I have been wondering all along,' he took up, 'what could be both neutral and life-enhancing. From us, so to speak. And distinctive but also connecting to others and other possibilities of direction. A fluidity of meaningfulness that has origins and outcomes.'

The VC wondered where all this nonsense was going. PVC Carter paused again.

'Think rivers,' he said, as if his imperative was also a flat statement of undeniable worth.

'Think rivers,' he said again.

'Those rivers which flow towards us, converge with others, mingle and swell in a confluence, run through us, carry forward their waters into the channels and seas of the world. Vein Wales from north to south, from east to west.'

And here he chanted as a plain song of deliverance: 'The Tâf or Taff, Rhondda Fawr and Rhondda Fach, the Cynon and Ely, the Aman and Rhymni, the Cleddau and the Tawe, Sirhowy and Towy, the Llynfi, Ebbw and Teifi, Afon Llwyd and Afon Gefenni.'

PVC Carter was relishing the liquescence of the moment, whispered in carefully enunciated Cymraeg.

'Colleagues, rivers are us, aren't they? And more so than our rooted singularity of place. Vice Chancellor, by moving with the rivers we leave the fraught implications of our historic location without wrenching up our rootedness, and we claim our wider destiny to the south, as once did that mineral wealth of these hills, by a process of titular infiltration of the territory of more fortunate others, and by an earlier nominal primogeniture.

'In other words, Vice Chancellor, your long-held wish and profound desire to have a city centre campus, too, and as of right, is not an outrageous land grab, as our educational rivals have labelled it, but a natural overspill from the banks which can no longer confine the torrent of our, your, ambition for our institution, for our students, for Wales itself. For, may I say in the language I am learning, Cymru Fydd.'

* * *

What had begun as a problem had been solved as a policy. The chair of governors made the public announcement at the beginning of the new academic year. No longer the stasis of alphabetised blocks but buildings nominated to recall the network of flow which was the pulse of the university's contemporary purpose, mingling its academic waters at the last in the nation's youthful capital city. She spoke in both of her tongues and licked the factional Present into fantasy shape with the seductive saliva which, everywhere nowadays in this shapeshifting country, lubricated the Past and the Future, or both the national tenses, as if it really was one continuous stream.

CLOSING ROUNDS

OUTWITH THE PEOPLE

The opening chapter of this book reconfigured twenty-five years on what was my purpose in 2000 as I then sketched out a century in Labour for a lecture, and subsequent pamphlet, *Out of the People*. I had wished to provoke debate about the nature of that people from whom Labour's political hegemony in Wales had sprung. Or rather, to be more precise, to examine the intricacies of social development and the organisation of political institutions within an overall culture and its whole way of life. It seemed an opportune moment: the 1997 vote had narrowly delivered an Assembly for Wales and it was more than likely that the political, or electoral, domination of Labour in Wales, not yet but soon to be 'Welsh Labour', would continue. What I wished to reveal, however, were the social and cultural fissures which had veined a century of political endeavour. All the more urgency needed, I thought, if the evidently consensual technocratic managerialism of New Labour was to be countered by a more historically informed conspectus on Labour's past and future prospect as a culturally rooted phenomenon. I was, then, still confident that if Labour 'pays attention to the past structures of feeling which gave it credibility it can connect, intimately, again, to a political constituency of imagination in Wales'.

A quarter of a century on, the jury is still out on that verdict because if the early signs of aspiration and endeavour were encouraging, if somewhat haphazard, the subsequent binding of people (as was) and politics (as maybe) has atrophied. It has become a wearisome mantra to repeat that in five successive Assembly/Senedd elections the overall percentage of eligible voters going to vote has never once reached 50 per cent. Wearying but devastatingly true. In Wales, all too often, the

Politics of Influence has replaced the Influence of Politics. Constitutional tinkering in these circumstances is akin to moving the deckchairs on the *Titanic* before the liner even leaves the dockyard. Meanwhile our navigational direction finders are so attuned to the GPS of identity politics that they have neglected social divisiveness and cultural fracture. We need a reset. Or rather Labour, especially Welsh Labour, should remind itself that it was not created to 'stand up' for Wales or any other such entity but to prioritise the lives and prospects of ordinary working people, its core supporters. For Labour, Class once trumped Nation, and still should.

* * *

In the first days of our newly devolved governance a discourse on culture, in the longer-term interest of the society and the government of Wales, became – in utero at least – central to the conception of what kind of a 'new nation' might evolve from this 'old country'. That was the unanimous opinion reached by a cross-party committee of the spanking-new Assembly for Wales as they presented a detailed report on the nuts and bolts of arts and culture across and for the polity of Wales – as it was and as it could be. The chief proposition of that committee was eye-wateringly, bravely apposite:

> Eighteen months after the establishment of the National Assembly for Wales we [Cynog Dafis, Plaid Cymru AM and the Post-16 Education Committee he had chaired] now see the publication of a report which lays out a provocative policy for the arts.
>
> [After] a thorough investigation held over a period of six months, committee members have become increasingly convinced that the arts are central to the process of social, cultural and economic renaissance promoted by the Assembly. Culture (of which the arts are only a part) is at the heart of our national enterprise.

The report was compiled by the arts practitioner and academic Ceri Sherlock who commissioned a thought-piece from me as one of two such annexes. Mine was entitled 'A Culture in Common' and was used as the report's overall titular mission. I was certainly singing from the same (proverbial) hymn sheet even if my linguistic emphasis was loudly Anglophone. Attached to a passionate plea for 'cultural revitalisation' to 'give the (Welsh) language new life', the report was adamant that 'the powerful and creative reality of English as one of the two main languages of Wales must also be recognised', alongside 'the notion of Welsh citizenship built on diversity (and a wider multilingualism) ... a strong sense of identity can be compatible with toleration, nay appreciation, of the strange and different'.

Written in advance of my reading of the whole report, my own contribution to it emphasised the historical sea change that had accompanied industrialisation, modernisation and urbanisation but I fell deliberately short of subsuming any such cultural side-stepping under the cheap catch-all rubric of Anglicisation. Something, as our literature and expressiveness in English readily revealed if only we could locate it, that was much more significant of any ongoing Welsh identity had occurred.

> This culture in common will affirm cherished identities for the Welsh, whether in linguistic or ethnic or landscape terms or in the informing of our tourist industry with insights beyond the imagery of advertising agencies, whilst never settling for separate identities that cannot intermingle or change. Indeed change will be of the essence for this cultural transformation since a culture, however rooted, without change will wither into the very construct that imprisons rather than releases its citizens. Contemporary Wales seems to have understood this precept in the case of an embattled Welsh language yet still shies away from the more vital embrace of the unsteady social foundations of its largely urban and industrial and monoglot people through an open-hearted appreciation of the culture they once created.
>
> Culture here is a bridge for those whose social and economic links with the best values of their communities – locally fixed but internationally fixated – have been snapped. Through all means available – print, broadcasting, education, sponsorship, the net

> and public installations from plaques to plinths – we should be saturating Wales with the knowledge that your place, your people, your dreams were described, painted, sculpted, played for, sung and discussed. What a legacy we leave rotting in the shade of our petty and divisive preoccupations for the local, whatever it is, is also the national and art is the space where what is universal and human and therefore best about our particular selves has been explored. *That* is a Wales we ought to be proclaiming to the world.
>
> It might seem unfair to burden this mewling and puking infant Assembly with such heavy demands, grandiose designs and idealistic projects. The reality will be that the Assembly as a political artefact will not fully emerge as mature and a social necessity unless it makes its own cultural connection with the people. The decision to locate in a new building of architectural purpose was a crucial first step in this learning curve. It makes the Assembly itself focal. Now, to build a true consensus beyond mere political agreement it needs to nurture a civic society where toleration the one of the other in a differentiated Wales actually requires dissent and disagreement to make our culture significantly worthwhile, fully human and held, truly, in common.

Aneurin Bevan had once coined the phrase 'imaginative tolerance' to reach out to (similar) others: and the support and subsidy, for example, which the Welsh language had increasingly been accorded within the monoglot culture of Bevan's Wales has been a remarkable, and ungrudgingly made, example of a mutual civic embrace. What was now being openly proposed as the twenty-first century began was for a full and equal accord, in a cultural sense (for politically and socially the balance had shifted irreparably anyway), to be given to the creative contribution, past and future, as made in the majority English tongue of the people of Wales. There were no dissenting voices. Perhaps, however, not all hearts and minds were so committed.

In 2003, drama was given new impetus in Welsh by the creation, and necessary subsidy, of Theatr Genedlaethol Cymru. In 2006, at long last, an embryonic National Theatre Wales was conceived by and soon exploded into being with an astonishing burst of creative energy from 2009, which, for a time, transformed all theatrical practice in Wales. In Welsh, fiction and poetry flourished as a new generation wrote freely in their primary tongue and, in a similar vein, Welsh writers could increasingly publish in English, their own primary tongue, under the auspices of publishers such as Seren and Parthian. All this, and much else in the fields of community arts and educational endeavours, was enabled by financial support from devolved administrations. The emergent culture committee listened to informed pleas led by M. Wynn Thomas at Swansea University, where a Centre for Research into English Writing had been established, and the government soon agreed to fund a Library of Wales to bring back into print those 'classic' works written in English from or about Wales which were, otherwise, unavailable. That lasted, with myself as series editor and fifty books published and sold, outside as well as inside Wales, until 2016 when the very success of the project attracted the ire of some who (falsely) portrayed it as the vehicle of gendered imbalance (instead of a historical reflection of literary and social reality) and sought an instrumental future purpose-based on identity in place of a purposeful rescue of the lived experience of the Welsh who had been and who, therefore, birthed our actual present existence in and through the articulation of our literature in English.

So, to be clear, advances were made, and even if direct financial subsidy was continuously exiguous there was, too, a sense of the dynamism which acknowledgement of the arts within our culture could bring to a connected-up sense of ourselves in this lopsided, emergent country. Rhodri Morgan, who had become Labour Party leader and then First Minister in Wales in 2000, certainly saw the propagation of cultural awareness as a pathway from community hesitancy to common regeneration which, he said in 2003, 'hinges upon widening access to the arts and culture of Wales [so] ... we will prioritise funding for community arts to those areas with the lowest levels of participation'. Former industrial areas and blighted urban communities were being invited to step forward. And, make no mistake, from

Valleys Kids in the Rhondda to NTW's globally resonant community play, Michael Sheen's *The Passion* in Port Talbot and Aberavon in 2011, the English tongue which the Welsh spoke would be the lingua franca of communication. It would not last.

To be blunt: at some point in the last decade the promise of a bilingual culture fuelled by both 'our main languages' was derailed by the drumbeat for a bilingual society-to-be in which Cymraeg would be prioritised across the board and Wales' alternative linguistic voice would be increasingly downplayed. There are multiple causes for this slide or slippage, not least high-grade intellectual trickery whereby the hard evidence of historical enquiry has been sidelined by the soft power of malleable textuality, but the major reason is the constant difficulty of engaging with a complex cultural process when it is so much easier to pin a badge of identity onto a well-worn lapel. Matters are further compounded when, as we move well into the 2020s, the official figures for Welsh speakers (readers and writers being even lower) have diminished (as at the 2021 census) whilst the Welsh Government hoists itself further onto the petard of attaining that rounded-up and plucked-out-of-the-air figure of one million speakers by 2050. This species of statistical box ticking, so far as bureaucracies are concerned, lends itself to that policy of authoritarianism and instrumentalization – command and effect – which shackles the freedom to invent, imagine, create, provoke and fail, delight and destroy that is the very DNA of the arts within our culture.

Where institutional influencing can be brought to bear, there is now no let-up in an attempted semiological leverage of modern Wales out of the actual past into a nominal future. An organised petition to the Senedd for debate proposed in 2024 that Wales itself be officially and only known as Cymru. In our schools the officially directed employment of everyday greetings or phrases in Welsh is the flashcard technique with which infants are accustomed to normative linguistic baths. Such incidental usage of Welsh is more than unlikely to ensure a fully bilingualised society by any date envisaged but it does make for a fictive veneer of normality to hide the more profound failures of educational endeavour and financial subsidy across the plywood board of the bilingual wish-world. Alarmed by the predictable shortfall in the number of fluent Welsh speakers envisaged by mid-century, the Welsh Government, in late 2024, proposed legislation to double the time spent on the Welsh language in primarily English-medium schools: to be 10 per cent of overall school time. It is likely that, for pupils and parents, enthusiasm for such imposed bilingual learning would be more readily energised if recognition of monolingual Welshness was simultaneously signalled as a cultural coping stone through the teaching of Welsh history, literature and art, with all duly appropriate linguistic and geographical emphases made. This stressed and unequivocal sense of belonging, in and through an unfolded history and articulated in that English tongue which became the Welsh articulation for all that, is the only route open to a future, and bilingual, Wales that is viable. However, as of now, the actual monocular signal being beamed out is a walleyed insistence removed from reality by an unimaginative, intellectualised reductiveness. A drumbeat usage has, in effect, forsaken the acceptably bilingual to replace names with a mapped-out singularity in an ironic echo of Brian Friel's marvellously nuanced play, *Translations* (1980), in which in the nineteenth century the naming of places, from Irish to English and round-about, was shown to be invariably subservient to actual historical and life experience.

If the nineteenth century saw nations stamped out of the ground by the rhythmic impulses of romantic verse and ideological imaginaries so our passports to a new Welsh nation are being summarily stamped by the border guards policing the portals of Welsh identity. For all of us, the familiarity of Snowdonia morphs into the purity of Eryri and the closeness of the Brecon Beacons is overcome by the exoticism of Bannau Brycheiniog. As yet Barry Island is only matched by Ynys y Barri and Cardiff still cosies up to Caerdydd, but this bandwagon is still rolling as an ersatz Cymru is paraded before us across Wales to subliminally persuade us of the inevitability of the echt Cymru to come. At the European Championships of 2022 the Football Association of Wales (founded as such on 2 February 1876) rebranded itself in almost every conceivable public fashion as 'Cymru' whilst its supporters, or most of them, continued to chant 'Wales! Wales!' in their customary support from the terraces. It is clear that an established bilingual presentation of Welsh international soccer would be overwhelmed, if possible, by a mono interpretation of the stereophonics of our sporting history. The candidates for linguistic lobotomy might yet be endless.

Assumptions underlie this tsunami of linguistic seepage. Not all of them are about a future to be invoked. Some purport to evoke a past of continuities in which memories allegedly lie deep and loyalties shudder into life even as extinction is threatened. In this version of the history of Wales, centuries collapse into one another like a compartmentalised concertina from which the original breath of life can be wheezily restored. This species of ancestor worship is surprisingly resilient and when rudely buffeted by the conceptualisation of historical context – the radical differentials of demography, economies, mores, beliefs – or by the undesirable shifts of lived experience – industry, migration, wars, secularism, technology, urbanisation – merely shrugs off the explanatory weight of history and reaches for the explication of bemusement, trickery and oppression as in the discredited, but oh so necessary, model of internal colonialism. That model serves to explicate the false consciousness of the Cymry who were 'colonised' by the English and lost the factors of national being which would have prevented their willing subservience.

Yet the North American sociologist Michael Hechter's 1975 book of that name has been taken apart, for both its theory and its evidence-based arguments, for almost fifty years by batteries of social scientists, economists, and, yes, historians who wearily point to the exploitation of the Welsh by the Welsh – coal owners, steel magnates, a shopocracy and a theocracy – and the absurdity of understanding a variegated 'England' as a monolith of state and capitalist overlordship. The telling alternatives of class exploitation and class solidarity, a historical reality across and within borders are summarily ignored. The notion, however, lingers and to dismiss it is, hysterically enough without any grounded counter argument, to be thought to be 'hysterical'. Assertion, called up from a cauldron of steamy myth making, is substituted for the rationale of analysis. M. Wynn Thomas in

Eutopia: Studies in Cultural Euro-Welshness, 1880–1980 (2021) rooted the undesirable vote for Brexit in Wales, a majority cast in the post-industrial 'Anglophone' areas, as being some kind of atavistic folk memory, and one spanning the centuries it would seem, of an attachment to the 'idea of Britain'. Against that, we are invited to contemplate the long-suppressed but revelatory qualities of the 'Welsh mind'. This is, indeed, Merlin redivivus along with Dragons whose forked tongues require a lingual soldering into one if we are ever to become Cymru (again).

My Welsh mind boggles at the scholarly scaffolding erected to create a contemporary platform for such century-spanning Hegelianism and woozy Herderian woodcraft. But, as Wynn Thomas so eloquently puts it: 'Those who wish a people to lose their identity cause them first to lose their memory.' Applied to the denizens and citizens of Wales, especially, of course, to dreaded and shapeshifted South Wales, his dictum takes on a different, uncanny relevance. It is felt history that is being lost for them, not any misty memory. One of the special ironies of this phase of the life of the 'Welsh mind' is that *Eutopia* appears in a series of studies of Writing Wales in English though it concentrates almost exclusively on Welsh-language writers and thinkers. There is Emyr Humphreys, Dylan Thomas and Vernon Watkins, to be sure, but not Richard Hughes nor the twentieth-century Welsh writer whose work was more translated and read across Europe – in Spanish, in Romanian, in German, in Italian, in Norwegian, in Russian, in Polish, in Hungarian, and in Bulgarian, as well as made available in English in the Netherlands and in Sweden – than any other writer from Wales. But then Gwyn Thomas, of course, was the chief literary witness to the reality of a Wales which had no need of Cymru as it remade itself as American Wales.

Those who lived beneath the radar of that particular nomenclature's deep significance for the nature of twentieth-century Welsh life were certainly aware, by grounded instinct as much as by direct knowledge, of what species of change was being widely experienced. There were plenty of clues around, enough to open the eyes (just a bit) of the most transient observer. One such was the journalist H. V. Morton who, on assignment for the

Daily Herald, went *In Search of Wales* in 1932 (Scotland, Ireland and England had already been sought and found) and stressed that he had 'explored the black valleys of the South as I have explored the green valleys of the North' (well, two out of twelve chapters did take in 'where the mass of the Welsh people earn their living'). Inevitably, 'the gloomy Rhondda valley' where he ends up and goes 'down a mine' is labelled, for its landscaped ugliness and its unemployed who 'can only stand about at street corners because they were born and bred to mine coal', as that 'heartbreak valley' whose only 'compensation' derives from 'a national gift' for 'song':

> They use their voices as a ladder to heaven. They are transfigured in song ... in many a Welsh miner's throat is something that can lift him from the darkness of a mine into regions that are not far from paradise.

And yet, conventional and heart-tugging in both sympathy and indignation as Morton was, he glimpsed something else that could not, amidst the economic misery and social waste, be gainsaid, and to his credit he saw it and said it:

> I would like to think, if I had entered a pit at the age of fourteen and I had grown to manhood in it, that I would retain the outlook and the intellectual curiosity of the average Welsh miner. His intellectual interests are remarkable. At a street corner in Tonypandy I heard two young miners discussing Einstein's theory of relativity. I know this was exceptional, but it is significant; and it is true.
>
> It will not seem out of the way to anyone who knows South Wales. It will be believed by the manager of Smith's bookshop in Cardiff, who recently delivered Murray's *Oxford English Dictionary* which cost £45, to the Workmen's Institute at Ton-yr-Efail. This £45 was saved by miners as twopences! And they followed it up by saving £39 for the *Encyclopaedia Britannica* [from 'the dole' or weekly wages of '£2 to £3.10']. These men know how to think.

A decade later a fourteen-year-old colliery boy (b. 1928) from Tonyrefail would visit his Uncle Evan (treasurer of the Coedely Lodge) after a shift underground to borrow a book from his 'little library'. Vernon Harding told me his first choice had been James Fenimore Cooper's *The Last of the Mohicans*. Vernon was an 'average Welsh miner' through whom the lines of force representative of 'American Wales' once literally intersected. That was in 1950 when he was the youngest of the three miners captured in an American photographer's iconic picture 'Three Generations of Miners' (now in the collection of the National Museum of Wales) after their shift at Coedely Colliery had finished. I was making a film for BBC Four, *The Lost Pictures of Eugene Smith* (his sojourn that election year being in South Wales), and we found, in 2005, that Vernon Harding, then seventy-seven, was still living in Tonyrefail. We became friends and, as I discovered more of his personal story, and of his own writing of it, I had his permission to highlight his exceptional understanding of the life and work he, and others, he stressed, had led within a society of extraordinary cultural impact. That story, my quizzing of him, and his own witnessing, formed a quintessential part of my book *In The Frame: Memory in Society, Wales 1910 to 2010* which I gave to him pre-publication but a draft of which with its cover photograph of the crowd of miners, including my grandfather, who were about to become Tonypandy rioters, he had previously seen. Vernon wrote me a wonderful letter, ostensibly a thank-you note but, in my opinion, a trumpet call from the past he had lived and I had come to study. Here it is, with me respectfully by his generation restored to 'David', and the lines of force limned and graphically present as unanswerable QED from Tonyrefail for American Wales.

Tonyrefail
Nr. Porth
Mid. Glam
16-11-2010

Dear David,

I'm writing to thank you for your gift and for the generous and numerous occasions you mentioned me in the book, I feel very proud, actually really chuffed, to know that when it's published and is on the shelf in our local libraries, friends and acquaintances will see my name, and on the fly-leaf no less.

When I came home from Llwynypia and showed Nora the book and told her that you had intended sending it to me at Christmastime she said that I shouldn't read it until then, to which I agreed. I'm afraid to say it didn't happen, a few glances through the pages turned into a full-scale assault and even a re-reading of certain passages several times, you know the ones I mean, my reading glasses seemed to mist up and I had to take them off to wipe them.

The first time I had seen the cover photograph on your book was when you sent me your initial draft of the first chapter and it was fairly blurred due to age. Since hearing your talks and also reading other sources concerning the riots I feel far more informed about the actual event and the reasons why it occurred. I agree with you, this was no spur of the moment, lashing out willy-nilly, blind rage of an uncontrolled mob. The cover photograph of the book, taken before the riot, has been enhanced and improved from the original, with the men's appearance and features more defined, there are no hoodies or scarves obscuring faces, no furtive looks down.

They are all clean shaven, apart from some with the fashionable moustache, dai caps set square on the heads of the older ones, at jaunty angles on the younger, a few wearing their bowler hats, their faces open, and looking straight ahead, their expressions unafraid. Study the eyes of the ones in the forefront, the men surrounding your grandfather, it's all there, wariness, distrust, scepticism, determination, and you can also see the intelligence. You can't tell me that those men would develop into an uncaring mob.

Your chapter, 'Boxing with Life', fancy you pulling out Ernest Hemingway's 'Fifty Grand'. That takes me back. Remember his 'The Killers', the basis for four or five films, the most notable one with Burt Lancaster as the Swede and Edmond O'Brien as the reporter tracing his back story until he discovered Ava Gardner was the double-crossing lover.

I read and enjoyed *Border Country* especially the little episode of the cantankerous railway employee who refused to work extra hours, thus enabling Raymond Williams' father to resume work. Their allotments at the railway station where they grew flowers to adorn the station. As you say in your biography of Raymond: he wasn't satisfied with the book, going back several times and writing different alternatives to parts of the story. I suppose a writer is able to do this, looking back, and we would all see instances where we would have acted differently, but I believe the person we were then is constrained by what we knew and experienced then.

Ron Berry's opening to 'The Tonypandy Kid' chapter, Judge's Hall and all the familiar names that fought there, like Nobby Baker who later trained young lads from the Tonypandy area. I enjoyed reading his exchanges of letters with Alun Richards. I only read one of Alun's books, *Ennal's Point*, but that was a long time ago and I remember very little about it, and only one of Ron's, 'Hector Bebb', in your Library of Wales re-issue.

I share Ron's views about Cormac McCarthy, there is a little of Hemingway in some of his sentences but Hemingway's scope was far broader. I also sympathise with the Spanish-Mexican words, you generally interpret the meaning of the odd word, but McCarthy would write whole sentences, with no explanation, so you would be left not knowing if you were missing something that was integral to the story. Yes, he does go off on muses of rhetoric with a touch of Gothic, more so in the two books completing the trilogy but, after *All the Pretty Horses* going to a film, his last two books are really stripped to the bone, with, I think, the film rights in mind, which duly followed. Ron is right he would 'drop the bomb' in *No Country for Old Men*. There is no hero, no sympathetic characters, so if you don't like it, tough, all he is doing is telling the story.

Alun is right, too, regarding John O'Hara's books and his characters' fixation on class, attending the right school and membership of a private club, with maybe *From the Terrace* the best example.

Ron Berry compares McCarthy to our own writers, but he is only one of many, and they had a vast canvas to work from. I have read some of what I consider to be the best, Damon

Runyon's wide-boys and grifters, Dashiell Hammett and Raymond Chandler's shamus and private eye, Budd Schulberg, *The Harder they Fall* and *On the Waterfront* but it was when I followed the white American's Manifest Destiny westward that I really found the greats. With Bernard De Voto, Brian Hall and a few other writers I have accompanied Merriwether Lewis and William Clark, leading their Corps of Discovery up the Mississippi to its headwaters and wintering with the Mandans, hiring Toussaint Charbonneau and his Shoshone wife Sacajawea to guide and interpret for them while crossing the Rockies before reaching the Pacific Ocean and then returning and recounting their findings to Thomas Jefferson. And later two members of that expedition, John Colter, hunter and trapper, reputed to be the first white American to see the natural wonders of Yellowstone National Park and Jedadiah Smith, who found South Pass, the easiest route through the Rockies, for the wagon trains heading for California. He is said to have stood astride a small rivulet in the heart of the Rockies, the backbone of the Continent, where all the rivers to the east flowed to the Atlantic, urinated in the stream and watched the water flowing westward to become the mighty Colorado on its way to the Pacific Ocean.

Dale Van Every, Conrad Richter, A. B. Guthrie Jr, Vardis Fisher, Walter Edmonds, and their stories of the early frontier. Kenneth Roberts with *Arundel*, *Rabble in Arms* and *Northwest Passage* his story of Roger's Rangers and their retaliatory raid on the Abenaki village of St Francis, near Quebec.

John Ehle, a prolific writer, and David Marion Wilkinson, among others, with the story of the Cherokee Nation, settled on their farms in Georgia and Tennessee being forced to leave, escorted by the Army on the Trail of Tears to a reservation in Oklahoma. Our old friend Howard Fast, *The Last Frontier*, telling the story of 300 of the Northern Cheyenne under the leadership of Dull Knife and Little Wolf escaping from their reservation in Oklahoma and returning to their homeland in Wyoming, being chased and killed by the Army, with about fifty reaching home and finally being left in peace. Dee Brown's *Bury My Heart at Wounded Knee*.

I have been with Wallace Stegner and John Vernon following

John Wesley Powell and his companions as they mapped the Grand Canyon section of the Colorado River.

Thomas Flanagan's trilogy of Ireland starting with *The Year of the French*, Madison Smartt Bell's trilogy of the slave revolt in Haiti led by Toussaint L'Ovourture and Desselines with the first book *All Souls Rising* very powerful. Shelby Foote's Trilogy *The Civil War*.

I fought with Captain Joshua Chamberlain of the 20th Maine defending Little Round Top in Michael Shaara's Pulitzer Prize winning novel *The Killer Angels* and watched Pickett's famous charge, that wasn't really a charge at all, just brave men walking over half a mile through cannon shell and grapeshot until they reached the breastworks, to finally die under the musket fire and bayonet of the Union troops.

And finally Donald McCaig's *Jacob Ladder* a novel of Virginia during the Civil War, published in 1998 to critical acclaim, a noted historian, he has written several other books. In 2007 his book *Canaan* was published, 'A saga of post-Civil War America, from the defeat of the Confederacy to the Battle of the Little Bighorn'. It has been on the to-read shelf of my little bookcase for three years, like a bottle of fine wine I'm loath to start it. I must begin, I'd hate to pop my clogs with it still unread. I'm enclosing a book by him I hope you like. Like 'The Fed' I found quite a 'few nuggets' when reading it. As Ron Berry said I hope you think 'it's a keeper'.

Again many thanks David and all the best.

Vernon

It is the social and economic demise of this American Wales which presented Welsh Labour with a cultural dilemma wrapped up as a political gift. Either in power or as lead partner in a coalition with Plaid Cymru or the Liberal Democrats, Welsh Labour could justifiably call itself the Party of Wales, stealing the pretension to that brand in the title of its nationalist rival, and so cause the vacuum of American Wales to be filled with the tribal attributes of political logos and conveniently solipsistic sentiments. If prioritising the existential survival of the Welsh language remained a sine qua non priority for Plaid, so embracing the Cymricisation of its profile, including implementing policies, was a no-brainer for a Labour Party with both a culturally diminished hinterland and yet still a strong legacy of historical identification with most of the people of Wales most of the time. The hegemony of early-twentieth-century Lib-Labism, progressive consensual politics under a pan-Wales umbrella, had given way to the domination of Labour as a class-focused social democratic organisation for most of the last century. Now, from 2000 on, it shaped for itself a new pan-Wales role with a strained rhetoric of cultural nationalism and an attenuated social mission. Almost as if a century in Labour had been rescinded. The limits of devolved power, and of finance, might well be just as much at fault in the mixed picture of the administration of health, education, and transport, and all the rest of the governmental portfolio, which we have seen undertaken since 2000: but there is no doubt, too, that the David Lloyd George of Cymru Fydd would find his place within this political circus horse more readily than would the provocatively creative force that was Aneurin Bevan.

The embrace of virtue-signalling policies and practice, as on every liberal and professional agenda from California to Cefn Gwlad, has elevated smug box-ticking to an art form to be effected behind closed and institutional doors. Meanwhile, increasingly outside those echo chambers, too many have turned away in despair at their own relative insignificance and far too many have heard the siren voices which lead to such as Brexit, and worse. When long-standing political connections, intertwined by mutual loyalties and acknowledged experiences, begin to fray, the final act of unravelling can be swift and fatal. Government by and for the Welsh as they were has slid down the agenda for social change whilst governance of Wales, a flailing about for a vehicular solution to stalled outcomes, has been inflated into a constitutional rescue package. We have allowed a deep concern for the state of the (Welsh) language to blind us to the equally necessitous and valid culture (in English) of the people of Wales who have never lived in Cymru and would cease to be the Welsh who they are if they ever had or did. It seems that if the people really cannot be dissolved so that we can elect another, then the political escapology of black holes will serve as an endlessly receding retreat from the press of historically defined, and recurring, realities. We need more than ever to measure the public and civic distances in and between our lives if we are all to come home, together.

OBIT PAGE

Obituaries had been commissioned. Some had even been written, and filed. An admirer had sent him one, updated to take account of his soon-expected death. He held it in his hands, and shrugged as he read it over again. Not for its accuracy - it was accurate enough as these things went - but for its banality, and not of the prose but of the life, his own, which it so scrupulously recorded. It even had a headline on the typescript, though doubtless the eventual newspaper would economise on that. It read: 'A Life in Politics: A Politic Life'.

He could feel, with an immediacy he no longer expected to hurt, the pain of the omission of the definer he would have wanted. It should have been, of course it should, 'A Political Life'. Two missing letters, and an epithet that damned rather than lauded. Well, that was how he felt about it. Others, accordingly, saw it differently, welcomed the judicious balance of the adjective they felt to be, even in political terms, the better one. Certainly, like his life, the more politic one.

It would make a half-page spread in the national broadsheets. Decent enough, and with a photograph, one of the early ones with his hair fashionably long, and perhaps his fist raised in mid-80s anger, one of the action shots Billy Maddox had taken during the Miners' Strike. Or perhaps that would not be politic enough. There was the usual Obit. Opening to set the scene:

> A political career that opened with much promise ended, if not with major practical achievements undertaken in office, then with superlative

> accomplishments recorded in his chosen literary forms: the essay and the biographical study.

How easily, though, it all read like someone else's life. Anyone else's life in its inability to evoke anything more than dates and offices held and ideas proposed. Most of the barebone facts were tabulated in a detached endnote.

> Born in 1944. School in the Valley and then in Birmingham from 1956 when his father gained a Headship.

Oxford, and then that surprising nomination for the Party when local squabbles and factions let a young, dark horse but native-born, academic through a crowded field and on to election in 1970. The rest, looking back on it forty years later, was a blur. Junior office at Trade and promotions in Defence when the Party came to power and the despond years that followed that first promising decade. He considered that he had been happy despite the waiting-room feel of the politics themselves, and despite, too, being overtaken and quickly sidelined by others more ruthless than him, when a return to government eventually came. He had led a life free from Westminster's too frequent family mishaps and his books and pamphlets and biographies had been carefully chiselled and respectfully received, even in the academia he had deserted, for the insights which his political practice had brought to them. On the Obit. page they were duly listed and respectfully weighed. It was for what, he reflected, he would be best remembered.

There had been such a lot of downtime in Westminster. Time to think as well as write. The fashion had been for hefty double-decker biographies, story-time narratives with the happy endings of definitive footnotes or, at least, fulsome acknowledgements and learned bibliographies. Jenkins on Asquith. Foot on Bevan. Always the leaders. Never the Led. History, he considered increasingly, as it was sieved, not how it had been lived. Instead he listened to Voices Off. He talked to those who Also Served. He contemplated a Culture for a Society. Over the years a trilogy of studies emerged. He turned to the Obit. proof to check if it had expressed more than a titular sense of them:

> His first book, *Vox Pop: A Vocal Culture* (1981), was an examination of the rhetoric and oratory of industrial South Wales - its excess, some in his Party were already concluding - through speech, accent, gesture and effect, but it slipped, intriguingly and often infuriatingly, into riffs on singing, choral and solo, onto disquisitions on humour on stage and in literature, through the roar of crowd behaviour to the antiphony of reserved silence in reading rooms and the cacophony of saloon bars. It met with a mixed reception but won a Welsh Arts Council Prize. Out of office and buffeted by the internal strife of the Foot and Kinnock years - he was a steadfast supporter of both - he wrote the biographical sketches published in book form as *Acolytes and Assassins* (1988). Here the intention, not always successfully achieved, was to throw light on major political or union careers by illuminating those who were waiting in the shadows, ready to assist or, as his provocative title indicated, to assassinate. So, instead of, say, a portrait of that Colossus, Nye Bevan, we had a brilliant sketch of his Famulus, Bevan's fixer and confidant, the diminutive and destructive (of others) Archie Lush. The spotlight was turned, for the once-powerful Communist Party, not on the ebullient and engaging Arthur Horner, President of the South Wales Miners' Federation in 1936, but on the

apparatchiks who always placed Party diktat before proletarian DNA. Then he swung to the right to put the egregious George Thomas, the ludicrously self-christened Viscount Tonypandy, in his sights: 'Of this Tartuffe, a study in sentiment and narcissism, let us say that the Sunday School superintendent was always more cross-bencher than cross-dresser for in this, too, he had the courage of every conviction but his own.' Many found the acid of such 'truth telling', if that is what it was, too scalding an element for their own political health at the hustings. Even his obituary of Will Paynter, the tough intellectualised comrade who had succeeded his own mentor, Horner, as general secretary of the NUM in 1959, had not resisted the temptation to speculate on exactly what a CP political commissar would have done in Spain in 1937. At the fever point pitch of the Miners' Strike this had not pleased the cheerleaders of 1984. Yet, in his final foray into this field, after Tony Blair had overlooked him for any kind of office in 1997, he wrote lightly and sunnily of those whom he had directly served for thirty years. *Epiphanies* appeared to muted acclaim in 2001, but we can now see it bears a classic status. Here, 'The Terraces', as he calls them, echoing the writer Gwyn Thomas, are laid before us as a landscape, one humanly fabricated and artfully framed by and for a people who had, he claims, once created a past fit for whatever future they might inhabit. How does he do this? By a set of interlocking cameos that take us from 'The Value of Allotments: The Alloting of Values' to 'The Cooked Dinner: Civilisation after the Club' and 'Standing not Sitting: Philosophy on the Bob Bank'. All linear lines and flat planes were rejected by the prismatic writing, a form that gave a crystalline light and a receding depth to the pastimes and dreams, but ones lived and relished, of a people he clearly feared were being bypassed by a more brutalist history and that history's political helpmeets, even those from within the ranks of Labour.

He let the obituary he would not live to see in print slip from his fingers onto the duvet. Not quite what he had meant his writing to say. But close enough, and praising enough, not to be begrudged. He resolved, again, to stop being grudging. It was, none of it was, anybody's fault. Not even his own. He would, without a grudge, accept the praise and accolades it helped them to give him. Particularly the family he had nurtured, and had, he knew, despite all, neglected more than he would have wished. They didn't seem to notice; perhaps they didn't feel it. He didn't know. They didn't say.

His son, who had developed an irksome habit of patting his hand as he sat propped up in bed so that he might look out of the picture window and over the Valley, kept telling him what 'A Great Life' he'd had and how he would 'not be forgotten'. He smiled and nodded, politic as ever, even managing a whispery 'Thank you, love' when his daughter, on the other side of the bed, reminded him how much he was 'Loved by Everybody'. It was true, he thought, that his wife, whom he'd met at Oxford had, in her own patrician way, 'loved' him and he'd sorrowed over her early death in the car smash she'd had with her parents when on holiday in Italy. He'd stayed home that summer on constituency work, intending to join them later. She had never felt 'At Home' in the Valley and had never hidden her disdain, her fear perhaps, of its inhabitants. Ironically, the sympathy he garnered with the death of the woman his supporters had privately called 'The Duchess' strengthened his control of the local party. He steered a middle course and, by the end, this end as he might now put it, he was consulted on all sides for his political nous, his historical grip and his experienced counsel. Oh, and for the colour copy his reminiscence of the Party's greats gave to journalists. He was restored. One of them. One of us. Ours.

Yet none of this was why he had come back for selection. And stayed as the elected member. He could barely explain it to himself sometimes. Yet he knew that there had been deep inside him political idealism, and an allied will to serve. He knew this to be true of himself even then. In his father's telling, the people of the Valley, his Valley, from which he had been wrenched so young, were mythic, generation by generation, and heroic, deed by deed. If it was an absurd generalisation, it was also vividly true. It had been bred into his political bone and so vitally that he had, and did always, feel it an honour to be elected to serve. But it was not that particular igniting spark which still flickered inside, and did not die even if he was dying and she was long gone. His thoughts were a junction box of random signals. Perhaps it was the morphine. Perhaps it was a dream. He half-smiled, ruefully, remembering a train journey he'd taken across country, to the west and some political function or other, just before the cancer had struck, less than a year ago. He had looked up at the information streamed up in electronic tickertape capitals at the end of the carriage, like a miniature mobile Times Square, he'd thought, as it ticked off the station stops to come, and what precautions you needed to take on arriving and alighting. Alighting. What a pompous, no pretentious, word. He had said it to himself, almost aloud, and, bored as dusk draped the crawling train, had looked up again at the flashcard red letters of information flowing left to right in their rectangular black box. Only this last time, the electrical charges had malfunctioned, had dropped letters and left spaces, and displayed, as the train pulled into the platform, in an illuminated reiteration of desire and warning, one he knew he had to heed:

personal be take their
longings with you personal be
take their longings with you

* * *

He had been twelve years old, sat on one of the back seats of the upstairs of a municipal double-decker bus. The bus, one of a fleet, swayed up the Valley from the grammar school, dropping pupils off at each of the straggling townships it touched. Every seat was taken. Downstairs, two or three prefects pretended to keep order, and everywhere there was noise and the deep, damp smell of sodden wool and the wet leather of satchels. Outside it rained as it seemed only to rain here. Swathes of wind-blown rain ballooning down from the mountains which hemmed them in and funnelled the rain into the streets. Rain tamping down onto the pavements. Rain bouncing off the roof of the bus and smacking against the windowpanes which steamed up inside, and outside turned the raindrops into never-ending rivulets which streamed drop by beaded drop as silvery snail trains. It was a cold rain. It swept in from the open platform at the back of the bus and carried its damp aftershock upstairs and into the soaked moquette seats. The caps of the boys and their black gabardine raincoats were heavy with rain, and the girls, barelegged and hatless, shivered in their pixie-hooded lovat-green mackintoshes. He had looked out of the window where, even at four o'clock, the lights were on in the shop windows and the few cars there were about stared back, with their headlamps unblinking warnings, out of the gloom. He had never felt more at one with everything. This was where he was and should always be.

One of the prefects, in the casual sports coats they were allowed to wear in the sixth form in place of their blazered uniform, came rattling up the iron-rimmed stairs and stood at the top. At the bottom was another prefect. The one at the top said, 'Right, now. One. Two. Three', and waved his arms whilst the one at the bottom began to sing. Then the whole bus, from top to bottom, began to sing, and some stood in the aisles as the bus seemed to half topple around a bend and up and over a steep hill, and some fell onto one another, satchels and caps scattering, laughing and singing and stamping all at the same time, singing, never happier, the blues that they would never feel more, and as if this moment could be held, forever.

Well, I never felt more like singin' the blues
'cause I never thought I'd ever lose
Your love, dear, why'd you do me this way?
Well, I never felt more like cryin' all night
'cause everythin's wrong, and nothing' ain't right
Without you, you got me singin' the blues.

The moon and stars no longer shine
The dream is gone I thought was mine
There's nothin' left for me to do
But cry-y-y-y over you (cry over you)
Well, I never felt more like runnin' away
But why should I go 'cause I couldn't stay
Without you, you got me singin' the blues.

And he looked to the back of the bus, all singing the lyric and shouting the refrain, and he saw the girl, his age, sitting, not singing, on the long seat across the aisle, at the back of the bus, and he saw her wet, plastered, black gloss of hair cut to frame her face with its shining eyes above her wet and reddened cheeks and as he did, stopping to sing the song that still rang all around him, unsmiling she looked straight back at him.

That was why, he knew, he had come back, and why he stayed and why, never known or spoken to or seen again, she would always be there. And there she would remain, loved and unknown, so long as hearts could still tell minds that they had 'never felt more'.

CARTOGRAPHERS AND SHERPAS

My map makers have been many and varied but none, for me, surer-footed as to known terrain and more enlightening as to unknown topography than were Eric Hobsbawm and Norman Mailer, both of whom I was able to quiz on our very own borderland at Hay-on-Wye thanks to that festival's then director, its incomparable founder Peter Florence. Closer still to Native Ground was Alun Richards whose voice we hear in this book, unusually for him, in a direct reflective manner but, elsewhere, whose subtle and probing fiction reminds us, too, that we need to gaze inwards and back if we are to aspire to look upwards and beyond ourselves. I wonder, however, in 2025, with 1985 as the earlier focal point for the theodolite's measuring of historical angles between the vertical and the horizontal, whether that injunction has been too difficult to implement in Wales. Perhaps it is because, as Gwyn A. Williams observed with a characteristically messianic warning note at that cusp time, the Welsh had run off their maps. All hitherto known ones, that is, as they lurched from one cul-de-sac to another – political and economic dead ends butting into social and cultural blind alleys – adrift from familiar markers, touchstones of assumed identity successively lost and the waiting abyss of the 1984–5 strike swallowing up a generation's sense of their own surety of footing.

As I finished this text I turned to recall exactly what Gwyn did say in the prophetic doomsaying volume he published in 1985 as *When Was Wales? A History of the Welsh*. Its prescience, even though the predicted outcomes were to be diverted or delayed, is shatteringly resonant in 2025:

> In response to a militant campaign [from the 1960s on] ... the British state, ruling a largely indifferent or hostile Welsh population, has countenanced and indeed subsidised cultural Welsh nationalism. Welsh is now officially, visibly, and audibly, a bilingual country... The issue of the Welsh language, in many fields

> of Welsh action, blots out all other political considerations. The consequences have been contradictory [positives and negatives]... It is, however, evidence of a much deeper malaise which is much more ominous: the denial of Welshness to the English-speaking Welsh... The adjective 'Welsh' is increasingly applied, outside and inside Wales, only to the Welsh-speaking component of the people, which is one fifth of the actual number. A new shadow-line runs across the face of Wales. Essentially English-speaking Welsh people are increasingly denied membership of Wales. Such people constitute four-fifths of the Welsh population and over two-thirds of those who would be considered biologically Welsh. What sort of Welsh nation or even Welsh people is going to survive this? Whom the Gods wish to destroy, they first afflict with a language problem. Or, to quote Thomas Paine on Edmund Burke, theorist of the organic community, 'He pities the plumage and forgets the dying bird.'

This was a heartfelt concern for recognition of an achieved culture – one largely dismissed for its intrinsic worth at that precise time across most official cultural and educational channels – which I shared with Gwyn as we worked together for a decade at Cardiff University. Coincidentally (sort of...) we contemporaneously made 'rival' television series exposing some of these fissures – my *Wales! Wales?* in 1984 for BBC Two/BBC Wales and his (with Wynford Vaughan Thomas) *The Dragon Has Two Tongues* in 1985 for HTV Wales/Channel 4. When Raymond Williams came to review the books spun from the series (*The Guardian* for Gwyn; The *London Review of Books* for mine) he struck a typically balanced note. Gwyn's was acclaimed for its range as a 'general history' and its stalwart refusal 'in loyalty to their own actual people ... to assimilate to singular and romantic national traditions'. But there was, too, just as typically, Raymond's own unwillingness to accept Gwyn's apocalyptic final words that 'we are now nothing but "a naked people under an acid rain" [for there is] evidence that it is being refused, and can be surpassed.' He wrote that in January 1985 as the NUM's nationwide strike ground on in self-consuming despair and an incandescence of hope. It was that precious measure of hope which Raymond wanted, as a fusion of class agency and community coherence, to cherish, and he said as much in his bookended consideration of my own (then) summation on the same publication day that very month:

> To accommodate the evident changes in Welsh life [into its industrial/modernising historical condition] ... there is a shift within the concept of continuity ... [shapeshifting as] potentially indicative of an observable historical process: at its weakest, the endless fantasies of a subjected people, magnifying past greatness or present uniqueness as forms of disguise not only from others but from hard-pressed selves; at its strongest, however, a capacity for active and flexible survival in which powers of a certain kind – hope, fidelity, eloquence – are repeatedly distilled from defeat. The test of the strongest sense would then be the welcoming admission of the latest shift: not as the abandonment of 'Welshness', in some singular and unitary form, but as the positive creating of a still distinctively Welsh, English-speaking working-class culture.

Raymond Williams had long (ante *Culture and Society*, 1958) understood the intricacies of that particular culture, especially its universality, but not as much, for how could he yet, its historicised specificities in all their telling detail. For the latter he would need to rely on literary texts, largely fiction, and indeed did so as his inaugural Gwyn Jones Lecture had testified before an enthralled audience at Cardiff University in 1978. That lecture series' establishment, by Gwyn A. Williams and myself, stemmed directly from the lack of any widespread provision for the scholarly study and propagation of what in 1985 Raymond would call 'the work of the English-language writers of industrial South Wales ... unmistakeably indigenous ... unmistakeably native writing and speech'. His own identification with and support for a cultural groundswell, including the impulse around Llafur as both society and as the journal for the study of Labour history, was gratifyingly clear and forthright. Further, he saluted 'the recent significant assertion, from what has been the nationalist tendency, that English is a Welsh language'.

Mapping the future, within and beyond the academy, seemed with cartographers like these to guide us, even in foggy times, an assured pathway on which we could be roped together as the reality of our destination opened up before the honest intellectual acceptance of the relative weight, or interlocked significances, of a lived history. For my part, in the various ways I have sketched in my autobiographical memoir *Off The Track* (2023), I was more than willing down to the early years of this century to act as a sherpa, pulling together different strands of understanding, or interpretation, across the fields of literary and cultural criticism, of historical enquiry and public communications to help in hauling them to new peaks of shared knowledge. Along the way we lost both Gwyn (1925–95) and Raymond (1921–88): to the incantatory former I paid my dues in an obituary essay in *History Workshop Journal* (1996) and to the resolute rootedness of the latter in my biography *Raymond Williams: A Warrior's Tale* (2008). That both would have welcomed the early cultural initiatives of the Assembly/Senedd, which neither lived to see, is, I believe, self-evident; as would have been Raymond's support for the Library of Wales series in which his novel *Border Country* (1960) made an early appearance. Indeed, if there was a topographical release valve for the pressure cooker that was, and is, the concept of Wales, then the limning of borders, on the ground and in the mind, would have been at the heart of its function. Everywhere in Daniel G. Williams' invaluable compilation of Raymond Williams' 'Welsh Essays' (*Raymond Williams: Who Speaks for Wales?* 2003/2011) there is a poised measure of necessary balance, or rather imbalance, between Welsh contradictions, one which never becomes a forced authorial weighting for current equity's sake. Any such contemporary rebalancing of the historical scales, he understood, would have been merely juristic. Shortcuts, constitutional and legalistic, without directional viewfinders, political and connective, would only short-circuit desired outcomes. Artificial impositions of conceptual frameworks onto the ley lines of actualised experience could be no workable substitute for those creative artifices required to translate ideas into feeling as the common good emerges from a culture held in common.

As this century drove on towards its quarter mark I could feel, despite a more and more diverse production of work across a scramble of genres, that age and practice had begun to confine me, too, to the spinning wheel of cartography whilst other sherpas hefted the off-cast load. If there are belvederes of insight in *Measuring the Distance* these foci owe much to what I have learned from these willing bearers of fresh and objective evidence (aka historians). A community of knowledge gatherers continue undaunted, even through debate and disagreement, to question what we mean by the tenses of Welsh existence. Too many to mention, one by one, here but two so related by subject matter and inclination to my own foremost questing that they must be singled out in thanks.

The first is one who fell to earth far too soon: in the very month of April 2024 when I was completing the first draft of this last book. Chris Williams was only sixty-one when he died without warning. The widespread grief which followed on from this shock said much about the impact his life and work had had, and especially, though not exclusively, so far as the history of Wales was concerned. I had first met him when he was a seventeen-year-old schoolboy (see my tribute for the Learned Society of Wales, 15 April 2024) and, thereafter, worked with him as successively my PhD student and then colleague at the universities of Cardiff and Glamorgan. He became, a generation younger than me, a firm friend with whom I conspired to make uncomfortable truths available even when they were not palatable. There was a map, of course, to be plotted out between us. Sometimes it could feel that an actual 'X' marked the spot as when in (almost) the last words of his superbly forensic book of 1996 *Democratic Rhondda: Politics and Society 1885–1951* he wrote:

> Had Rhondda been typical or representative it would not have had the force and energy that enabled it to lead South Wales for seventy years. Rhondda acted instead as a beacon to the rest of the coalfield, signalling its history. It could be believed that what Rhondda experienced today, other parts of South Wales and Britain with similar, working class 'definitions of community'

> would experience tomorrow, even if that 'experience' was to be confined to the realm of political thought and debate, to capturing the imagination of theoretical advance. In an important sense that realm had greater vitality and relevance than anything achieved on the ground, because it contributed to a collectivist, universalist definition of working class, and indeed, Welsh identity that defied the linguistically exclusive 'Welshness' of a privileged minority. If those self-blinded visionaries had looked, they would have seen Wales not in Penyberth but in Penygraig, where national identity was if not irrelevant, then marginal compared to an intermeshing of class and community solidarities whose horizons truly were international.

I would happily take that, then and now, as an epitaph for the histories I was, in tandem, writing. Only, those were his trumpet sounds of engagement, not his endnote of careful consideration. That he had reserved for a challenging duo of footnotes, the very last in his book, in which the map was spread out for further exploration, a historian's challenging calculus to be figured out into the future:

> Footnote 19. As Dai Smith 'The Valleys: Landscape and Mindscape' (1988) suggests Rhondda might also have spoken in a very different way, had the visions of ... D. A. Thomas, Lord Rhondda been realised. Thomas represented the leading edge of capitalist advancement, his Liberalism, rooted as it was in 'American Wales', having shaken off the sentimental trappings of Cymru Fydd and the remainder of the ideological props of Welsh-speaking Liberal Wales. The future which Thomas represented was curtailed: by his own death in 1918, and by the collapse of the coalfield's economic fortunes between the wars. With this 'alternative' of an indigenous, present South Wales capitalist leadership wrenched out of history, and with the self-serving deceits of Welsh Liberal Nonconformity exposed by the blood and violence of 1910, there was no 'alternative' to the working-class leadership of coalfield communities, in defeat as much as in victory.

> Footnote 20. And in this sense Rhondda was an 'alternative culture', a 'society within'.

Or stressed another way, as in the title of his 1998 commentary-cum-documents *Capitalism, Community, Conflict: The South Wales Coalfield 1898–1947*, the standoff between an expansive then crippled capitalism and a nascent then dominant Social Democracy took place in the birthing pool of a cultural structure we may indeed imagine as 'American Wales'. It took Daryl Leeworthy, a generation on, to reassert this fundamental issue in the history of Wales, and for which there is still in Bevan's blunt assertion 'No Democracy of Facts'. This passage comes towards the end of his coruscatingly brilliant and boldly excursive book of 2018 *Labour Country*:

> Attempts by recent revisionist scholarship to demolish this understanding of the past – or to cloak it with questions of identity, constitutionalism, and nationhood – offer little meaningful alteration to those fundamental terms. South Wales may now find itself reduced in rank to a lower-case geographical expression but its upper-case vitality remains apparent in the historical record. It was as South Wales, not south Wales, that this social democracy was envisaged and thought and written about. There is much to be gained from a revival of the capital.

* * *

And from that vantage point of rest, all measured as best can be for now, the baggage carried thereto can be unpacked with thanks. To the National Library of Wales and to the Hay International Festival of Literature under whose respective auspices 'Out of the People' and the interviews with Eric Hobsbawm and Norman Mailer were first aired orally. The Rhys Davies Trust with the (then) University of Glamorgan hosted Alun Richards' Lecture (The Writers at my Elbow) which appears here with the permission of Jessica, Steve and Daniel Richards. The essay 'Rhys Davies and his "Turbulent Valley"', now revised, was originally in *Rhys Davies: Decoding the Hare* (Ed. Meic

Stephens, 2001). Assistance with some material used in 'John Hopla: The Tonypandy Revolt' came from the indefatigable David Maddox. Lord Kenneth Morgan commissioned 'Tonypandy: Churchill's Nemesis' for the volume on *Churchill and Wales* which he edited for the International Churchill Society in 2021. 'Obit. Page' was a part of my novel *Dream On* in 2013 and the short stories – 'The Bailey Report' and 'Counteractual' – were collected in my *All That Lies Beneath* in 2016. The monologue 'Pass (it) On' was commissioned by Dylan Moore for *The Welsh Agenda* in 2017. The story 'Aliens' owes some reported factual matter to my former graduate student Colin Hughes in his delightful *Lime, Lemon, Sarsaparilla: The Italian Community in South Wales 1881–1945* (1991). 'Maximum Boyce' was first written as a review essay around a compendium of his work in 2022 for *Wales Arts Review*. My aria to Shirley Bassey was sung for one book only (now two) in *Hymns and Arias* (Eds. Trevor Herbert and Peter Stead, 2000). Finally, for technical nous, editorial interventions, and the digital dynamics of his own forthcoming book, *American Wales*, my deep gratitude and comradely salutation to Daryl Leeworthy, who continues to show the way. Of course, where we go from here will not be the prerogative of this 'exile' in this present time but, then again, I have always considered going up the mountain to gain perspective secondary to coming down to earth again to tell of what has been seen. And there is hope. The Welsh Government in the autumn of 2024, by establishing an Expert Advisory Group to guide specific operational policy, reaffirmed its commitment to improving the teaching of Welsh history in all 'its diversity and complexity' as a mandatory part of the Welsh school curriculum. Those twinned watchwords could serve as the essence of this book which, in turn, I hope will help promote and sustain their past truth and ongoing purpose.

THIS MONGREL BREED

When the Future
Did not arrive
They just invented
Whatever they could.
(Cymru for Wales)

When linguistic fluency
Stuttered and stalled
They just changed
The Rules of the Game.
(Speakers not Learners)

When the political Map
Blushed populous red
They highlighted green
Territory bottom to top.
(Grass not Class)

When leftover people
Withdrew from voting
They altered the compelling
To make it just compulsory.
(Populace in dissolution)

When everything devolved
Nosedived out of sight
They just double downed
Fast in a consensual tailspin.
(Constitutional Parachuting)

When schooled language drills
Drifted to playground anarchy
They policed the neglected
Precincts of impure academies.
(Numbers trump Words)

When the Past of Wales as was
Proved too embarrassing now
They fudged Public Memory
Dismissed the burden of meaning.
(Identity trumps Culture)

When lived experience was forgotten
Complexities lost in Civic Dementia
They branded the Present as Cymric
Burying Welsh remains in the grave.
(Colonised Internally)

When the Future was subtitled
They ensured the Past was mute
Only trivia escaped the Network
Banners flapped silent in the wind
(Mouths stuffed with mold)

When I cried out in anger
"Over my dead body!"
They made especially for me
One more coffin of secrecy.
(The Alone to the Alone)

****

No Brit here
Nor Cymro either
Will ever lie.
Just Pure Welsh.
(Mongrel History)

****

When the dust had settled
  New voices were heard,
  History inflecting each note,
  Learning to sing in harmony.
    (Cymru fydd Wales)

When choral unity came overall
Discord was its needed virtue,
  Dissonance its courteous exchange.
  Tribal solipsism a misplaced fart.
    (Dialectic for Wales)

Modern Wales by Parthian Books

The Modern Wales Series, edited by Dai Smith and supported by the Rhys Davies Trust, was launched in 2017. The Series offers an extensive list of biography, memoir, history and politics which reflect and analyse the development of Wales as a modernised society into contemporary times. It engages widely across places and people, encompasses imagery and the construction of iconography, dissects historiography and recounts plain stories, all in order to elucidate the kaleidoscopic pattern which has shaped and changed the complex culture and society of Wales and the Welsh.

the RHYS DAVIES TRUST

PARTHIAN

TO HEAR THE SKYLARK'S SONG

Huw Lewis

To Hear the Skylark's Song is a memoir about how Aberfan survived and eventually thrived after the terrible disaster of the 21st of October 1966.

'A thoughtful and passionate memoir, moving and respectful.'
– Tessa Hadley

PB / £8.99
978-1-912109-72-2

ROCKING THE BOAT

Angela V. John

This insightful and revealing collection of essays focuses on seven Welsh women who, in a range of imaginative ways, resisted the status quo in Wales, England and beyond during the nineteenth and twentieth centuries.

PB / £11.99
978-1-912681-44-0

TURNING THE TIDE

Angela V. John

This rich biography tells the remarkable tale of Margaret Haig Thomas (1883-1958) who became the second Viscountess Rhondda. She was a Welsh suffragette, held important posts during the First World War and survived the sinking of the *Lusitania*.

PB / £17.99
978-1-909844-72-8

BRENDA CHAMBERLAIN, ARTIST & WRITER

Jill Piercy

The first full-length biography of Brenda Chamberlain chronicles the life of an artist and writer whose work was strongly affected by the places she lived, most famously Bardsey Island and the Greek island of Hydra.

PB / £11.99
978-1-912681-06-8

PARTHIAN

RAYMOND WILLIAMS: A WARRIOR'S TALE

Dai Smith

Raymond Williams (1921-1998) was the most influential socialist writer and thinker in post-war Britain. Now, for the first time, making use of Williams's private and unpublished papers and by placing him in a wide social and cultural landscape, Dai Smith, in this highly original and much praised biography, uncovers how Williams's life to 1961 is an explanation of his immense intellectual achievement.

'Becomes at once the authoritative account... Smith has done all that we can ask the historian as biographer to do.'
– Stefan Collini, *London Review of Books*

PB / £16.99
978-1-913640-08-8

BETWEEN WORLDS: A QUEER BOY FROM THE VALLEYS

Jeffrey Weeks

A man's own story from the Rhondda. Jeffrey Weeks was born in the Rhondda in 1945, of mining stock. As he grew up he increasingly felt an outsider in the intensely community-minded valleys, a feeling intensified as he became aware of his gayness. Escape came through education. He left for London, to university, and to realise his sexuality. He has been described as the 'most significant British intellectual working on sexuality to emerge from the radical sexual movements of the 1970s.'

HB / £20
978-1-912681-88-4

PARTHIAN

BEHIND THE SCENES: THE DRAMATIC LIVES OF PHILIP BURTON

Angela V. John

BELONGING

Patricia James

THE EXTRA TEST: THE STORY OF GLAMORGAN PLAYING THE BEST 1875-2025

Andrew Hignell